GOD AT THE GRASS ROOTS, 1996

Religious Forces in the Modern Political World
General Editor Allen D. Hertzke, The Carl Albert Center, University of Oklahoma at Norman

Religious Forces in the Modern Political World features books on religious forces in politics, both in the United States and abroad. The authors examine the complex interplay between religious faith and politics in the modern world, emphasizing its impact on contemporary political developments. This new series spans a diverse range of methodological interpretations, philosophical approaches, and substantive concerns. Titles include:

GOD AT THE GRASS ROOTS, 1996

The Christian Right in the American Elections

*Edited by Mark J. Rozell
and Clyde Wilcox*

ROWMAN & LITTLEFIELD PUBLISHERS, INC.
Lanham • Boulder • New York • Oxford

ROWMAN & LITTLEFIELD PUBLISHERS, INC.

Published in the United States of America
by Rowman & Littlefield Publishers, Inc.
4720 Boston Way, Lanham, Maryland 20706

12 Hid's Copse Road
Cummor Hill, Oxford OX29JJ, England

British Library Cataloguing in Publication Information Available

Library of Congress Cataloging-in-Publication Data

God at the grass roots, 1996 : the Christian right in the American
  elections / edited by Mark J. Rozell and Clyde Wilcox.
      p.   cm. — (Religious forces in the modern political world)
    Includes bibliographical references and index.
    ISBN 0–8476–8610–8 (alk. paper). — ISBN 0-8476-8611–6 (paper :
  alk. paper)
      1. Conservatism—religious aspects—Christianity—History—20th
  century. 2. Elections—United States. 3. United States—Politics
  and government—1993–. 4. United States—Church history—20th
  century. I. Rozell, Mark J. II. Wilcox, Cyde, 1953   .
  III. Series.
  BR526.G625   1997
  324.973'0929'088204—dc21   97–19042
                                                                 CIP

ISBN 0–8476–8610–8 (cloth : alk. paper)
ISBN 0–8476–8611–6 (pbk. : alk. paper)

Printed in the United States of America

♾ ™ The paper used in this publication meets the minimum requirements of
American National Standard for Information Sciences—Permanence of Paper for
Printed Library Materials, ANSI Z39.48–1984.

To James S. Fleming

and

Adamae Conrad

Contents

viii *Contents*

Preface

In the wake of the historic 1994 elections, many analysts speculated about the future impact of the Christian Right movement in both electoral and policy terms. Indeed, the Christian Right had supplied substantial energy and grass-roots support for conservative GOP candidates throughout the country, and many political observers credited the Christian Right in large part for the electoral success of the GOP in 1994. As has often been the case with the Christian Right, many of the analyses of the success of the movement in 1994 offered very broad generalizations without much regard to important contextual factors. We set out to provide a first cut at a more systematic and scholarly account of the role of the Christian Right in the elections; the result was the publication of *God at the Grass Roots: The Christian Right in the 1994 Elections* (Rowman & Littlefield, 1995). That volume was composed of the insights of a number of leading scholars of the Christian Right and of state politics.

Yet insights gleaned from a single election do not tell the full story. Although many observers credited the Christian Right as an essential ingredient in the GOP electoral victories in 1994, representatives of the movement were conspicuously absent from the Republican presidential convention stage in San Diego in 1996. The essays in this volume show the successes and failures of the movement in 1996 at the state and national levels.

God at the Grass Roots, 1996 is made up of all new chapters. Many of these studies focus on the same states as the earlier book and are written by the same authors. This allows us to trace the movement at the grass roots, where the Christian Right has focused its energy. In addition, we have added new states to the current volume, including ones where the Christian Right is not a major political force. The outline of this volume is the same as that of the earlier one, however: an overview of the Christian Right in the elections, a state-by-state analysis of the role of the Christian Right in the elections, and a concluding assessment of the successes, failures, and prospects of the Christian Right.

As was the case in 1994, the Christian Right in 1996 had substantial influence in some states and moderate or little influence in others. The chapters that follow provide considerable detail on the power of the Christian Right in each state and offer explanations for the presence of, or lack of influence by, the movement. Ultimately, case studies are useful only if they can lead to broader generalizations, and we think that these cases can provide some insight into the factors that make the Christian Right more influential in some areas of the country than in others and in some election years than in others. In his introductory essay, John C. Green makes an important contribution to our understanding by systematically exploring the factors that appear to be most critical to the success of the Christian Right.

Compared to 1994, the 1996 elections were a letdown for the Christian Right. But despite some significant setbacks, the movement had its successes and remains a formidable player in the Republican Party and in the policy process at different levels of government. As the following essays show, the Christian Right is resilient and will be a vocal and instrumental part of the American political landscape for a long time.

We wish to express our thanks to acquisitions editor Steve Wrinn who took on the initial *God at the Grass Roots* volume and encouraged us to follow up with a new version of the book about the 1996 elections. We also thank our colleague John C. Green for once again going beyond the "call of duty" not only to contribute the integrative introductory essay but also to comment on the individual chapters. We appreciate the efforts of Wesley Joe, who prepared the index.

We dedicate this book to two model teachers who made an important difference to us at critical junctures in our career paths: James S. Fleming (for Mark Rozell) and Adamae Conrad (for Clyde Wilcox).

1

The Christian Right and the 1996 Elections: An Overview

John C. Green

For the Christian Right, 1996 was a mixed year in every sense of the word, from the movement's political prowess to ballot box results. Largely because of its impact in the 1994 campaign (see Rozell and Wilcox 1995), the Christian Right was widely recognized as a significant political force. And unlike previous years, this new status was not diminished by the vicissitudes of the presidential campaign (Green 1995). But having "arrived" on the political stage, the Christian Right faced new obstacles, including legal questions about the operations of its flagship organization and increasingly effective countermobilization by opponents. The Christian Right enjoyed some significant victories at the polls in 1996, helping Republicans retain control of Congress. But the movement also suffered serious defeats, with key candidates and ballot propositions failing across the nation. All told, the 1996 campaign suggests that the Christian Right has found a small but prominent niche in national politics.

The essays in this volume are state-level case studies of the Christian Right in the 1996 elections, and taken together they describe the movement's niche in some detail. First, the movement's status and activities have put it in contention in many states, allowing it to participate in politics at an unprecedented level. This expanded level of participation has not been uniformly successful, however. In some states (such as South Carolina and Texas), the Christian Right has become part of a consolidated Republican coalition to the benefit of movement and party alike, while in other states (such as Oregon and Minnesota), the Christian Right has provoked bitter confrontations within the GOP to the detriment of all. Still other states (such as Virginia and California) fall in between, with elements of both consolidation and confrontation. Finally, there are states (including Maine and West Virginia) where the movement is not yet in contention and may never be.

Understanding the Christian Right

To understand better the impact of the Christian Right in 1996, it is useful to begin with a catalogue of its strengths and weaknesses and the roles it can play in electoral politics. The Christian Right is a social movement dedicated to restoring "traditional values" in public policy by mobilizing evangelical Protestants and other conservative religious people to political action (Green et al. 1996). Like other movements, the Christian Right can be usefully described by different strata of activity, with leaders and movement organizations at the top, sets of activists in the middle, and a group of potential voters at the bottom. From this perspective, the Christian Right, properly so called, is all three strata set in movement politically. Such movement has focused on grassroots efforts in elections, the primary concern of the case studies. However, the movement has increasingly confronted the challenges of policy making, a topic that is reviewed in the final chapter of the book.

Strengths

The Christian Right's strengths derive primarily from the vitality of evangelical Protestantism (Jorstad 1993). Of particular importance is the internal structure of evangelicalism, which combines orthodox Christian beliefs with intense individualism, resulting in a highly decentralized set of religious organizations, including thousands of small denominations, parachurch groups, and independent churches. Even the largest bodies, such as the giant Southern Baptist Convention (the largest Protestant denomination in the country), are actually voluntary alliances of the component institutions. This environment puts a premium on aggressive, entrepreneurial leaders who are adept at recognizing discontent among religious people, identifying opportunities to respond to such discontent, and organizing the resources to bring the two together (Green et al. 1996, chap. 9).

These leadership skills can be effectively applied to politics if the opportunity presents itself, as has happened in recent times. Over the last generation, social and economic forces have increasingly brought evangelicals into contact with lifestyles and worldviews they find abhorrent (Wilcox 1992). Government policies directed at protecting, extending, and enforcing these rival values have been particularly galling, especially when they deal with matters easily linked to traditional morality: sexual conduct, abortion, women's roles, family arrangements, education, crime, and the legal status of religion itself.

These discontents have allowed leaders to recruit a corps of zealous activists, which could, on the one hand, provide the resources for movement organizations and, on the other, engage in political activity (Leege 1992). Like other politically involved Americans, these activists are largely middle class, with the personal skills and resources necessary to be effective in politics (Green et al. 1994, chap. 5). While churches themselves are rarely a formal part of the movement's organization, they are key to its success: the close-knit religious communities and related communication networks are a fertile source of activists and a potent forum for their activities.

A final movement strength is the relative size and cohesiveness of evangelicalism in the mass public (Green et al. 1996, chaps. 14, 15). Nationally, white evangelicals make up about one-quarter of the adult American population and are more numerous in southern and midwestern states. The high degree of religious commitment among them allows for effective mobilization on the basis of moral appeals, religious communities, and networks. By way of reference, evangelicals are about as numerous as Roman Catholics and outnumber mainline Protestants and the secular population. Although they are hardly a political monolith, mobilizing just one-half of this large tradition would produce a voting bloc more numerous than African American voters and roughly ten times larger than Jews or Episcopalians (cf. Leege and Kellstedt 1993). When combined, these strengths can be quite formidable.

Weaknesses

The nature of evangelical Protestantism also generates weaknesses for the Christian Right. For one thing, evangelicals have been very difficult to organize, even at the elite level (Jelen 1992). One special problem has been the otherworldly orientation of these deeply religious people, many of whom have had little interest in politics, while others have been outright hostile to it. An equally serious problem has been religious particularism: long-standing theological differences among evangelicals have inhibited political cooperation. It has been even harder to reach out beyond evangelicalism to members of other religious traditions who might share political concerns, particularly Catholics and African Americans. And the entrepreneurial tendencies among evangelical leaders have been a further drag on cooperation, as each leader looks out for his or her own interests.

Another weakness is the intense and sometimes extreme views of movement activists. The very opinions that motivate these people to engage in politics often make them difficult to work with. This problem has seriously interfered with political alliances with secular conservatives. Central to these difficulties is the movement's social-issues agenda, which is controversial in many quarters. Attempts to set priorities, broaden the movement's goals, or compromise on such issues can become a source of conflict. The division between purists and pragmatists is common in movement politics, of course, but may be especially problematic in the Christian Right because of the movement's religious dimension (Green et al. 1994).

Finally, the Christian Right's activities and agenda can produce intense countermobilization by opponents, particularly liberal social movements, many of which draw on the natural opponents of evangelicals: religious progressives and the secular population (Wilcox 1994). In addition, many important social institutions, including the news media, the entertainment industry, public and higher education, and the professions, are also often critical of the Christian Right's agenda. And key elements of the movement's agenda are not popular with the public, making it possible to mobilize large blocs of voters in opposition. When combined, all these weaknesses can present formidable obstacles to the movement.

Potential Results

The Christian Right can fit into the political process in at least three ways (Wilcox, Green, and Rozell 1995). First, the movement must be in contention: it must exploit its strengths and overcome its weaknesses sufficiently to permit it to participate in the political process with some hope of success. Or put another way, if the movement is not in contention, it is of little consequence. Indeed, much of the literature on the Christian Right tells how the movement gathered momentum over the last two decades, reaching the point where it could be sufficiently active in enough places to matter politically (Rozell and Wilcox 1996).

Having the ability to participate in politics begs the question of the results of such participation, and here we can imagine two opposite situations. On the one hand, the Christian Right can be consolidated into a broader political coalition and thus contribute to victories at the polls and to policy making after the election. Consolidation is most likely to occur when the Christian Right is strong, adopts a pragmatic style, and operates in a political context that is both competitive and conservative (Green, Guth, and Hill 1993).

On the other hand, the Christian Right can participate in confrontation, warring with would-be allies and preventing the development of broader coalitions. Confrontation can produce defeat at the polls and thus limit influence on subsequent policy making. Confrontation is most likely to occur when the Christian Right is weaker, adopts a purist style, and operates in a political context that is both competitive and diverse. Consolidation and confrontation are not mutually exclusive categories, of course, and elements of both can occur together.

Movement contention, consolidation, and confrontation take place in the context of candidate-centered politics. In contemporary American elections, candidates themselves are the most dynamic element of campaigns, and their quality and efforts are usually decisive (cf. Salmore and Salmore 1989). Thus, the impact of the Christian Right comes chiefly from its association with candidates: strong candidacies help the movement succeed at the polls and poor ones produce high rates of failure. Once the Christian Right is in contention, consolidation increases the probability that it will be associated with strong candidates and effective campaigns, while confrontation reduces these prospects.

Movement Strengths and Weaknesses in 1996

How did the Christian Right cope with its strengths and weaknesses in 1996? Overall, the movement further exploited the former and overcame some of the latter. Other weaknesses still hampered its efforts, however, and new ones appeared. These trends can be seen in a brief review of the movement's three strata.

Leadership and Organization

In 1996, the Christian Coalition was the preeminent movement organization, and its executive director, Ralph Reed, its chief strategist. The success of the Coalition appeared to derive in equal measure from its effective organization and its pragmatic style. Its resources continued to expand in 1996, with the organization reporting a membership of 1.9 million and some two thousand local chapters in all fifty states. The other major movement organizations, Concerned Women for America and Focus on the Family, appear to have maintained their size and activity level, together perhaps equaling those of the Coalition. In addition, numerous smaller organizations were active, many organized at the state or local level. Most of these groups appear to have also maintained their size and activity level, although some, such as the Oregon Citizens Alliance, suffered a decline, and others, such as Maine's Christian Civic League, were quite weak.

The case studies reveal this organizational diversity. The Christian Coalition was prominent in nearly all the states covered but was stronger in some places (South Carolina, Texas, and Georgia) and weaker in others (Michigan and Oregon). Concerned Women and the Focus on the Family affiliates were the next most common groups, followed by several organizations associated with schools, such as Citizens for Excellence in Education and home schooling groups. Prominent regional or state groups included the American Family Association in South Carolina, the Traditional Values Coalition in California,

Citizens for Traditional Values in Michigan, and the Citizens Alliances in Oregon and Washington. The case studies also note the importance of organizations routinely allied with the Christian Right, including the Right to Life committees and the Eagle Forum.

This mix of organizations allowed the Christian Right and its allies to develop and deploy extensive electoral resources. The movement seems to have exploited its religious base among evangelical Protestants with increasing success. These gains resulted in part from the diminution of two weaknesses that have long troubled the movement. Evangelicals have become increasingly accepting of political activity (Pew Research Center 1996), and the effects of religious particularism have declined, allowing for fuller cooperation among different kinds of evangelicals (Wilcox, Rozell, and Gunn 1997). South Carolina and Texas are good examples of these trends.

Other weaknesses remain. For instance, competitive tendencies among evangelical leaders were problematic, and the multiple movement organizations often either failed to cooperate or openly conflicted with one another. Michigan is a good example of the former and Minnesota an example of the latter. The movement organizations also continue to have difficulty recruiting support from nonevangelicals, despite high-profile efforts among blacks, Hispanics, and Catholics. In fact, as the Florida and California cases reveal, the movement may have further alienated these groups by opposing immigration.

In the summer of 1996, Christian Right organizations confronted a new obstacle: the federal government. In response to a complaint by the Democratic National Committee, the Federal Election Commission (FEC) filed a civil suit against the Christian Coalition alleging violations of the campaign finance laws (Marcus 1996). The Coalition was accused of making illegal corporate contributions to Republican candidates and illegally coordinating its activities with Republican campaigns. Both of these claims revolve around the strong GOP bias in the Coalition's "nonpartisan" voter guides. Should the FEC prevail, the Coalition would be required to operate as a political action committee, subject to disclosure requirements and other regulations. Such a decision might well imperil the Coalition's tax-exempt status and that of cooperating churches. Although the lawsuit probably had only modest effects on the 1996 campaign (McCord 1996), an FEC victory could affect the movement's effectiveness.

Activists

As in 1994, the Christian Right deployed an extensive activist corps during the campaign. While the exact numbers are not known, a careful review of group claims, conservative mailing lists, and comments by reliable observers suggests that overall, the activist corps probably numbered a little over 200,000 nationwide, up modestly from 1994. Some of these activists were part of well-coordinated local chapters and others were less sophisticated solo operators (Berkowitz and Green 1996). They were active in a variety of settings, from Christian Right operations to party committees to candidate organizations. The major activity was the distribution of voter guides, often in association with churches (Niebuhr 1996). For instance, the Christian Coalition claimed to have given out some 45 million voter guides in the fall campaign involving some 125,000 churches. Other organizations also distributed voter guides, so the total may have been significantly higher.

The dedication and intensity of Christian Right activists have become legendary, and they are mentioned in nearly all of the case studies. The activist corps appears to have been most numerous in states that have large populations of evangelicals and that have become politically competitive in recent times, such as South Carolina. Highly competitive states with smaller evangelical populations—for example, Minnesota and Oregon—appear to have had fewer activists. And in some states the level of activism was very modest. In Maine, for example, the small number of evangelicals, combined with a liberal culture and a tradition of political independence, has limited the movement's activist corps. In West Virginia, the lack of political competition and the dominance of economic issues have kept a large evangelical population from becoming mobilized.

The movement activists are also known for their zealotry and sometimes extreme views. Not surprisingly, conflict with other activists, particularly moderate Republicans, is a staple of the case studies. Such conflicts were common even in places where the Christian Right was relatively strong, such as Texas, and were especially sharp in states where the movement was weaker, such as Virginia. Clearly, pragmatism helped reduce the level of conflict, as in Washington State, and purism intensified disagreements, as in Oregon. The pragmatism-purism divide ran deep in the movement activist corps— observers identified four significant factions in 1996 (Penning and Smidt 1996)—weakening the movement's overall effectiveness. The disappointments of the presidential campaign may exacerbate these disagreements in the future.

Opponents of the Christian Right were much better organized and more vocal in 1996 than in 1994. Groups critical of the movement, such as People for the American Way, Americans United for Separation of Church and State, and the Institute for First Amendment Studies, produced a steady stream of information on, and criticism of, movement activities. A favorite target in 1996 was the voter guides of the Christian Coalition, which were attacked for inaccuracy and partisan bias (People for the American Way 1996). These efforts were often part of "shadow campaigns" run by labor unions and environmental and women's groups against conservative Republican candidates, who were also supported by the Christian Right (see the North Carolina case study, chap. 5).

The most interesting aspect of the opposition to the Christian Right was the emergence of a "Christian Left" at the grass roots, including the Call for Renewal, an effort of liberal and moderate evangelicals, and the Interfaith Alliance, an ecumenical group with substantial support among mainline Protestants. The latter took a page out of the Christian Coalition's playbook, developing 109 local chapters in thirty-six states with some 40,000 members and using this structure to distribute some 5 million voter guides (*Norfolk Virginian-Pilot* 1996). Interestingly, the development of the Interfaith Alliance parallels the emergence of the Christian Right in some important respects. It was inspired by secular liberals and launched with assistance from the Democratic Party, much as the original Christian Right groups were proposed by secular conservatives and assisted by the GOP. Like the original Christian Right groups, the Interfaith Alliance was initially led by, and directed at, favorably disposed clergy. And its grassroots organization was an afterthought, arising from a strong local response to the group's public activities, much as occurred with the Christian Right. If these efforts prosper, the Christian Right may face stiff opposition from moderate and liberal Christians in the near future.

Mass Support

What about support for the movement in the mass public in 1996? A survey taken before the fall election suggests that the movement faced both challenges and opportunities in this regard (Kellstedt et al. 1997). Overall, the mass public was divided on the movement, with 32 percent expressing a positive and 33 percent a negative view, figures that are largely unchanged from 1994. The Christian Right was much more popular among white evangelicals (55 percent favorable to 19 percent unfavorable) and similarly unpopular in the secular population (14 percent to 56 percent). All told, the core constituency of the movement remained somewhere between one-sixth and one-fifth of the electorate, depending on how movement support is measured. The public was also divided on the social issues that are central to the Christian Right's agenda, with the movement's positions often quite unpopular.

Consolidation and Confrontation in 1996

When the foregoing evidence on leadership and organization, activists, and public support is examined, it is clear that the Christian Right was in contention in many, though not all, parts of the country in 1996. But how well did the movement fare in the actual campaigns under consideration? Once in contention, the Christian Right can influence candidacies in at least three ways: by recruiting candidates, participating in the nominating process, and participating in the general election campaigns. As in 1994, the Christian Right was active in all three ways, with its weaknesses most evident at the level of candidate recruitment and its strengths clearer in direct voter mobilization. The movement's weaknesses in these processes frequently provoked confrontation, whereas its strengths tended to have the opposite effect.

Candidate Recruitment

Like other movements, the Christian Right can have the most influence in candidate-centered politics when it participates in the actual recruitment of candidates. But candidate recruitment creates a classic dilemma for the movement: whether to back candidates who best articulate the movement's values and goals or to support candidates who have the best chance of being elected. Movement purists tend to advocate the former, while pragmatists are at least equally concerned with electability. This dilemma becomes especially intense when candidates arise from within the movement itself.

More often than not "self-starting" candidates bring the Christian Right's weaknesses to the fore, including its internal divisions, extreme views, and unpopular positions. Even when pragmatic leaders advise against it, the activist corps is often impressed by such candidates' commitment to the movement's agenda. Beside having unpopular positions on issues, self-starters frequently lack other credentials, such as previous political experience or government service and a well-developed agenda on other issues of concern to voters. Not surprisingly, such candidates are rarely successful. Few obtain major party nominations, and those who do tend to lose by large margins. The combination of unpopular positions and lack of electability can generate ferocious confrontations between Christian Rightists and other activists.

All told, there were probably fewer movement self-starters in 1996 than in 1994, but there were several good examples. For instance, Monti Moreno in Minnesota and Clint Day in Georgia were classic self-starters, and both had an impact on the election outcomes. Perhaps the best example, however, was Ellen Craswell in Washington State. Craswell was active in Republican politics before she became associated with the Christian Right and performed yeoman service for the movement. Thus, when she chose to run for the GOP gubernatorial nomination, she had enough support to succeed despite her weaknesses as a candidate in the general election, where she was defeated by the less-than-formidable Democratic candidate. A number of movement self-starters who were swept into office in 1994 were defeated in 1996, including Andrea Seastrand in California, Steve Stockman in Texas, Randy Tate in Washington State, and David Funderburk in North Carolina.

However, good candidates do arise from time to time from within the movement, and under the right circumstances, they can succeed. Jim Ryun of Kansas was a good example in 1996, as was Todd Tiahrt, another Kansan, who was elected in 1994 and reelected in 1996. Other candidates associated with the Christian Right were also reelected in 1996, including Steve Largent in Oklahoma, Jon Christensen in Nebraska, Linda Smith in Washington State, and Helen Chenoweth in Idaho. However, the defeat of Robert Dornan in California, a longtime supporter of the movement, surely ranked as a major setback.

As the case studies of Oregon and California report, the Christian Right has been very active in ballot issues as well. Politically, a referendum on a single issue in the movement's agenda resembles the situation of a self-starting movement candidate. And as with self-starters, such efforts frequently fail, largely because they present an unpopular issue in isolation. In 1996, the movement had high hopes of a "parental rights" referendum in Colorado, which was soundly defeated (Havermann 1996). The movement had more success in opposing gambling initiatives, and it was crucial to the passage of Proposition 209, an anti–affirmative action amendment, in California.

Nomination Politics

More pragmatic Christian Rightists have sought to minimize the problems of movement self-starters by becoming involved in the rough-and-tumble of nomination politics. In some cases, movement activists have helped recruit credible candidates who shared their goals, but mostly they have supported candidates recruited by other means. This process is quite informal and mostly local, involving three-way contacts between candidates, activists, and leaders. Under the best circumstances, this kind of involvement reduces the risks to the movement, since the disagreements between purists and pragmatists can be negotiated around a particular candidate. This seems to have happened with David Beasley in South Carolina and Rod Grams in Minnesota, both elected in 1994. Examples in 1996 include Sam Brownback in Kansas, Tim Hutchinson in Arkansas, and Jeff Sessions in Alabama.

There is no guarantee, of course, that such a process will succeed: even when self-starters are avoided, movement activists may back less viable candidates. Good examples of this problem occurred in 1994 with Oliver North in Virginia and Allen Quist in Minnesota. Less dramatic but equally unsuccessful examples were seen in Georgia and North Carolina in 1996, where the Republicans passed over more competitive candidates and ended up losing close races. Similar scenarios were played out in Louisiana with Woody Jenkins and in several congressional races in Georgia. Such cases can produce a "double whammy": bitter confrontations over nominations and defeat in the general election. Of course, this problem works both ways. More moderate Republicans can lose elections if they alienate movement activists, such as may have happened with Rudy Boschwitz in Minnesota.

Overall, the Christian Right seems to have been less pragmatic in 1996 than in 1994, when the movement backed successful mainstream conservatives such as John Engler in Michigan, Pete Wilson in California, and George W. Bush in Texas. As several of the case studies point out, the Christian Right does best when it is part of a broader consolidated coalition led by a mainstream conservative candidate.

These case studies starkly reveal the importance of nomination rules. For example, the use of a state convention in Virginia allowed the Christian Right to help nominate Oliver North in 1994, but in 1996 the use of a primary election allowed John Warner to overcome vehement opposition by the movement. Similarly, the "jungle" primary in Washington State allowed Ellen Craswell to win the nomination. Clearly, rules that benefit the Christian Right do not necessarily benefit the party.

The Christian Right's involvement in nomination politics parallels its involvement in Republican Party organizations. Partly for ideological reasons and partly for strategic ones, the Christian Right has chosen to focus on the GOP. The case studies strongly suggest that the movement has gained considerable influence in Republican organizations (see Persinos 1994). However, these gains yield mixed results. The South Carolina and Kansas cases show that influence in the party can pay off, at least in the short run, but the California and Florida cases reveal that the opposite result is equally likely. And the case of West Virginia reveals the costs of a one-party strategy. (For a review of Christian Right involvement in the presidential campaign, see the final chapter.)

Campaign Support

Once candidates are nominated, the Christian Right can campaign on their behalf. If nomination struggles reveal the movement's weaknesses, then general election activities reveal its strengths. All of the case studies point to the positive effects of the movement's grassroots activities. In most cases, the distribution of voter guides was the centerpiece of these activities, but movement activists performed a wide variety of other roles, including raising funds for favored candidates. These efforts can be critical to Republican candidates, even those who are strongly at odds with the movement. For example, John Warner benefited from the general election efforts of the Christian Coalition, despite having been targeted for defeat in the primary. This case surely represents one of the most ironic results of the 1996 election.

However, too close a connection to the Christian Right can hurt even mainstream conservatives in the general election. A good example is Gordon Smith in Oregon. He lost a very close special Senate election in 1995 in part because of the endorsement of the Oregon Citizens Alliance, but in 1996 he won a close race for the state's other Senate seat after having publicly disassociated himself from the Alliance while retaining strong support from conservative Christian voters.

How important were conservative Christians on election day? Overall, they clearly helped the Republicans, and probably more so than in 1994. The postelection poll cited earlier showed that white evangelicals accounted for 28 percent of the congressional vote, two-thirds of which went for the GOP. A more restrictive definition of the Christian Right's mass constituency in exit polls reveals that its adherents made up 17 percent of the votes cast, and almost three-quarters voted Republican. Indeed, all the case studies reveal that white evangelicals were a critical constituency for the GOP. It is worth noting, however, that in none of the cases did the evangelical vote constitute a majority of GOP votes. Clearly, GOP candidates must build broader coalitions to win, even in states where the movement is strong and evangelical voters numerous. Consolidation makes this result possible; confrontation reduces the chances of success.

The Christian Right in 1996

Table 1.1 offers a brief summary of the Christian Right's role in the case studies that follow. The movement was clearly in contention in the first twelve states, where its role varied from consolidation to confrontation. At one extreme are South Carolina and Texas, where the movement has made itself a key constituency in the state Republican parties. In Georgia and North Carolina, the movement was less comfortably part of the GOP, while in Virginia, Florida, Michigan, and California, the Christian Right had a mixed relationship with the party. Oregon and Washington State were a step more confrontational, and full-scale confrontation occurred in Minnesota and Kansas. Finally, the Christian Right was not in contention in Maine or West Virginia.

These case studies reveal a fascinating web of factors that contribute to the impact of the Christian Right. However, the foregoing discussion suggests several factors that underlie the pattern shown in table 1.1. First, the movement's

Table 1.1
The Christian Right in 1996: Summary of Case Studies

Movement in Contention					
Consolidation ....Mixed..Confrontation					
South Carolina	Georgia	Virginia	Michigan	Oregon	Minnesota
Texas	North Carolina	Florida	California	Washington	Kansas
Movement Not in Contention					
West Virginia					
Maine					

ability to be a player is related to the successful exploitation of its strengths and minimization of its weaknesses in the context of political competition; the absence of contention seems to be related to severe movement weaknesses or the lack of political competition. Second, once the movement is in contention, consolidation is most likely where movement strengths are great and the political context is conservative, such as in southern states. Third, confrontation is most likely where movement weaknesses are great and the political context diverse, such as in the Midwest and on the West Coast. And finally, mixed situations occur where the movement is relatively strong and the context relatively diverse. Overall, then, the Christian Right has found a small but prominent niche in national politics.

References

Berkowitz, Laura, and John C. Green. 1996. "Charting the Coalition: The Local Chapters of the Ohio Christian Coalition." In *Sojourners in the Wilderness: The Christian Right in Comparative Perspective,* ed. Corwin E. Smidt and James M. Penning. Lanham, Md.: Rowman & Littlefield.

Green, John C. 1995. "The Christian Right and the 1994 Elections: An Overview." Chap. 1 in *God at the Grass Roots,* ed. Mark J. Rozell and Clyde Wilcox. Lanham, Md.: Rowman & Littlefield.

Green, John C., James L. Guth, and Kevin Hill. 1993. "Faith and Election: The Christian Right in Congressional Campaigns 1978–1988." *Journal of Politics* 55:80–91.

Green, John C., James L. Guth, Lyman A. Kellstedt, and Corwin E. Smidt. 1994. "Uncivil Challenges? Support for Civil Liberties among Religious Activists." *Journal of Political Science* 22:25–50.

Green, John C., James L. Guth, Corwin E. Smidt, and Lyman A. Kellstedt. 1996. *Religion and the Culture Wars: Dispatches from the Front.* Lanham, Md.: Rowman & Littlefield.

Havemann, Judith. 1996. "Coloradans Reject Parental Rights Issue." *Washington Post* (7 November): A41.

Jelen, Ted G. 1991. *The Political Mobilization of Religious Belief.* Westport, Conn.: Praeger.

Jorstad, Erling. 1993. *Popular Religion in America.* Westport, Conn.: Greenwood Press.

Kellstedt, Lyman A., John C. Green, James L. Guth, and Corwin Smidt. 1997. "The 49 Percent Solution: Religion in the 1996 Election." *Books and Culture* 3(2): 24–25.

Leege, David C. 1992. "Coalitions, Cues, Strategic Politics, and the Staying Power of the Religious Right." *PS* 25: 198–204.

Leege, David C., and Lyman A. Kellstedt, eds. 1993. *Rediscovering the Religious Factor in American Politics.* Armonk, N.Y.: M. E. Sharpe.

Marcus, Ruth. 1996. "FEC Details Case against Christian Coalition." *Washington Post* (1 August): A10.

McCord, Julia. 1996. "Election Guide Suit Sparks Debate." *Omaha World Herald* (25 August).

Niebuhr, Gustav. 1996. "At Churches across the Nation, Christian Coalition Flexes Political Muscle." *New York Times* (29 October): A12.

Norfolk Virginian-Pilot. 1996. "Religious Blocs Rally to Dull Christian Coalition." (29 October): A2.

Penning, James M., and Corwin Smidt. 1996. "What Coalition?" *Christian Century* (15 January): 37–38.

People for the American Way. 1996. "State-by-State Analysis of Christian Coalition Voter Guides in the 1996 Election." Washington, D.C.: People for the American Way.

Persinos, John F. 1994. "Has the Christian Right Taken Over the Republican Party?" *Campaigns and Elections,* 21 September, 21–24.

Pew Research Center. 1996. *The Diminishing Divide: American Churches, American Politics.* Washington, D.C.: Pew Research Center.

Rozell, Mark J., and Clyde Wilcox. 1995. *God at the Grass Roots: The Christian Right in the 1994 Elections.* Lanham, Md.: Rowman & Littlefield.

———. 1996. *Second Coming: The New Christian Right in Virginia Politics.* Baltimore: Johns Hopkins University Press.

Salmore, Barbara G., and Stephen A. Salmore. 1989. *Candidates, Parties, and Campaigns.* 2d ed. Washington D.C.: Congressional Quarterly Press.

Wilcox, Clyde. 1992. *God's Warriors.* Baltimore: Johns Hopkins University Press.

———. 1994. "Premillennialists at the Millennium: Some Reflections on the Christian Right in the Twenty-first Century." *Sociology of Religion* 55: 243–62.

Wilcox, Clyde, John C. Green, and Mark J. Rozell. 1995. "Faith, Hope, and Conflict: The Christian Right and the Republican Party." Paper presented at the annual meeting of the American Sociological Association, Washington, D.C.

Wilcox, Clyde, Mark J. Rozell, and Ronald Gunn. 1996. "Religious Coalitions in the New Christian Right." *Social Science Quarterly* 77: 543–58.

2

South Carolina Christian Right: Just Part of the Family Now?

James L. Guth and Oran P. Smith

South Carolina presents an excellent opportunity to look at the development of the Christian Right in a most favorable environment. Not only has the movement been active in South Carolina longer than in other states, but it is almost a microcosm of the national movement. The state GOP saw an infusion of separatist fundamentalists into the party between 1964 and 1976, a movement that has now become part of the party establishment. In addition, the Falwell Moral Majority had a very modest presence during the early 1980s, but it left little impression. This first "fundamentalist" phase was followed by the mobilization of charismatic and Pentecostal Protestants during the 1988 presidential campaign of Marion G. "Pat" Robertson, a drive that had little effect on the electorate but resulted in a strong organizational challenge to GOP autonomy. The migration to the right of the state's largest religious constituency, Southern Baptists, has also had important long-term political effects. In addition, other organized manifestations of the Christian Right, including the American Family Association and Focus on the Family, are represented by state lobbies, filling out the cast of actors. Despite the familiar cast, South Carolina religious politics has many unique features and, to paraphrase Tip O'Neill, "All religious politics is local."

Perhaps it is not surprising, then, that many analysts consider the South Carolina Republican organization to be dominated by the Christian Right. The reality, however, is much more complex, revealing many of the fissures within the movement and within the state Republican Party. The full picture should warn us against easy generalizations about either the Christian Right as a political movement or its likely effect on the prospects of the Republican Party.

Prologue: The Religious Context

Like several other states, South Carolina has long laid claim to being the "buckle" of the southern Bible Belt. Although economic development and consequent in-migration from other parts of the country (and the world) have begun to diversify the population, especially in the state's three major metropolitan areas, the population is still dominated by conservative Protestants, especially Southern Baptists, the state's (and nation's) largest Protestant denomination. Indeed, Southern Baptists constituted over 40 percent of the church members in South Carolina in 1990. The state also has a large number of adherents to mainline Protestant churches, such as the United Methodist Church (14 percent), the Presbyterian Church in the U.S.A. (4 percent), and the Evangelical Lutheran and Episcopal denominations (3 and 2 percent respectively). There are also numerous (and mostly uncounted) independent fundamentalist congregations, usually Baptist, and a growing number of independent charismatic churches, often quite large, located in the major suburban areas. Other evangelical denominations, such as the Presbyterian Church in America, have enjoyed considerable growth and have begun to play a noticeable political role. The African American community is served by various black Baptist denominations (16 percent of the state's church members) and many other historically black churches such as the African Methodist Episcopal Church Zion (Bradley et al. 1992, 31). These churches and their leaders continue to play an important role in African American politics.

For most of the twentieth century, the centrality of the racial issue in South Carolina politics precluded any large role for religion in party politics (see Guth 1995). But this began to change in the 1960s and 1970s, as the Republican Party first challenged the Democrats' dominance of state politics. The rising GOP of the 1950s and early 1960s reflected the religious background of its new urban, often "immigrant," leadership: traditionally upper-status mainline Protestants such as Episcopalians, Presbyterians, Methodists, and some "First Church" Southern Baptists. But other religious forces soon crashed the party, mobilized by political movements affecting the GOP.

The First Wave of Christian Right Activism

The first encroachment by the Christian Right came in the 1960s as the Goldwater movement attracted many independent fundamentalists, especially those owing allegiance to Bob Jones University (BJU) in Greenville, a leading training ground for the strictest wing of the movement. This initial infusion of religious activists was largely uncoordinated, but in 1976 two BJU loyalists, Elmer Rumminger of Greenville, a faculty member at the university, and Orrin Briggs of Columbia, a BJU alumnus and lawyer for the South Carolina Association of Christian Schools, masterminded a takeover of GOP precinct committees and, as a result, captured the Greenville County GOP, the bulwark of the state's staunchest metropolitan Republican stronghold. The objectives of the new activists were mixed: some wanted to advance the candidacy of challenger Ronald Reagan against incumbent president Gerald Ford, others wanted to push the entire GOP platform to the right, and many were concerned with the Carter administration's "attacks" on Christian schools (see Smith 1997).

The BJU infiltration met strong resistance from regular Republicans, accustomed to running their own show without interference. The two factions certainly had somewhat different agendas, personal styles, and social backgrounds. Many religious activists were little inclined to tolerate even modest religious deviation by other Republicans: one BJU enthusiast at a county convention demanded to know of future governor Carroll Campbell, then a state senate candidate, *when* he had been "born again." For a time the regulars threatened to defect, but the electoral defeat suffered by the GOP in 1976 soon forced the two factions back together.

The subsequent assimilation of the "BJU crowd" into the state GOP reflected several factors. First, the BJU forces were not numerous enough to control local party organizations in most of the state, although they established their presence in many areas. Even in areas they dominated, however, almost all the candidates they ran for local offices lost. Second, party leaders such as Fourth District congressman Carroll Campbell and Governor James Edwards played critical roles in cultivating support among the BJU contingent, patiently mediating intraparty disputes and rewarding cooperative behavior. At the same time, the university's leadership apparently decided to forgo further organized political efforts, preferring to emphasize BJU's spiritual mission. Thus, although the "Bob Jones Republicans" remained prominent in the South Carolina GOP, they were active primarily as individuals; many eventually attained important party and elected positions. In any event, this strategic decision by the university meant that the BJU crowd was soon dominated by savvy and strategic politicians, rather than by amateur religious enthusiasts, permitting easier accommodation with the regulars, who were inclined to trade platform concessions to the BJU forces in return for loyal support. Although the fundamentalists were often more concerned with moral issues than their regular counterparts, the day-to-day political or governmental implications of this difference were sometimes hard to detect, and many BJU politicos gained the respect even of their ideological and partisan opponents (Hammond and Gladfelter 1996). By the mid-1980s, the BJU Republicans were a distinct but fairly well integrated part of the state party. As Terry Haskins, an influential member of the BJU contingent, told journalist Alan Ehrenhalt, the fundamentalists and the regulars "agreed on everything except where to go to church" (Ehrenhalt 1991, 98).

The role of the BJU conservatives in South Carolina was a unique feature of Christian Right politics, tied to the location of the university. Although BJU graduates have appeared in national Christian Right leadership roles, been elected to Congress and legislatures in other states, and provided a considerable corps of activists in other regions, this portion of the fundamentalist movement has refrained from national political organization. In South Carolina, however, BJU forces have played a role out of all proportion to their numbers in GOP politics, supplying a large cadre of skilled activists, who usually support the most conservative candidate in the GOP primaries, unless that candidate has clearly unacceptable religious tendencies (such as charismatic or Pentecostal beliefs), but invariably behaving as pragmatic tacticians, supporting the ultimate Republican candidate in the general election, thereby winning the gratitude of party leaders (Smith 1997).

The dominance of BJU fundamentalists did, however, preempt any major involvement by Jerry Falwell's Moral Majority in South Carolina Republican politics. Although the Moral Majority had little grassroots organization anywhere, it had virtually none in South Carolina, aside from a couple of megachurches affiliated with Falwell's Baptist Bible Fellowship. And the few candidates with Falwell connections usually failed at the polls, especially in BJU precincts. The animosity between the Joneses and Falwell precluded any merger of forces. This antagonism was spurred in part by organizational competition, as their respective fundamentalist universities competed for many of the same potential students, but the differences were ultimately theological: as true separatists, the Joneses rejected Falwell's eagerness to work with anyone—Catholics, Jews, Mormons—who agreed with his political perspective, and they distrusted the seeming centrality of politics over religion in Falwell's empire. In any event, the Moral Majority never represented a threat to GOP harmony in South Carolina.

Just about the time when the state and local Republican organizations had managed to incorporate the BJU contingent, the charismatic and Pentecostal forces of religious broadcaster Pat Robertson presented a far more serious challenge. Although these religious communities represented only a small, if growing, part of the state's population, the Robertson organization, as in other states, mobilized contingents large enough to capture poorly attended GOP precinct meetings and almost control the state convention in 1987, in preparation for the 1988 presidential primary. They were narrowly repelled by the regulars (with the help of BJU allies) only through astute maneuvering supported by friendly judges. Robertson's organizational near victories were not repeated in the 1988 presidential primary, however, where he finished a poor third, with only a fifth of the vote, far behind winner George Bush and runner-up Bob Dole. Robertson had failed to expand his religious base much beyond its original charismatic and Pentecostal core. The BJU Republicans favored Jack Kemp, but most of the state's large contingent of born-again Christians voted for Vice President George Bush, including most Southern Baptist clergy and a majority of their congregations. To keep peace in the party, Governor Campbell, acting on behalf of the Bush campaign, gave the Robertson supporters some party offices and influence, including many delegate slots to the 1988 GOP national convention.

Nevertheless, the integration of the Robertson forces into the state GOP did not go smoothly. After three years of inactivity, Robertson loyalists were reorganized in 1991 as the South Carolina Christian Coalition, led by chairwoman Roberta Combs. Although the Christian Coalition's national leader, Ralph Reed, was often criticized by other Christian Right leaders as being far too accommodating to Republican leaders, hoping to win a "place at the table," the South Carolina organization under Combs was often much more belligerent, going for organizational control. In its first political outing in the 1992 elections, the Coalition distributed hundreds of thousands of voter guides, helping George Bush carry the state handily and assisting GOP congressional candidates as well. Indeed, the Coalition's involvement in Fourth District congressional challenger Bob Inglis's upset victory over incumbent Liz Patterson eventually attracted a suit against the Coalition by the Federal Election Commission (Hoover 1996c), although Inglis's surprising victory was probably more the result of his own grassroots campaign, support from the BJU crowd, and the work of activists from his own Presbyterian Church in America.

Still, buoyed by such victories, continued organizing in the state's three major metropolitan areas, and some success in recruiting Southern Baptists and other conservative Protestants, especially those active in local antiabortion groups, the Christian Coalition flooded the 1993 GOP precinct meetings, narrowly controlled the state Republican convention, and helped elect Henry McMaster as state GOP chairman over Greenville Republican Knox White, a Campbell protégé and moderate conservative who had nevertheless built strong ties with the BJU Republicans (Graham, Moore, and Petrusak 1994). As a former Republican appointee as U.S. attorney, organizer of Jack Kemp's 1988 campaign in the state, and an unsuccessful U.S. Senate nominee, McMaster had a good bit of support among party regulars as well. Upon his election he attempted to recognize all factions of the party in his staff selections, thereby adding Coalition activists to the state party organization. After a series of embarrassing incidents involving the Christian Coalition's objectives and operatives, however, McMaster sought to distance himself from the Christian Right organization, staving off Coalition efforts to gain operational control of the state GOP executive committee. He also worked hard, with considerable success, to keep disgruntled regulars, led by his predecessor, Barry Wynn, from setting up an alternative organization. Within a year or so, he had won the gratitude of many party regulars, putting himself in an almost impregnable position for reelection, despite the hostility of some erstwhile religious allies (Smith 1997).

The Gathering of the Forces: The 1994 Gubernatorial Campaign

The culmination of two decades of Christian Right development in South Carolina came in 1994, with the election of David Beasley as governor. Beasley demonstrated the electoral advantage of being part of the state's largest religious constituency, Southern Baptists, while cultivating the less numerous but more politicized fundamentalist and Pentecostal groups. Born to a wealthy and politically influential banking family, Beasley was elected to the state legislature at age twenty-one and rose quickly to become Democratic majority leader in the House. Brought up as a "Methodist-Presbyterian," he underwent a religious conversion in 1985 and found that his Democratic identity clashed with his new "born-again" conservatism on both social and economic issues. He became an outspoken advocate for antiabortion legislation and, in 1991, crossed over to the GOP (Bursey 1994).

During the next three years Beasley ran a quiet, two-tiered campaign for governor. First, he recounted his religious conversion to myriad conservative churches, a stump speech that was distributed via audiotape and religious TV stations all over the state. Although he spoke frequently in Pentecostal and charismatic churches, he also cultivated the BJU crowd and certainly was one of the few speakers welcomed in both venues. But his main focus was on congregations and pastors of his own new denomination in the South Carolina Baptist Convention (SCBC). Perhaps because of his favored status with Pat Robertson's forces, many South Carolinians assumed that Beasley himself was a part of the Christian Coalition's religious constituency. Recognizing the importance of the Southern Baptist vote, Beasley got the word of his own membership out among Baptist churches. As he told one of the authors, this meant bypassing SCBC bureaucrats, many of whom were closet political moderates and even Democrats, and appealing to the more conservative elected leaders and Baptist laity who had come to dominate the state convention's recent proceedings. All these efforts, in Beasley's judgment, had considerable effect (Smith 1997). At the same time, Beasley pursued traditional Republican constituencies, cultivating business groups, fellow GOP state legislators, and, most important, Governor Campbell's formidable electoral machine, which had carried the state for George Bush in two presidential primaries and two general elections.

Thus, as the 1994 campaign started, Beasley was the candidate both of religious insurgency and of much (but not all) of the GOP establishment, eventually defeating two veteran Republican competitors in the primary and a runoff, despite the efforts of both to make his association with the Christian Right an issue. Beasley's vote was highest in counties with the largest populations of Southern Baptists and Pentecostals, while his rivals did better in areas where these groups were less numerous. First Impressions Research, Inc. found that Beasley won 66 percent of the (largely Southern) Baptist vote, carried only a narrow majority of Methodists and a plurality of Presbyterians, and had a minority among Episcopalians, Lutherans, and other mainline Protestants, as well as the state's small Catholic population. In a similar vein, Beasley won 61 percent of Republican voters who attended church every week, slipping to a 43 percent plurality among those who attended most weeks, and doing very poorly among nonattenders. The results by voters' religious self-identification followed a similar pattern: Beasley captured 75 percent of charismatics, 67 percent of evangelicals, 66 percent of fundamentalists, but only 43 percent of mainline Christians (Smith 1997). Very similar patterns appeared in the runoff primary, which Beasley won easily with 58 percent of the vote.

Not all Christian Right candidates did so well in the 1994 primaries, however, especially those who lacked support from Republican regulars (Guth 1995). The vote totals in other races suggested that the Christian Coalition and other conservative religious groups could muster only 35 to 40 percent of Republican primary voters when "pure" Christian Right types ran against GOP regulars. Whatever the result, the political maturation of the Christian Right groups was demonstrated by the subsequent willingness of most of the losing candidates to fall in behind the GOP regulars for the general election.

In the November general election, Beasley faced a formidable Democratic figure, Lieutenant Governor Nick Theodore of Greenville. During the campaign, both Beasley and Theodore stressed economic development, but from that point they diverged: Beasley emphasized family values and crime, advocated tax cuts, opposed a state lottery (a hot-button issue for religious conservatives), and suggested consideration of educational vouchers, while Theodore endorsed a state lottery to increase education funding (for public schools only), took a strong pro-choice stance on abortion (Beasley tried to downplay the issue), and constantly attacked Beasley's connection to the "extremist" Coalition. Thus, most of the issues that dominated the campaign had strong religious or moral overtones.

During the fall campaign, the Christian Coalition was again much in evidence, distributing guides and contacting friendly voters through phone banks.

But there was also a broader Christian Right effort that received much less coverage in the press: the BJU crowd turned out an overwhelming vote for Beasley, and the Palmetto Family Council (associated with James Dobson's Focus on the Family), the American Family Association of South Carolina, and a growing number of local religious groups also issued voter guides and worked in races for state, county, and school board offices (Guth 1995). Indeed, the strength of the movement was such that several mainline Protestant and Catholic leaders issued strong warnings on the danger of identifying the Christian faith with partisan (i.e., Republican) agendas.

On 8 November, Beasley won the governorship with 51 percent of the vote to Theodore's 48 percent. Whatever other factors may have been involved, the results suggest that Beasley benefited from a united Christian conservative effort. Although the BJU fundamentalists, the Christian Coalition, and Southern Baptists might not worship together, they certainly combined behind the Republican ticket. Overall, Beasley won 70 percent among white born-again Christians, who constitute a majority of the state's population. Although he did less well among white mainline Protestants, he still drew considerable statewide support from establishment Republicans. Evidently Beasley's open and prominent identification with the Christian Coalition did not turn away most mainstream Republicans, although he did trail slightly behind other Republican winners.

Once in office, the new governor moved quickly to shore up his religious base, using religious rhetoric in his public pronouncements, putting some moral issues on the agenda, and appointing a number of outspoken Christian activists to his administration, including BJU, Christian Coalition, and Southern Baptist adherents. None was exactly a puppet of the Christian Coalition, but all were new and different enough to make the Republican establishment nervous (Smith 1997). Beasley often touched base with Christian Right leaders, was a star at the 1995 Christian Coalition national meeting, and also appeared on Pat Robertson's *700 Club,* raising fear among some regular Republicans that he was cutting off his ties to the old party establishment. In any event, Beasley and the Christian Right groups would be major actors in the critical 1996 South Carolina presidential primary.

The 1996 Republican Primaries

The 1996 Republican presidential primary, then, represented the first national contest that would test the strength of various forces in the state GOP, both religious and regular. As in 1988 and 1992, the South Carolina GOP primary had a crucial position on the schedule, coming on Saturday, 2 March, just three days before eight state primaries on 5 March, the New York contest on 7 March, and another mass of seven primaries the following Tuesday. As in the 1988 campaign, South Carolina was a critical state for all the GOP contenders, but especially for front-runner Bob Dole and his major challenger, Pat Buchanan (Sack 1996; Gray 1996). Each made important overtures to Christian Right forces, which were arguing over their own strategies (Berke 1996).

The most critical maneuvering was that between the GOP candidates and the Christian Coalition. For its part, the Christian Coalition seemed determined to have a foot in the door of each potential nominee, or at least was resigned to the fact that its activists were divided over their initial choices. Roberta Combs's behavior suggested that the Coalition favored Senator Dole, the apparent choice of national Coalition leader Ralph Reed. Dole was also the candidate endorsed by both former governor Carroll Campbell and Governor Beasley, the Coalition's hero (Reed 1996, 243). Other Coalition leaders signed onto the Buchanan and Gramm campaigns, however, and Combs herself offered to provide all the acceptable candidates with key contacts and advice on how to win over Coalition activists. Nevertheless, more Coalition resources were available to Dole, who was perceived as the likely winner of the primary and eventual GOP nominee. Activists at the Coalition's preelection rally in Columbia gave Buchanan's stump speech a rousing ovation, but Dole's defense of his "100 percent" Christian Coalition voting record, his consistent antiabortion stance, and his emotional retelling of his life story were seen by many observers as a turning point in the campaign for Christian Right support (Reed 1996, 242).

The BJU forces were also divided, but they were even more frustrated by the development of the campaign. In the preliminary candidate maneuvering, the BJU leadership was clearly in the camp of Senator Phil Gramm of Texas (Wyman 1995; Broder 1996b). Although Gramm had antagonized some national Christian Right leaders by refusing to feature moral issues in his campaign, he found a much warmer reception on the campus of BJU and among other Christian conservatives in the Upstate, where he campaigned in the company of well-known Christian financial adviser and radio show host Larry Burkett. The BJU Republicans were left without a candidate, however, when, after poor showings in Iowa and New Hampshire, Gramm withdrew from the race and endorsed Dole. Most BJU activists then gravitated to the Buchanan camp. This was not an entirely unfamiliar location, as many had supported his quixotic challenge to President George Bush in the 1992 GOP primary, and the BJU precincts in Greenville had actually given Buchanan a majority over the incumbent president.

This support for the Catholic Buchanan might seem quite surprising to those familiar with the history of the fundamentalist movement, always fiercely anti-Catholic in both theology and religious rhetoric. The BJU enthusiasm for Buchanan reflected gratitude for his long-standing support for the university in its ongoing tax-status battles with the Internal Revenue Service and agreement with his strong moral traditionalism, as well as a certain sympathy for his strident nationalism. Nevertheless, the willingness of separatist fundamentalists to support a Catholic presidential candidate was certainly a major development in Christian Right politics. Charismatic and Pentecostal Christians have moved in the same direction, creating an ironic situation in which activists in each evangelical movement have backed a Catholic candidate but have not usually exhibited similar tolerance for the other's "nominees." In any event, one of Buchanan's most successful rallies in South Carolina took place at the Evangel Cathedral, a charismatic megachurch just off Interstate 85 in the Upstate. Although Buchanan did not win over all the evangelical faithful in attendance, his warm reception was another indicator of declining religious particularism on the Christian Right. As Houston Miles, the church's politically activist pastor noted, in the Pentecostal tradition, clergy historically "preached against two things: Communists and Catholics" (Brownstein 1996). But that had changed: a Buchanan supporter at the rally said that he once thought that Catholic candidacies were "a horrible thing, but now I think that a person can be a Catholic and still be a believer, still go to heaven, as long as he has faith in God" (Feldman 1996). Thus, the national Christian Coalition's well-advertised efforts to build a "Catholic Alliance" were reflected in the tentative alliance between Buchanan and part of the Christian Coalition's Pentecostal base.

Eventually, then, Buchanan stitched together a coalition with some strong religious elements (Hoover and Hammond 1996). His state steering committee included several Bob Jones activists, most notably state representative Terry Haskins, who initially headed the Gramm campaign, as well as several Christian Coalition county leaders, who rejected Ralph Reed's and Roberta Combs's dalliance with Dole. Henry Jordan, a veteran GOP activist and political candidate who led Pat Robertson's 1988 campaign in the state, was a vice chair of the Buchanan committee and sought to activate Christian Right forces. And the state's leading antiabortion movement figures were also well represented in the Buchanan camp. The committee also included representatives of anti–free trade groups, gun enthusiasts, and many former Perot supporters.

Thus, both the first and second wave Christian Right activists were deeply involved in the primary contest, although in rather complex formations. It is more difficult to assess the third Christian Right force in the state, the vote-rich South Carolina Baptists. Although the state Baptist convention, like those elsewhere, had moved to the right politically, it was not centrally organized for electoral involvement. Many South Carolina Baptists were active in the antiabortion movement and on a variety of other social issues, such as pornography, gay rights, and education, but lacked any central organizing forum. Many prominent Baptist lay leaders were successful business and professional people with close ties to the party establishment represented by Carroll Campbell and, to some extent, Governor Beasley. And most evidence points to a great deal of support for Senator Dole among the denomination's clerical leadership. A survey of South Carolina Baptist ministers by one of the authors reveals that even more than their counterparts in other states, an overwhelming majority of South Carolina Baptist clergy considered themselves Republicans. They felt close to most organizations of the Christian Right— but not the Christian Coalition—but almost unanimously voted for Dole in the GOP primary, although many reported a preference for a more conservative, but unelectable, candidate such as antiabortion spokesman Alan Keyes. Thus, as in 1988, when Baptist clergy strongly supported George Bush over Christian Right candidate Pat Robertson (and Bob Dole), South Carolina's conservative religious establishment supported the candidate of the state's GOP establishment (Guth 1996).

Ironically, although Buchanan's Catholicism may still have presented a problem to some evangelicals, it was not his major obstacle. Nor was his lack of establishment endorsements. Rather, Buchanan's political style and issue positions turned many potential supporters away. Some Christian conservatives disliked his strident rhetoric, while others rejected his critical attitude toward Israel, always an important symbol in evangelical Protestant eschatology. Even more problematic were his perceived ties with white-supremacist organizations and leaders, which represented a real threat both to Christian Right attempts to build an African American base and to budding efforts by evangelical clergy and laity to reduce divisions in a state with continuing racial tensions. Many also were skeptical of his trade policy, preferring the free-trade orientation pushed by the state Republican establishment, including Governor Beasley. Above all, many conservative Protestants doubted Buchanan's electoral strength against Southern Baptists Bill Clinton and Al Gore, an extremely unpopular ticket among many Baptist clergy and laity.

The South Carolina primary was ultimately reduced to a fight between Dole and Buchanan, as Steve Forbes relied on television ads, and former Tennessee governor Lamar Alexander generated little excitement. Buchanan emphasized personal campaigning, especially in economically depressed textile communities, where he pushed his anti–free trade views, and before church groups, where social issues came to the fore. He also advertised heavily on the state's omnipresent Christian radio stations. Dole, on the other hand, continued to rely on television ads featuring Carroll Campbell and Governor Beasley, the vigorous support of the state GOP establishment, especially elected officials, and phone banks targeting Christian conservatives with Dole's conservative voting record on abortion and other moral issues. Henry Hyde, the Illinois Republican congressman whose name is synonymous with antiabortion legislation, lobbied pro-life groups on Dole's behalf. Elizabeth Dole, herself an evangelical Christian from neighboring North Carolina, spent much time in the state, addressing the religious side of the issues in explicit ways her husband usually avoided.

As Dole's strategists hoped, South Carolina turned the tide in his direction at just the right time. He carried almost half of the state's GOP voters (45 percent), with Buchanan a distant second (29 percent). Steve Forbes (13 percent) and Lamar Alexander (10 percent) broke into double digits, but their prospects of continuing the race were severely damaged (Hoover 1996d). Dole's religious strategy was critical to his victory. Depending on the poll used, between one-third and two-fifths of the GOP primary voters considered themselves "religious conservatives" or part of the "religious right," while a strong majority (60 percent) had a favorable view of the movement. Although Buchanan won these voters (44 percent to 40 percent among the "religious right" voters in the networks' Voter News Service exit poll), Dole's strong showing among Christian Right voters and his much larger margin among other Republicans combined for his decisive victory. The media and many activists immediately credited the Campbell organization with lining up GOP loyalists and Governor Beasley with mobilizing a critical bloc of his own Christian conservative base on behalf of a mainstream candidate (Apple 1996; Broder 1996a; Balz 1996). By several accounts, however, the governor experienced some backlash from Christian supporters for his choice, which nevertheless improved his position with party regulars.

Although the Christian Coalition and the regular Republican forces led by Campbell had eventually coalesced around Dole, the tension between the religious conservatives and the old establishment appeared once again at the state Republican convention in May, where nineteen of the thirty-seven delegates to the national GOP convention would actually be selected (Hoover 1996a). (Eighteen were previously chosen by congressional district meetings.) Prior to the state convention, Governor Beasley, his aides, and Roberta Combs met several times and exchanged conference calls to assemble a gubernatorial/Christian Coalition slate, representing a cross section of the party, including elected officials, but favoring Christian conservatives. Some saw this as a concession to Beasley, as the Coalition had controlled enough precinct meetings and county conventions the previous year to dictate the result. At the state convention, however, the agreement fell apart. The consensus slate was distributed to all delegates, but to Beasley's surprise, each county Coalition leader provided followers with a different list, composed only of Coalition activists and "friends" (including Upstate BJU activists), with the exception of slots for Beasley and Senator Strom Thurmond. Former governor Campbell was excluded, as was a leader in the Southern Baptist right, Cyndi Mosteller, a Beasley appointee to the state health board and chair of the convention platform committee.

The results clearly showed the Coalition's clout. Several Coalition unknowns outpolled former governor Campbell, who placed twelfth in the balloting, and GOP congressman Floyd Spence, even further down the line. One of the four GOP congressmen had to settle for an alternate's slot. The state's incumbent Republican national committeewoman and committeeman not only were excluded from the delegation but were defeated in bids to retain their party posts. On the whole, the resulting delegation was staunchly conservative, lukewarm toward Bob Dole, and very "Christian Right." All thirty-seven delegates were white and only four of the alternates were black (Hoover and Perry 1996; Hoover 1996e). To add insult to injury, several Christian Coalition leaders and activists also complained publicly about the possibility that Carroll Campbell might emerge as Dole's running mate, an action that elicited an angry dismissal of the Coalition by Campbell, once again raising the prospects of intraparty feuds, especially should Campbell return to state politics in the near future (Edsall 1996; Hoover 1996b).

The general election contest in South Carolina was relatively quiet and failed to excite much interest from voters or religious activists. Although Democratic strategists made brave remarks about carrying the state for President Clinton, they assumed, with most observers, that if Bob Dole carried only a few states in the union, South Carolina would be one of them. Thus, the presidential campaign was notable by its absence: there were virtually no visits by members of the presidential tickets, minimal TV and radio advertising, and little overt activism by Christian Right organizations. The Christian Coalition, as expected, did distribute voter guides in churches the Sunday before the election (Hoover 1996c), religious radio stations carried some discussions of the campaign, and many conservative clergy quietly supported the Republican ticket. Dole carried the state with 50.1 percent of the vote to Bill Clinton's 44.3 percent and Ross Perot's 5.6 percent. Dole enjoyed a more than comfortable edge among the state's conservative white Protestants, with his highest vote percentage (80 percent) among the substantial bloc of voters who considered themselves part of the religious right; indeed, Dole's showing among this group in South Carolina was even stronger than that among the same group in the national electorate. Other Republicans fared well, as ninety-three-year-old Senator Strom Thurmond was reelected, all four Republican U.S. House members were easily returned to Washington, and the GOP gained two South Carolina house seats but lost two in the state senate (Karr 1996b). Thurmond received 82 percent of the votes of white members of the religious right, but only 47 percent of the votes of other white voters, with challenger Eliot Close winning a 51 percent majority in that constituency. All four GOP congressional victors also received at least some Christian Right help, assistance that was quite substantial, but totally unnecessary, in two House districts. One heavily supported U.S. House candidate failed to unseat a vulnerable Democratic incumbent, however.

Indeed, not all Christian Right candidates and issues were triumphant, as somewhat mixed results came in from local races. With the outcome of national races not in doubt, much Christian Right organizational activity centered around local contests. One of the most closely watched involved the school board in Greenville County, the state's largest school system, which had been dominated by a coalition of conservative Christian activists for two years. Countermobilization by opponents was successful, however, and three conservative board members were unseated, along with one of their board opponents, moving the board back to the right-center. At the same time, however, other leading Christian conservatives won seats handily on the Greenville County Council.

Aftermath

In 1996, Christian Right forces certainly demonstrated their influence in South Carolina politics, especially within the Republican Party. They played a major role in the primary campaigns of both Bob Dole and Patrick Buchanan, provided the organizational energy for local and state Republican institutions, and supplied many activists for the GOP in the fall campaign. No Republican could any longer win a statewide race in South Carolina without support from some part of the Christian Right. Still, not all elements of the Christian Right always moved in concert; indeed, in 1996, prominent BJU, Christian Coalition, and Southern Baptist conservatives could be found in the camp of every Republican contender, although most had lined up behind either Dole or Buchanan by the end of the campaign. Such diversity sometimes represented a strategy designed to provide access to whatever candidate emerged victorious, but more often it was the natural result of activists' differing assessments of the candidates' character, religious acceptability, position on important issues, and electability. This situation provided openings for almost all the Republican candidates to make potentially telling appeals to Christian Right activists and voters. Of course, the diversity of activist choices may also demonstrate a certain intractability of Christian Right activists, brought up in the inherently individualistic training grounds of independent fundamentalist, Pentecostal, or charismatic churches. Neither the BJU leadership nor even the Christian Coalition could achieve total consensus on favored presidential candidates.

What is the future of the Christian Right in South Carolina? Will the various elements be integrated into the party, losing their distinctive markings? To some extent this will occur, as illustrated by the Bob Jones case, but it is likely that Christian conservatives will continue to have a somewhat different agenda from their regular counterparts. During 1996 and 1997, for example, a wide range of issues, many of them new to the state, elicited activity by conservative Christians, suggesting that the impetus behind the movement would remain strong. Gay rights became prominent as never before when the Greenville County Council condemned gay lifestyles, eliciting an outpouring of protest from more liberal forces and boycotts of the area by the Olympic torch during the summer of 1996. The state legislature also passed, and Governor Beasley signed, the Defense of Marriage Act, a major legislative priority of the Christian Right groups, especially the American Family Association and the Palmetto Family Council (Karr 1996a). In addition, other state and local policies, ranging from the Beasley administration's new regulations on abortion clinics, to the ending of free condom distribution by the state department of health (Breckenridge 1997), to local ordinances and state laws regulating adult entertainment, became front-page news, energizing Christian Right forces.

On many of these moral issues, the Christian Right was unified, but in early 1997 a major issue divided conservative Protestants: Governor Beasley's effort to remove the Confederate battle flag from the state capitol building in Columbia. Although the governor had pledged during his 1994 campaign to keep the flag flying, after much prayer, he said, he felt God was telling him that the symbol of racial division should be removed to another place on the capitol grounds. (More cynical observers attributed his turnabout to pressure from the business community to "modernize" South Carolina's image.) His switch not only elicited a firestorm within the Republican Party, as many of the governor's own partisans in the legislature refused to follow his lead, but it divided the state's religious establishment as well. For several weeks, hundreds of clergy from all over the state lined up on opposite sides, expressing themselves through marches, full-page newspaper advertisements, and well-scripted news conferences. Mainline Protestant, Catholic, and Jewish religious leaders were joined by African American clergy in supporting Beasley's plan, but a great many conservative Southern Baptists, Pentecostals, and charismatics also stood behind "their" governor. Other Christian Right clergy, however, vocally opposed the governor's plan and warned that his action threatened religious support for his reelection campaign in 1998. Indeed, the South Carolina Baptist Convention was so divided that it failed to take a clear position and merely published opposing views in the *Baptist Courier.* Once again, the issue of race has bedeviled Southern politics (Key 1949), this time within the ranks of the Republican Party and its allies on the Christian Right.

References

Apple, R. W., Jr. 1996. "Dole Fulfills His Promise in a Contest in the South." *New York Times* (4 March): A12.

Balz, Dan. 1996. "Dole Nomination Drive Gets Seven-State 'Super' Push." *Washington Post* (13 March): A1.

Berke, Richard. 1996. "GOP Unites in Cultivating Religious Right." *New York Times* (2 March): 1.

Bradley, Martin, Norman M. Green Jr., Dale E. Jones, Mac Lynn, and Lou McNeil. 1992. *Churches and Church Membership in the United States, 1990.* Atlanta: Glenmary Research Center.

Breckenridge, Mona. 1997. "Beasley Gets State to Abstain from Condom Handouts." *Greenville News* (10 January): 10.

Broder, David. 1996a. "Dole Sweeps Aside Rivals in Eight States." *Washington Post* (6 March): A1.

———. 1996b. "South Carolina on Their Minds." *Washington Post National Weekly Edition* (15–21 January): 13.

Brownstein, Ronald. 1996. "Buchanan Tumbles Old Walls of Religion." *Los Angeles Times* (2 March): A1.

Bursey, Brett. 1994. "David Beasley." *Point,* October, 4-6, 19.

Edsall, Thomas B. 1996. "Putting GOP Delegates to the Loyalty Test on Abortion." *Washington Post National Weekly Edition* (17–23 June): 15-16.

Ehrenhalt, Alan. 1991. *The United States of Ambition.* New York: Random House.

Feldman, Linda. 1996. "Carolina Vote Tests Role of Religion in Politics of South." *Christian Science Monitor* (3 March): 1.

Graham, Cole Blease, Jr., William V. Moore, and Frank T. Petrusak. 1994. "Praise the Lord and Join the Republicans: The Christian Coalition and the Republican Party in South Carolina." Paper presented at the annual meeting of the Western Political Science Association, Albuquerque, N.M.

Gray, Jerry. 1996. "Dole Counts on a Surge of Support in the South." *New York Times* (28 February): A11.

Guth, James L. 1995. "South Carolina: The Christian Right Wins One." Chap. 7 in *God at the Grass Roots: The Christian Right in the 1994 Elections,* ed. Mark J. Rozell and Clyde Wilcox. Lanham, Md.: Rowman & Littlefield.

———. 1996. "The Bully Pulpit: Southern Baptist Clergy and Political Activism, 1980-1992." In *Religion and the Culture Wars: Dispatches from the Front,* ed. John C. Green, James L. Guth, Corwin E. Smidt, and Lyman A. Kellstedt. Lanham, Md.: Rowman & Littlefield.

Hammond, James T., and Melinda Gladfelter. 1996. "State Rep. Herdklotz Dies at 55." *Greenville News* (5 July): 1A.

Hoover, Dan. 1996a. "Christian Coalition Cements Control of State GOP." *Greenville News* (5 May): 3B.

———. 1996b. "Christian Coalition Cool to Campbell as Dole VP Choice." *Greenville News* (9 August): 2A.

———. 1996c. "Democrats Upset about Christian Coalition Voter Guides." *Greenville News* (29 October): 3D.

———. 1996d. "Dole Roars Past GOP Field." *Greenville News* (3 March): 1A.

———. 1996e. "Powell Urges GOP to be Compassionate." *Greenville News* (13 August): 1A .

Hoover, Dan, and James T. Hammond. 1996. "Conservative Coalition Unites behind Buchanan." *Greenville News* (27 February): A1.

Hoover, Dan, and Dale Perry. 1996. "South Carolina Delegates Eager to Hit the Floor." *Greenville News* (11 August): 4F.

Karr, Gary. 1996a. "Beasley Signs Measure Banning Same-Sex Marriages." *Greenville News* (21 May): 2D.

———. 1996b. "Election Changes Little in Columbia." *Greenville News* (10 November): 3D.

Key, V. O., Jr. 1949. *Southern Politics in State and Nation.* New York: Knopf.

Reed, Ralph. 1996. *Active Faith: How Christians Are Changing the Soul of American Politics.* New York: Free Press.

Sack, Kevin. 1996. "South Carolina Is a Crossroads for the GOP." *New York Times* (29 February): A1.

Smith, Oran P. 1997. *The Rise of Baptist Republicanism.* New York: New York University Press, forthcoming.

Wyman, Scott. 1995. "Gramm Campaigns in Greenville at BJU." *Greenville News* (10 October): 1D.

3

Texas: A Success Story, at Least for Now

John M. Bruce

In the 1996 election cycle the Christian Right solidified its previous gains in Texas politics. There was increased activity by conservative Christian groups in this election, as well as increased influence within the Republican Party, although the movement had only limited success in winning new offices around the state. Candidates throughout the state stressed issues associated with the Christian Right. It is clear that the mobilization of Christian conservatives has significantly moved Texas politics. In this light, the Christian Right has "won" politically in Texas, at least for now. However, the shine of this success is somewhat tarnished by some striking failures of the movement, as well as an emerging backlash against the new political power of conservative Christians. There are enough mixed signals to make the durability of this victory uncertain.

The Situation Leading Up to 1996

In order to place the success of the Christian Right in some context, it is useful to consider three key factors in the state prior to this election cycle: its demographics, the nature of politics in Texas, and the recent history of the Christian Right in the state.

The most relevant demographic characteristic of the state is that Texas is home to many conservative churches, especially Baptists and independent evangelical and fundamentalist churches. These congregations have been fertile ground for mobilization by the Christian Right. Texas also has a large Catholic population (estimated to be between 5 and 5.5 million), some 65 to 70 percent of which is Hispanic. This group has been more Democratic than Republican. Such large numbers make the recruitment of Catholics a tempting goal, and the Christian Coalition has tried to attract these Catholics through its affiliated Catholic Alliance. In Texas, the results of this campaign are mixed. There are Catholics (including some Hispanics) involved with the Christian Right, but they are relatively few in number. The Democratic tendencies of Hispanics in Texas make this a difficult population to recruit.

When it comes to politics, Texas is generally typical of the southern states. In the period following Reconstruction, the state was overwhelmingly Democratic (see Key 1949), and no viable Republican Party was present in the state for nearly one hundred years. One-party domination of the state continued through the New Deal period into the 1960s. As the national Democratic Party began to address civil rights concerns, the tension between this agenda and the values of the conservative Texan Democrats grew. By the time of the Nixon administration, Texas was quickly trending to the GOP at the national level in both presidential and congressional contests. In 1978, the first Republican governor since Reconstruction was elected. At the same time, the number of Republicans in the state legislature began to rise. Just as had been the case in other southern states, the pattern of Republican voting was visible first in federal elections, followed by emerging strength at the state and local levels. Going into 1996, the Democrats held majorities in both legislative chambers, with the governorship, both U.S. Senate seats, and eleven of thirty U.S. House seats held by Republicans.

It was in this rapidly changing political world that the Christian Right emerged as a force in the state. While there have always been politically active social conservatives in the state, the sense of a real movement can be traced to the rise of the Christian Coalition. A Texas chapter of the Christian Coalition had existed before 1991, but the organization had been weak and ineffectual. It was at this point that Dick Weinhold was selected to lead the state chapter. Weinhold was not new to the Coalition: he had been the chief fundraiser for Pat Robertson's 1988 presidential campaign and had been involved with the national chapter for some time. Weinhold brought strong organizational and political skills to the state, and his presence marked the beginning of a dramatic conversion. Weinhold's tenure has seen a striking growth in the membership rolls of the Texas Christian Coalition, which grew from fewer than 10,000 members in 1991 to more than 120,000 in 1996.

It may seem unfair to credit the actions of one organization for the overall rise of the influence of the Christian Right. After all, many other religious, socially conservative organizations were active in the state before Weinhold took over the Christian Coalition. However, Weinhold took one particular step that enhanced the overall power of conservative Christian politics in Texas: he organized a regular meeting among leaders of various groups in order to coordinate activity. This meeting served as a vehicle for various pro-family organizations in the state to share information and coordinate actions. Looking back at the rapid increase in the movement's political clout in Texas, the value of this sort of coordination should not be underestimated.

The goal of the Texas Christian Coalition, according to Weinhold, is "to equip Christians to have an effective voice in our government again" (Roser 1996).[1] Prior to 1996, to what degree was this goal met for the Christian Right in general? The Christian Right (and the Christian Coalition in particular) did have an effective voice in government, or at least in parts of government. Conservative Christians had been active at all levels of politics in the state and had been very good at bringing their issues to the forefront. At the elite level, numerous candidacies were associated with, or supportive of, the Christian Right. At the mass level, individuals supported the Christian Right by giving money, time, and electoral support to like-minded candidates. By the 1996 elections, no Republican candidate could seek nomination to office without paying attention to this newly mobilized group. The Christian Right's ties to social conservatives in the Democratic Party were much weaker than those to Republicans, but a conservative Democrat would certainly have to be aware of this voting bloc.

The Christian Right has developed its influence in the state primarily through the state's Republican Party. In past years, the Christian Coalition has sponsored training sessions on how to get elected as a precinct chair (a non-partisan training process, the effects of which were felt almost exclusively in the GOP). Through this process, the selection of conservative delegates to the state convention was assured.[2]

Social conservatives were prominent at the 1992 and 1994 state Republican conventions. Their strength at the 1994 convention was striking. Of the six thousand delegates and six thousand alternates, some 60 to 65 percent were evangelical Christians. Over half of these delegates had never attended a polit-ical convention before, suggesting that the movement had mobilized a new constituency in Texas politics. The best evidence of their strength that year was seen in their ability to drive the sitting party chair from office. The incumbent chair, Fred Meyer, withdrew in the face of opposition from conservative Chris-tians. This prompted the head of Texans United for Life to note that "the major victory has already been won."[3] The resulting open contest had three contes-tants: sitting member of Congress Joe Barton, lawyer and former Reagan White House official Tom Pauken, and businesswoman Dolly Madison McKenna. Barton was the pick of Meyer and Senators Gramm and Hutchison. McKenna's moderate policy stands and open concern about the role of the Christian Right in the party reduced her campaign to little more than a symbol. Pauken, on the other hand, had received support from Weinhold. Both Barton and McKenna withdrew in the face of support for Pauken, allowing him to win an uncontested vote. Beyond the selection of the new chair, the overall tone of the convention in 1994 was very conservative. The lower-level conventions had passed many conservative resolutions, some of which made it to the state level. A resolution acknowledging that Republicans have a range of views on any given issue was proposed by moderates and was soundly defeated. When the gavel dropped to close the convention that year, there was little doubt that the Christian Right had made dramatic and influential marks on the Republican Party in the state.

Fertile Ground for Christian Right Gains

Not surprisingly, the political activities of the Christian Right continued in 1996. The state political arena is now home to representatives of all the major national organizations in the movement, as well as a variety of groups native to the state. Yet it would not be difficult to argue that the Texas Christian Coalition is the most important group in the statewide movement. Weinhold's leadership has placed it at the heart of conservative political discussion. Still, the influence of the Christian Coalition is enhanced by the presence of a number of other groups. The American Family Association has a chapter in Texas.[4] Concerned Women of America has a number of local chapters in the state. Typical of others present in the mix are Eagle Forum, Associated Conservatives of Texas (PAC), Concerned Texans, Texas Home School Coalition, and Citizens for Excellence in Education. The impressive accomplishment in the Texas case is the degree to which these various organizations find ways to work together. This cooperation certainly has limits, but the general theme is one of collective action toward common goals. This approach allows the Christian Right movement to be more efficient than it might otherwise be, increasing the potential influence of the movement.

The Christian Right in Texas has begun to make the transition from outside agitator to political power broker. The process of any campaign or movement maturing into a player in the normal routine of politics can be difficult. In this case, the difficulty is compounded by the near impossibility of compromise on many of the social issues being pursued by the Christian Right. In James Q. Wilson's language, those in this movement tend to be "amateurs" (Wilson 1960). When faced with the choice of compromising one's ideals and winning or holding steadfast to one's beliefs and being defeated, amateurs are more likely to opt for the latter outcome. As the Christian Right has grown into a real political force, its adherents have found themselves in a new position. Where they could once be uncompromising in the advocacy of their beliefs, their newfound political clout makes this more difficult. Issue advocates can easily be pure, while political leaders must compromise to survive. The task for the leaders of this movement has been to decide when and where compromise is possible or prudent. While there has not been, and is not likely to be, any such compromise on the hot-button issues of the right, the movement's willingness to work with a moderate Republican governor has been impressive. It has had significantly less success working with the more moderate (and pro-choice) Senator Kay Bailey Hutchison, who was backed by the Christian Coalition in her 1992 election.

Entering into the 1996 election cycle, there existed in the state a set of socially conservative organizations with some experience at working together. These organizations, along with the generally receptive audience for a conservative message,[5] set the stage for the Christian Right to have a potentially enormous impact in the elections.

The 1996 Elections: Standing Fast or Gaining Power?

The Christian Right in Texas during the 1996 election worked hard and generated results. The movment's activities during the election can be broken into three broad categories. There were some tasks aimed at influencing the mass public (or at least those sympathetic to the aims of the Christian Right). Similarly, there were concentrated efforts to train and mobilize political activists at the precinct level and beyond. Finally, there were activities that were aimed at benefiting candidates directly. Each of these broad classes of activities will be discussed in turn, as they will shed some light on the nature of the influence the Christian Right had during the 1996 election.

The principal means of mobilizing sympathetic voters is also perhaps the most widely reported activity of the movement, the distribution of voter guides. In Texas, these guides came primarily from the Christian Coalition. They were produced for the primaries and the general election. At least five million of these voter guides were distributed in Texas during 1996, largely through churches.[6]

Within the state, the voter guides created two distinct controversies during 1996. The first spark erupted when the national Christian Coalition mailed sample guides to churches in Texas, encouraging them to obtain the guides for distribution within their respective congregations. In the sample guide, the candidate who agreed with the Coalition's positions was white, while the candidate who disagreed was black. This led the Texas state conference of NAACP branches and a variety of ministers to denounce this as "race-baiting" and "conduct unbecoming of those who carry the identity of Christians" (Palomo 1996b). The national office of the Coalition took full responsibility for the mailing, attributing it to a series of missteps in the production process. Regardless of the origin of the problem, the result was bad press just before the election about the Christian Coalition and its main voter education project.

The second controversy involved the basic question of voter guide distribution. A number of clergy in the state came together under the guise of the Texas Faith Network to ask that churches not distribute the materials. They argued that the Christian Coalition was a tool of Pat Robertson and worked for the Republican Party. This group of clergy did not oppose political involvement by religious leaders but did oppose actions that appeared partisan. The guides, they said, included issues "far afield from core issues of faith" (Palomo 1996b). The Texas Christian Coalition obviously disagreed, describing itself and the voter guide as nonpartisan. The overall impact of this request was probably quite small. However, it was yet another bit of negative coverage of the Christian Coalition's work during the fall campaign.

The second broad group of activities undertaken by the Christian Right during the election cycle was aimed at the mobilization and education of political activists. This process started at the precinct level and went all the way to the Texas delegation to the Republican National Convention. The principal goal was not to secure electoral victory but rather to gain control of, or at least to influence, the party apparatus and agenda.

At the precinct level, the goal was to educate activists on how to become precinct chairs. From this position, supporters could select the delegates to the next level of convention. The end product of controlling the precincts was the ability to set the tone of the state party convention and platform. This training was nonpartisan (indeed, the head of the Christian Coalition's training program was a Democrat), but the bulk of those trained seemed likely to direct their focus within the Republican Party.[7] The Christian Coalition ran at least twenty-five training sessions around the state.[8] One GOP activist estimated that Coalition-backed candidates ran for 80 percent of the precinct chairs around the state (Roser 1996). This strategy, which worked so well in 1994, set the stage for the Christian Right to have a major say in the Republican Party again in 1996.

The successful effort to maximize the number of precinct chairs sympathetic to the movement meant that the individuals selected to go to the state senatorial district conventions were sure to be socially conservative. Likewise, control of the senatorial district conventions meant that the delegate-selection process for the state convention was sure to produce a delegate slate sympathetic to the Christian Right. Two significant events came from this control of the delegate-selection process. First, the task of writing the Republican Party platform in the state was now left to social conservatives. Second, the selection of delegates to the national convention was controlled by activists who did not have great enthusiasm for the Republican presidential nominee. Repercussions of these events were felt in both state and national politics.

The Republican Party in Texas has always been rather conservative on economic affairs and has grown increasingly so on social matters. In particular, the party appeared to shift sharply to the right on social issues after 1992. Much of this shift can be credited to the Christian Right's influence on the delegate process in 1994. The platform passed at the 1996 state convention continued this trend. Perhaps the most dramatic example of this is seen in the party's treatment of abortion. In 1994, the party passed a platform that opposed abortion except to save the life of the mother or in other very rare instances. The 1996 platform encouraged a total ban on abortions with no exceptions for the life of the mother, rape, incest, or anything else.[9] The chair of the state party, Tom Pauken, said this was done so that the state's platform would conform to the expected national platform (Robison and Bernstein 1996). The state platform also encouraged the state legislature to outlaw the distribution of birth control to minors. In an interesting twist, the 1996 platform reversed one longtime proposal that had been backed by the GOP: the use of initiative and referendum. The new platform did not encourage the implementation of these policy-making procedures. Observers read this step as concern by the Christian Right that this sort of democratic procedure could produce laws that the movement opposes (Robison and Bernstein 1996). From a political perspective, it means that the movement feels stronger in its ability to influence legislators than in its ability to hold public opinion.

While the passage of a very conservative platform was noteworthy, the contest over the selection of delegates to the national convention involved an old-fashioned political battle. This conflict pitted established state political figures against the very conservative delegates at the convention. The results not only indicated how powerful the Christian Right was at the convention but also highlighted the difficulty facing the movement now that it is a major political force.

The Dole campaign had put forth a slate of recommended delegates to the national convention. The campaign had made these recommendations to screening committees in the various congressional district caucuses. Each of the 30 caucuses was to select 3 delegates and 3 alternates to the San Diego meeting. Additionally, there were to be 33 at-large delegates from Texas. As a result of primary voting, all but 2 of the 123 delegates were pledged to support Dole at the national convention. The actions of the delegates at the state convention quickly dashed any expectations held by the Dole camp that they might be able to control the Texas delegation in San Diego. Across the various caucuses, the state delegates rejected many of the Dole nominees, replacing them with strong social conservatives.[10] The resulting delegation was much more socially conservative than it would have been if the Dole list had been accepted. The number of social conservatives seated among the delegates to the national convention was estimated to be 72 of the 90 district delegates, plus about one-half of the at-large delegates. While some of these individuals may also have been on the Dole slate, the overall presence of social conservatives is striking.

One of the most intriguing political facets of the rejection of the Dole delegates is that the state convention delegates showed no reluctance to reject mainstream Republican political figures in the state. Among those who were nominated but denied status as a delegate from the various district caucuses were former state party chair Fred Meyer, U.S. Congressman Henry Bonilla, U.S. Congressman Mac Thornberry, and the Texas cochair of the Dole campaign, Richard Collins (Collins was later selected as an at-large delegate). U.S. Senator Kay Bailey Hutchison was given status as an at-large delegate only after the intervention of Governor Bush, Senators Dole and Gramm, and party chair Pauken. Her nomination had been stridently opposed by antiabortion activists among the delegates. Among those selected to be at-large delegates were Texas Christian Coalition chair Dick Weinhold, conservative activist Steve Hotze,[11] state board of education member Donna Ballard; Cathie Adams, leader of the Texas Eagle Forum, and Tim Lambert, president of the Texas Home School Coalition.

The preference for social conservatives over other Republicans was also visible in the people selected to fill other positions. Governor Bush was rejected as chair of the delegation to the national convention in favor of state party chair Pauken. Bush was named honorary chair of the delegation. The selection of Pauken appears likely to have been a way of punishing Bush for his more moderate views; Pauken, who had been selected as chair by the very conservative delegates at the 1994 state convention, was a more comfortable pick for the 1996 delegates. The vice chair of the Texas delegation to San Diego was none other than Weinhold. The power of the conservatives was also seen in the selection of Lambert as one of the two Texas representatives to the Republican National Committee.

The ability of the Christian Right to influence politics in Texas was very visible within the realm of Republican activists. From the precinct convention all the way to the floor of the Republican National Convention, these activists were mobilized and trained to maximize their influence. They produced a very conservative state platform, selected a very conservative slate of delegates at every step of the process, and placed sympathetic and socially conservative voices in positions of authority within the party structure. Much of this was done in the face of contrary wishes by the Dole campaign. The results made it very clear that the state's Republican Party is heavily influenced by the Christian Right.[12]

A final set of activities undertaken by the Christian Right in the state was aimed at directly benefiting certain candidates. Under IRS rules, organizations such as the Christian Coalition are limited in what they can do on this front.[13] The Coalition's voter guides are technically "voter education," but in laying out the candidates' stands on issues dear to the Coalition, they grow very similar to endorsements. In that light, they may be construed as beneficial to certain candidates. Other types of organizations, however, were able to take more direct actions. For example, the American Family Association/Texas (AFA/Texas) chapter has a political action committee, the Texas American Family Action Committee (TAFAC), which was active in at least six state house races, six state senate races, three state board of education races, and numerous other contests (including the campaigns of both successful candidates for the Republican National Committee). This PAC provided a range of resources, including direct financial contributions, in-kind contributions, publicity, advertising, and database work. TAFAC allowed AFA/Texas to become directly involved in the campaigns.[14]

State Board of Education: Battleground of the Year

While the Christian Right was active in the board of education races in 1994, its presence was more pronounced in 1996. Just as in numerous other states and localities, public education has mobilized many conservatives in Texas. There is strong support for local control of education within the state. Among conservative Christians, animosity is particularly strong toward the federally funded Goals 2000 program, which brought $29 million into the state during the 1995–1996 school year. The state board of education's vote to accept the federal money after receiving a waiver from the Department of Education's usual guidelines was strongly criticized by social conservatives around the state, who argued that this would lead to the distribution of birth control on campuses, as well as giving the federal government entry to Texas schools (Brooks 1996a). Acceptance of these federal funds was an issue in some of the 1996 board contests. Other issues on the table as the board elections grew near included phonics versus "whole language" teaching methods, "moral relativism," textbooks that were perceived as too liberal in their discussion of the environment, the content of sex education courses, and the ability to use public school dollars at private or religious institutions through vouchers (Brooks 1996a, Markley 1996).

Before the 1996 elections, Republicans held nine of the fifteen seats on the state board; of these nine, five were supporters of the Christian Coalition. Thus, while the Republicans held a majority on the board, there were not enough votes to ensure victory on the issues of the Christian Right. Opportunity to pick up the three votes needed to control the board came from the eight seats being contested in 1996. Candidates supportive of the Christian Coalition contested at least six of those eight elections. Two of these contests are worthy of detailed discussion. The current chair of the board, Republican Jack Christie, was challenged in the primaries by a former teacher, Terri Leo. Christie was supported by the governor, while Leo was supported by many conservative Christians. This contest involved no unusual issues or concerns. The striking difference between the two campaigns can be found in the funding levels and sources. The incumbent, Christie, raised less than $4,000 between July 1995 and the week prior to the election. Challenger Leo raised more than $50,000 for the contest, over $30,000 of it in the last month and a half before the election. A large amount came from a PAC controlled by businessman James Leininger. She also raised money from TAFAC; the Eagle Forum's Cathie Adams; Eugene Fontenot, an unsuccessful candidate for Congress and conservative social activist;[15] and Margaret Hotze, the mother of Steve Hotze, who manages several conservative Christian political organizations. This large funding differential did little to help Leo, as she lost in the primary by a significant margin.

The second key board of education race was the battle to select the Republican nominee to challenge Democratic incumbent Will Davis. There were three candidates in the Republican battle, two of whom (Charlie Weaver and Cynthia Thorton) supported the Christian Coalition's education agenda. Both Weaver and Thorton said that they would oppose taking Goals 2000 money, while the third, Donald Clark, was willing to take it: "When you get $30 million from the government, take advantage of it" (Brooks 1996a). Clark's willingness to take federal funds may not have been responsible for the election results, but he did finish third in the primary. Thorton received the most votes and faced a runoff with Weaver. Their one-two finish in the primary did not reflect the funds they had used in their campaign. Weaver had raised more than $20,000 for the primary, while Thorton reported raising less than $500. The runoff campaign between Thorton and Weaver also offered something unique. The five sitting members of the state board of education who were sympathetic to the Christian Coalition endorsed Weaver's candidacy—in a Republican primary to challenge a sitting Democrat. This unusual action produced some negative attention for the board and the Christian Coalition, but it may have contributed to Weaver's victory in the runoff.

The Christian Right's goal of gaining a majority on the board of education receded after the primaries. With losses by several of the candidates aligned with the Christian Coalition, the odds of gaining three seats were strikingly long. On election day, the bloc of Coalition supporters on the board increased by a single seat. Weaver lost to the incumbent Democrat, while two other Coalition-backed candidates won their contests. One of the sitting members of the board, part of the five-vote bloc supportive of the Christian Right, lost to a Democratic challenger in the general election (Brooks 1996b). Holding six seats on the board, the Coalition needs to pull two additional votes (most likely from the other three Republicans on the board) in order to advance its agenda.

The failure to reach a majority on the board does not reflect a lack of organization or resources. Indeed, candidates affiliated with the conservative Christian movement were often much better funded than the others. The sources of these funds tended to be in other socially conservative circles. One source, James Leininger, is worthy of additional consideration. Leininger had been involved with board of education races in the past. In 1994, his PAC, Texans for Governmental Integrity, paid for a mailing used in two campaigns in conservative East Texas. The material depicted an interracial homosexual couple kissing and argued that the current school system promoted homosexuality, lesbians' right to adoption, and the use of condoms. The impact of these mailings was estimated to be significant to the election outcome (Walt 1996b). In the 1996 contests, Leininger's new PAC, A+PAC for Parental School Choice, gave vast amounts of money to conservative board candidates.[16] Through his PACs and personally, Leininger gave about $300,000 to conservative board candidates in 1996. This kind of high-level funding makes it possible for challengers to run unexpectedly strong campaigns. In this case, it also seems very likely to ensure support for school vouchers among conservatives on the board. The volume of cash flowing into the board contests added a new dimension to Christian Right activities. Conventional wisdom was that support from this movement would bring the candidate people and passion. The ability to raise money at a phenomenal rate, if replicated for other offices, would alter the way that conservative Christians have traditionally participated in the system.

Looking Ahead

Forecasting politics in Texas, as in most places, is a dicey enterprise. Crises, scandals, charismatic leaders, or even the whims of the public can lead politics in unexpected directions. Still, it is not much of a risk to conclude that the Christian Right will continue to have significant influence in the state for some time to come. It moves toward the end of this century with a strong organization, impressive resources, and sympathetic friends in government and party positions. This sort of situation is obviously conducive to political clout.

The key elements of the Christian Right's influence in Texas politics are holding control of the GOP and continuing public support for Republican concerns. Yet support for a Republican agenda does not translate directly into a conservative Christian political agenda. There is broad support for economically conservative policies in Texas, so the Republican Party in the state would likely have done very well without a Christian Right movement. In some fashion, the movement was simply able to place itself on the leading edge of a wave. By occupying grassroots positions within the party, it was able to influence the platform and other party operations. As long as the GOP continues to work toward the conservative economic goals supported by so many in the state, the Christian Right will be able to advance its socially conservative issues. The Republican Party wins, for it now has a cadre of highly mobilized and dedicated activists and candidates. The conservative Christian movement wins, as it now has an avenue through which to pursue its agenda. The crucial question that must be asked involves the durability of this winning position. Two primary threats to continued success are any possible decay in the relationship between the GOP and the Christian Right and any significant shift in public opinion toward issues that fall outside the realm of the Christian Right. Should either develop, the recent victories could be but memories of a bygone golden era.

Coming out of the 1996 elections, it is difficult to say that the relationship between the Christian Right and the rest of the Republican Party is in any jeopardy. The overlap in ideological focus, issue concerns, activist pools, and mass support is enormous. The Christian Coalition's and other groups' claims to be nonpartisan ring hollow in the face of consistently partisan behavior. The Christian Right has found a comfortable home in Texas, and that home is within the GOP. Moderate Republicans have largely either left the party or simply been defeated.[17] Some elements of the party have been more resistant to influence than others. One example is the Texas Federation of Republican Women, an affiliated group that has been dominated by more moderate Republican voices, although in the last two years this may have started to change. The main party structure, however, is dominated by the Christian Right, from the precinct chairs to the state chair to the state representatives to the national committee. This extraordinary presence will not be undone in a year or two but may well be present for a decade or more.

For all the success that the Christian Right has seen in the state, the population has certain moderate, albeit Republican, tendencies.[18] Although there is support for conservative economic policy, preferences in the social realm move toward the center. For example, there is support for an increased governmental role in education, even if it comes from the federal government (Herrick 1996). One of the best examples of the moderately conservative views of so many Texans was the election of George W. Bush as governor. A candidate who was dramatically conservative on social issues would not have had the same success. The governor is an interesting case, in that he meets the Christian Right's critical litmus test of being pro-life but does make a broader and more moderate ideological pitch than do most in the movement. His moderately conservative actions have preserved his popularity. From the perspective of the Christian Coalition and others, Bush is a mixed blessing. He is a much more sympathetic ear than was the previous governor, Ann Richards, but he does not endorse the full agenda of the Coalition. The less-than-perfect fit with the social conservative movement is rarely visible in public, but the occasional tension is surely present.[19] Should the governor raise issues that are unpopular with the Christian Right, he would likely be able to generate strong popular support. This likelihood points out the risks facing the conservative Christian movement. If the Republican agenda places an emphasis on issue positions that are endorsed by the general public but opposed by the Christian Right, the movement may find itself marginalized.

The Beginning of a Backlash: How Big a Threat?

A more immediate threat to the Christian Right is the emergence of a counter-movement. The Christian Coalition and other such groups have enjoyed a period of little or no organized opposition. This honeymoon period is over, for there now exists such organized opposition. In the aftermath of the 1994 elections, the Texas Freedom Network was formed to counter the influence of the Christian Right.[20] According to its executive director, the organization was created with four aims: (1) to be a grassroots-level resource on the Christian Right in the state; (2) through public relations work, to provide an alternative voice in media coverage; (3) to train people to identify and combat the Christian Right; and (4) to provide policy alternatives to the conservative Christian agenda. During 1996, an additional task was added through the development of an offshoot organization, the Texas Faith Network. Made up of about six hundred members of the clergy, it seeks to provide an alternative religious voice in the policy realm.

The Texas Freedom Network is a small organization. There are fewer than three thousand contributors to the network, and the contributions are nearly all small and in-state. The group has three full-time staff members and is run on a lean budget. In spite of the modest start, the Freedom Network has made some progress on its original aims. The most dramatic change has come in the nature of media coverage. Not as much progress has been made toward the goals of becoming a grassroots resource and training people statewide. The Freedom Network is also engaged in promoting policy alternatives. Also in the realm of advocacy, the Texas Freedom Network, in conjunction with numerous other organizations in the state,[21] created the Texas Mainstream Voters project. The major accomplishment of this project in 1996 was the production of voter guides. In this election year, however, the guides were produced only for the state board of education races.

During the 1996 election cycle, the Freedom Network often made the news. The bulk of this coverage involved the state board of education races, where the network concentrated its activities. The overall impact of the Texas Freedom Network (as well as the Faith Network and the Mainstream Voters project) is difficult to assess. The organization is young and pales in comparison to the Christian Right. Still, the development of this sort of group has had one major effect: it has challenged the views and actions of the Christian Right, which for so long went without real organized challenge. The Texas Freedom Network spent time identifying the candidates and issues of the conservative Christian movement.[22] This information changed the way the election was covered in the media. Numerous stories were published in 1996 that set the Freedom Network up against, for example, the Christian Coalition. This sort of story makes it more difficult for the Christian Right to get its views out in an uncontested form. The sort of information distributed by the Freedom Network also could generate a public backlash, especially if the Christian Right's agenda is perceived as extreme. The massive fund-raising by the Christian Coalition–backed candidates in state board of education races provided an opportunity for Richards and others to criticize the Christian Right's attempt to buy control of the system. It is easy to disagree about the effect that organizations such as the Texas Freedom Network may have on elections or policy. One thing is clear, however, and that is that the Christian Coalition and others like it now must deal with organized political opposition.[23] The degree to which opposition groups are successful will play a large role in determining whether the Christian Right's recent success is short term or long term.

Conclusion

The Christian Right made dramatic gains in Texas during 1994. Its adherents picked the chair of the state Republican Party, guided several candidates to electoral victory, and turned the Republican Party sharply to the right. The movement had a new moderate Republican governor with whom to work and essentially owned the party organizational structure as of that year. The 1996 elections were the first where the Republican Party was under the de facto control of the Christian Right throughout the election cycle. Perhaps the best analogy is that of a student graduating from school: the 1994 elections were the commencement ceremony, and 1996 was the first time the Christian Right was able to act on its own in a significant way. There can be no debate about its success in this first turn. Various actors from the Christian Right controlled the process of selecting Republican delegates at every level. This not only produced a very conservative state platform but also made continued control of the party structure likely.

All this said, the leaders of the Christian Right in Texas probably should not grow too complacent about their success. Their control of the Republican Party, which is unquestionable, does not automatically translate into success at the polls. In fact, the 1996 elections saw many candidates of the Christian Right soundly defeated. One Republican who defeated a Coalition-backed candidate in a state house primary said, "What it means is that the Christian Coalition is great at organizing, at taking over the party, which they've done here, but they aren't worth a hoot, they aren't worth a tinker's damn, at winning elections" (Gamboa 1996). While this candidate may have overstated the case, his point is valid. The positions of the Christian Right are not held by the majority of people in the state. The movement's success so far has come within the more hospitable confines of the Republican Party, with larger success coming from exceptional organization and mobilization. There is, indeed, a significant difference between fighting to gain control of one party and fighting to win general elections.

Anyone who expects the Christian Right to disappear from Texas anytime soon is wrong. At the same time, anyone who expects an unbroken string of successes is also mistaken. The Christian Coalition and others are now faced with the difficult task of governing. There now exists organized opposition to the agenda of the Christian Right. Perhaps most important, the Christian Right faces a public that, while conservative, is not wholly in agreement with the social conservative agenda. Ironically, the past success of the Christian Right will make its future more difficult. Only when Christian Right candidates began to win office and party leadership positions did any real opposition develop. The state of Texas is too receptive an environment for the Christian Right to fail outright, but the success it now claims may represent the height of its ascent in state politics.

Notes

1. According to its home page on the World Wide Web:

The mission of Texas Christian Coalition is to organize, educate, and involve conservative people of faith to impact effectively the political process in our state and nation with Godly principles. We operate out of a set of values based on shared beliefs.

We believe Christians hold dual citizenship in the kingdom of God and the United States of America. As citizens, Christians have a sacred responsibility to influence their culture for righteousness. One means of influence is through government. Texas Christian Coalition represents over 120,000 people of faith committed to returning integrity to the government of this state and nation.

2. Some time prior to the 1994 convention, Pat Robertson sent a letter to supporters in the state, seeking support for what he called "Operation Precinct" (*Dallas Morning News*, 22 May 1994). This letter was the start of the campaign to educate activists on how to win control of the precincts.

3. Quoted in the *Dallas Morning News*, 22 May 1994.

4. AFA Texas also has created a lobbying arm and a PAC to push its pro-family agenda.

5. A poll conducted at the start of the year showed strong support for conservative economic issues usually associated with the GOP (such as government spending and the deficit). There is little particular evidence, pro or con, on support for the more controversial social issues associated with the Christian Right (Herrick 1996).

6. Not all churches were receptive to the guides. For example, the bishop of the Roman Catholic Diocese of Austin told his priests not to allow the distribution of materials that rated candidates or summarized their positions on the issues. Under those rules, the Coalition's voter guides would not be allowed (Palomo 1996a).

7. The Democratic Party was concerned about a "takeover" by the Christian Coalition, however. In a November 1995 letter to members of the Texas Christian Coalition, chairman Dick Weinhold urged members to attend precinct conventions of both parties. He argued for placing "people of faith" as precinct chairs in both major parties. This letter prompted the chair of the state Democratic Party to warn precinct officials of this "radical" group. Weinhold, on the other hand, said he was simply trying to increase the involvement of religious citizens (Bernstein 1996).

8. The level of information provided at these sessions was impressive. According to one attendee, the Coalition passed out copies of the state form that must be filled out in order to run for precinct chair. The form, perhaps not surprisingly, is a dense collection of boxes to be filled. The Coalition had reproduced the form, printing critical boxes in a different color to alert the candidate to information that must be provided to file successfully.

9. One indicator of how far apart the delegates and the larger pool of Republicans were was the abortion question. While the platform contained a "no exceptions" proposal, a majority of Republicans surveyed in the primary exit poll said they felt that the platform should not contain such a call (Ratcliffe 1996).

10. Dole had never been particularly popular with the Christian Right in the state. He won 56 percent of the primary vote, with Buchanan coming in second with 21 percent. About four out of ten Republican voters identified themselves as Christian Conservatives in primary exit polls, with Dole and Buchanan splitting these votes (Voter News Service results as reported in Ratcliffe 1996). One leader of the social conservative movement in Texas said: "The marriage of the Christian Right and the Dole cam-

paign has always been a shotgun wedding. There is definitely the feeling that Dole had to be dragged to the altar, and it's beginning to show"(Benjaminson 1996).

11. For information on some of Hotze's past political activity, see Bruce 1995.

12. Of course, the various players in the Christian Right may have their own agendas, including showing off their power. Jeff Fisher, the executive director of the Texas Christian Coalition, advised Texas delegates to the national convention not to answer any issue questionnaires or media polls. Fisher's argument was that these answers would be used to create an incorrect "stereotype" of the movement. Others offered a more cynical interpretation, suggesting that the Coalition sought to establish itself as the voice of the delegation (Robison 1996).

13. The controversy over the voter guides and the FEC suit in this matter indicate that the Christian Coalition may be moving rather close to the limit of what is allowed.

14. In the races where TAFAC was involved, the results were not particularly strong. TAFAC backed one winner in the state house races, three in the state senate races, and one in the board of education contests.

15. See Bruce 1995, n. 34 for more on Fontenot.

16. The sources of contributions to Leininger's PAC are interesting. John Walton, son of Wal-Mart founder Sam Walton and an Arkansas resident, gave at least $100,000. The political group associated with the California-based Coalition to Educate America gave $10,000. From Pennsylvania, Robert Cone gave $100,000, while Indianapolis resident John Rooney gave $50,000. Not all big donations were from out of state, of course. Leininger himself gave at least $140,000 (Stutz 1996; Walt 1996a).

17. This is not to say that there are no moderate Republicans in the state. It is not difficult to find a Republican who bemoans the loss of the party to the Christian Right. These unhappy partisans, however, seem incapable of regaining the party at this point.

18. Some evidence of the Republican tendencies in the state can be seen in the increase in congressional seats held by the GOP to thirteen of thirty after 1996.

19. Recall the designation of Bush as honorary chair of the state's delegation to the national Republican convention.

20. The bulk of information about the Texas Freedom Network was gathered from Peppel (1997) and Richards (1997).

21. The other organizations included such groups as the American Association of University Women, the American Civil Liberties Union, Americans United, and various teachers' groups.

22. The Texas Freedom Network works with the Texas chapter of the People for the American Way on monitoring the Christian Right.

23. The executive director of AFA/Texas reacted strongly to the presence of the Texas Freedom Network, making it the subject of a rather critical mass mailing.

References

Benjaminson, Wendy. 1996. "Dole's Conservative Support." *Houston Chronicle Interactive* (13 October).

Bernstein, Alan. 1996. "State Democrats Warned about Religious Right." *Houston Chronicle Interactive* (21 February).

Brooks, A. Phillips. 1996a. "Christian Coalition Setting Its Sights on Education Board." *Austin American-Statesman* (29 February): B4.

———. 1996b. "Religious Right Gains Board of Education Seat." *Austin American-Statesman* (7 November): A13.

Bruce, John M. 1995. "Texas: The Emergence of the Christian Right." Chap. 4 in *God at the Grass Roots: The Christian Right in the 1994 Elections,* ed. Mark J. Rozell and Clyde Wilcox. Lanham, Md.: Rowman & Littlefield.

Gamboa, Suzanne. 1996. "Keel, Rayburn Victors in Legislative Runoffs." *Austin American-Statesman* (10 April): A11.

Herrick, Thaddeus. 1996. "Poll Finds Texans Favoring GOP's Agenda for America." *Houston Chronicle Interactive* (12 January).

Key, V. O., Jr. 1949. *Southern Politics in State and Nation.* New York: Knopf.

Markley, Melanie. 1996. "Education Board Blasted in Bid to Topple Incumbent." *Houston Chronicle Interactive* (30 January).

Palomo, Juan R. 1996a. "Christian Coalition's Voter Guide Called Racist." *Austin American-Statesman* (11 October): B1.

———. 1996b. "Clergy Group Wants No Voter Guides in Churches." *Austin American-Statesman* (28 September): B3.

Peppel, Harriet. 1997. Telephone interview by author, 13 March.

Ratcliffe, R. G. 1996. "Texas Gives Big Boost to GOP Front-Runner." *Houston Chronicle Interactive* (13 March).

Richards, Cecile. 1997. Telephone interview by author, 14 March.

Robison, Clay. 1996. "Don't Talk to Strangers." *Houston Chronicle Interactive* (9 August).

Robison, Clay, and Alan Bernstein. 1996. "GOP Conservatives Flex Muscles." *Houston Chronicle Interactive* (22 June).

Roser, Mary Ann. 1996. "Might Makes Right." *Austin American-Statesman* (25 February): A1.

Stutz, Terrence. 1996. "$200,000 Raised for Candidates." *Dallas Morning News* (16 October): A1.

Walt, Kathy. 1996a. "Religious Right Donators Create a Cash Splash in Legislative Races." *Houston Chronicle Interactive* (2 November).

———. 1996b. "Religious Right Roaring into Race." *Houston Chronicle Interactive* (8 March).

Wilson, James Q. 1960. *The Amateur Democrat.* Chicago: University of Chicago Press.

4

Georgia: Purists, Pragmatists, and Electoral Outcomes

Charles S. Bullock III and Mark C. Smith

Although the rate of ascent slowed in 1996, GOP gains in Georgia continued. Republicans netted seven more state house seats and one senate seat, picked up a clutch of local offices, retained a seat on the public service commission, and put the state in Bob Dole's column. Republicans failed, however, in their top-priority objective of capturing the seat of retiring Senator Sam Nunn. The GOP also came up short in several coveted state legislative contests.

Christian conservatives played prominent roles in the fortunes of Georgia Republicans. This component of the party did not just contribute important votes, they often ended up in the camp of the winner of the GOP nomination. The Christian Right played an especially prominent role in selecting the Republican standard-bearer in the Senate contest.

Christian Coalition Activities

The Christian Coalition is the major organization in the Christian Right in Georgia. As in 1994, the Coalition's most significant role was the wide dissemination of two publications designed to guide the faithful as they pondered whom to support. One item, *The 1996 Georgia Legislative Scorecard,* rated each legislator on selected roll-call votes cast in 1995–1996. Senators were scored on eight votes; ten votes were used for representatives. Unlike in 1994 when computational errors in support scores were rife (Bullock and Grant 1995), 1996 calculations were accurate, although in 1996, as in 1994, Democrats criticized the Christian Coalition for some of the items chosen for inclusion. Some Democrats who felt that they had been improperly portrayed in 1994 attempted to inoculate themselves by determining which issues the Coalition was likely to include and then voting for the Christian Right's position. Of course, that kind of behavior promoted the Christian Coalition policy agenda.

Second, voter guides were prepared for the primary, runoff, and general elections. These publications reported candidate stands on a handful of issues, usually no more than ten. Different versions were prepared in different parts of the state so that they could contain evaluations of the stands taken by statewide candidates along with the positions of candidates for Congress, the state legislature, and, at times, local offices. The national office selected issues on which to compare congressional candidates, while the state office, sometimes working with local members, chose issues for state legislative and local races (Gibbs 1997). Voter guides were distributed primarily through churches, often the Sunday before the primary, although in some communities volunteers passed out copies at shopping centers and fast food outlets.

Political publications were not the extent of Coalition activities. The organization's second in command, Jack Gibbs, sponsored fifty-three sessions throughout Georgia during the spring aimed at preparing activists for the upcoming campaign and training first-time candidates (Gibbs 1996). He estimates that some fifteen hundred people attended these sessions, where they received information about issues dear to the sponsor and learned of recent activities of the general assembly. By concentrating on communities in which the organization had little strength, he recruited people to disseminate voter guides and scorecards; also, those who attended might become sufficiently motivated to start or revitalize a chapter.

The Coalition and other Christian conservatives launched a voter registration drive. The Citizenship Sunday program took advantage of the "motor voter" legislation and boasted of signing up between thirty thousand and fifty thousand voters. At least one hundred churches participated, with congregants filling out forms at Sunday school.

Size of the Christian Right

The Christian Right does not have a clearly defined membership, so all estimates of the ranks of Christian conservatives include guesswork. One method by which to approximate the size of the Christian Right is to examine votes for candidates who it is believed drew almost exclusively on the evangelical community for support, such as Paul Broun, a U.S. Senate candidate in the GOP primary. Even when one candidate has a special appeal to social conservatives, rarely is he or she the only recipient of support from this community. Therefore the twelve thousand votes for Broun were not a full enumeration of Christian Right supporters, many of whom voted for Clint Day, who aggressively courted them, or for primary front-runner Guy Millner. On the other hand, to sum the votes for these three candidates, all of whom had substantial support from the

Christian Right, would substantially overestimate the movement's ranks.

An alternative method examines the share of the electorate that identifies with the Christian Right. The Voter News Service exit poll of participants in Georgia's March presidential primary found that 38 percent of the respondents professed membership in the "religious right." The November exit poll found that among white voters, 21 to 22 percent acknowledged being part of the religious right.[1] Given the strong preference of Christian conservatives for Republican candidates, we expect to find that these voters constitute a larger share of the Republican primary electorate than of the general election electorate, even when we restrict the latter set of voters to whites. The percentage of "religious right" identifiers in the GOP presidential primary electorate is in line with figures for other southern states (Bullock forthcoming). The 38 percent identified in the presidential primary closely approximates the 40 percent figures that some have used when estimating the share of the GOP that belongs to the Christian Right (Foskett 1996).

The numbers of identifiers far exceed the ranks of the "dues-paying" members. The largest of the groups in Georgia, the Christian Coalition, is reported to be sixty thousand members strong (Pettys 1996). While the numbers of adherents have grown, the distribution of active chapters of the Christian Coalition has not spread as rapidly as former executive director Pat Gartland had hoped when interviewed in 1995. At that time, he wanted branches in 120 to 125 counties (Bullock and Grant 1995). By the November election, the Christian Coalition had only sixty chapters, but it had a presence in a greater number of counties since some chapters were multicounty.

Christian Right Preferences and Voting Power

As shown in table 4.1, the Christian Coalition legislative scorecard tended to evaluate Republicans more positively than Democrats. In the state senate no Democrat exceeded 50 percent, while the median Republican score was 80 percent and no Republican fell below 50 percent. Although not as skewed as the senate, house scores show Democrats clustered below 50 percent, with the median being 33 percent. While one Republican's score was 20 percent, only three members of the GOP fell below 78 percent and the GOP median was 100 percent, a score attained by three-fifths of the Republicans but by fewer than one in twenty Democrats.

The voter guides also portrayed Republicans as more supportive than Democrats of stands embraced by the Christian Coalition. While the position of the Christian Right in the general election often seemed to be that any Republican is preferable to any Democrat, the Coalition evaluated some GOP

Table 4.1
Distribution of Favorable Scores from the Christian Coalition Legislative Scorecard
by Chamber, 1995–1996 (in percent)

Chamber	0-50%	51-74%	75–89%	90–100%	N
Senate					
Democrats	100	0	0	0	35
Republicans	0	23.8	52.4	23.8	21
House					
Democrats	72.6	18.6	4.4	4.4	113
Republicans	3.0	1.5	25.8	69.7	66

Source: Compiled by the authors from data in *Georgia Legislative Scorecard.*

primary candidates more highly than others. Some Republican candidates actively courted Christian conservatives, while others were favorably received by this component of the electorate because of stands they had taken. Frequently, the candidate who proposes the most restrictive conditions on abortion has received Christian Right support.

In two high-profile statewide GOP primaries, certain candidates were widely perceived to be particularly favored or opposed by conservative religious activists. In the six-person Senate primary, three candidates made special appeals to religious conservatives. Paul Broun, a south Georgia physician who had two unsuccessful congressional bids behind him, was generally seen as having staked out the most restrictive antiabortion stand. Two more formidable candidates competed with Broun for support from the Christian Right by opposing abortion under most conditions. These two candidates offered the advantage that they had realistic opportunities to secure the nomination, and if nominated, they were expected to provide credible alternatives to Max Cleland, the former secretary of state who was unopposed for the Democratic nomination.

One of the better-funded GOP candidates seeking Christian conservative support, Clint Day, had served two terms in the state senate. The son of prominent Democratic contributors who had founded the Days Inn motel chain, Day boasted the presence of the former head of Georgia's Christian Coalition branch, Pat Gartland, on his staff. Day would allow abortions only to protect the life of the mother. The voter guide scored Day as the most conservative candidate in the primary field (Foskett 1996), and he was believed to be the favorite of single-issue, right-to-life voters.

While many Christian social conservatives liked Day, he faced opposition from Guy Millner, the multimillionaire founder of the Norrell temporary help firm, who had come within one percentage point of winning the governorship in 1994. Millner had not been the first choice of the Christian Right in 1994, but he had received strong support from this quarter once he beat their preferred candidate in the GOP runoff. Christian Right support had provided a significant increment to Millner's vote share in the general election (Bullock and Grant 1996).

Political realists saw a certain inevitability to Millner's nomination, and his campaign claimed to have the inside track with the Christian Coalition. He had vowed not to lose because of miserly spending, and his wealth guaranteed that he could buy massive amounts of media advertising even in Atlanta's pricey market. Millner and his wife publicized their participation in prayer groups and their opposition to abortion. However, ghosts from Millner's past gave pause to some of the devout. Did the businessman's two divorces undercut his professed support for a family-values agenda? As a further challenge to his family-values credentials, opponents noted that he had once invested in a casino. In challenging the depth of Millner's commitment to opposing abortion, critics pointed out that he had been landlord to an abortion clinic. Hard-liners found Millner less desirable than Day since Millner would permit abortions to end pregnancies produced by rape or incest as well as to protect the life of the mother—a wider range than was acceptable to Day.

While two of the leading candidates, Millner and Day, vied for Christian Right support, the third major player, Johnny Isakson, a seasoned state legislator and 1990 GOP gubernatorial nominee, took the bold step of going moderate on abortion. Isakson embraced a middle-ground stand similar to that taken by many Republicans and Democrats in the past, but now uncommon in GOP intramural contests in the South. In his television ad, he appeared with his wife and twenty-year-old daughter, and stated, "I don't believe our government should fund, teach or promote abortion, but I will not vote to amend the Constitution to make criminals of women and their doctors. I trust my wife, my daughter and the women of Georgia to make the right choice" (Alexander 1996b). The executive director of the Christian Coalition observed of Isakson's stand, "He's drawn a line in the sand with this" (Alexander 1996b).

The other statewide GOP primary chose a nominee to fill the remaining two years of the post of secretary of state, occupied on an interim basis by a Democrat appointed to succeed Democratic Senate candidate Cleland. Two of the four candidates had realistic chances at the nomination. Angling for the inside track with the Christian Right was Dave Shafer, who had stepped down as state party chair to manage Millner's gubernatorial campaign. His main opposition came from state representative Willou Smith, a personal friend of Isakson who staged campaign events with the moderate senatorial candidate.

Because of Christian social conservatives' preference for the GOP, we expect that statewide they participated disproportionately in that party's primary. (In parts of rural Georgia where Democrats dominate local officialdom, a desire to influence the choice of the sheriff or to help a neighbor win a seat on the county commission or school board undoubtedly prompted some Christian social conservatives who would vote for Republicans in statewide general elections to ask for Democratic primary ballots.)[2] We examine whether the candidates who sought Christian Right votes appeared to benefit and whether Isakson paid a price among Christian social conservatives.

Determining the number of Christian conservatives in an area is a bit difficult. Our approach is to assume that certain denominations may be more likely to flock to candidates who receive positive reviews from the Christian Right either from the pulpit or in publications such as the voter guides. The unit of analysis is the county. The measure of evangelicals comes from Bradley et al. 1990.[3]

Controls are introduced with region dichotomized since Republicans usually run better in north Georgia. The urbanization variable is also dichotomized since Republicans have done better in urban than in rural counties. Urban counties are those that are part of metropolitan areas, for it is here that Republicans have shown greatest strength. While the models in table 4.2 focus on primary elections, a measure of partisan strength is included to see whether some candidates ran better in counties that have shown GOP strength in the past. There have been conflicts between traditional Republicans and the new recruits of the Christian Right (cf. Guth and Green 1989). We use a measure of partisan strength computed by the GOP. This technique, pioneered by an analyst with the Texas-based campaign consulting group headed up by Lance Tarrance, uses results of multiple past, recent elections to compute an expected GOP vote share.

Table 4.2 shows that candidates who courted the religious community generally fared better in counties with large percentages of evangelicals than did candidates who lacked close ties with conservative religious voters. In the Senate primary, Isakson ran significantly worse in counties that had concentrations of evangelicals. His chief foe, Millner, did significantly better in these counties. Day, who probably counted on evangelical support more than any of the other, stronger senatorial aspirants, did perform better in counties with high percentages of evangelicals, although the slope just misses the .05 threshold using a one-tailed test. Broun, despite being the furthest right on abortion, did no better in counties with concentrations of evangelicals than elsewhere.

In the secretary of state primary, Smith, like Isakson, paid a penalty where evangelicals were numerous. While the evangelical slope for Shafer was positive, it was small and not significant.

The linkage between voting behavior and concentrations of evangelicals was much stronger in the runoff than in the primary. In both runoffs, the candidate closer to religious conservatives ran significantly better, with the slopes

Table 4.2
Support for Major Candidates in GOP Primary and Runoff, 1996

	a	Evangelical	Urban	Region	Party	Adj. R²	F
			Senate Primary				
Broun	.152	.038	-.023	-0.27*	-.211**	.09	5.02**
		(.88)†	(-.15)	(-2.10)	(-2.61)		
Day	.025	.088	-.019	.114***	.065	.30	17.6***
		(1.61)	(0.10)	(7.05)	(.630)		
Isakson	.166	-.217***	.043	.020	.348***	.21	11.4***
		(-3.79)	(2.08)	(1.21)	(3.31)		
Millner	.568	.145*	-.012	-.093***	-.168	.15	7.9***
		(1.95)	(-.427)	(-4.21)	(-1.19)		
			Secretary of State Primary				
Shafer	.268	.045	.034	.082***	-.111	.16	8.57***
		(.735)	(1.53)	(4.59)	(-.967)		
Smith	.091	-.242**	-.047	-.012	.826***	.12	6.19***
		(-2.70)	(-1.41)	(-.453)	(4.87)		
			Senate Runoff				
Millner	.347	.258***	-.039	-.004	-.275*	.10	5.20**
		(3.37)	(-1.38)	(-.182)	(-1.90)		
			Secretary of State Runoff				
Shafer	.763	.294***	.063*	.040	-.849***	.15	7.85***
		(3.49)	(2.00)	(1.605)	(-5.33)		

†T-tests in parentheses
*$p > .05$ **$p > .01$ ***$p > .001$

for Millner and Shafer exceeding .25. These results support observations that Christian conservatives are most influential in low-participation contests, since turnout dropped from the primary to the runoff. The magnitude of the relationship in the gubernatorial runoff and the increase in the slope for Millner from the primary to the runoff fit nicely with the dynamics of the campaign.

In one hundred thousand letters sent to supporters and others announcing his choice in the runoff, third-place finisher Day urged his 18 percent share of primary voters to transfer their allegiance to Millner. Jerry Keen, chair of Georgia's Christian Coalition, wrote to forty thousand members of his organization endorsing the former head of the Norrell Corporation. The leader of the Georgia branch of the American Family Association wrote members warning that Millner's defeat of Isakson was a "matter of life or death" (Alexander 1996c).

The runoff voter guide compared Millner and Isakson on ten issues and reported opposing stands on four items. Three of these issues had abortion overtones, with Millner more restrictive on allowing abortions and opposing the RU-486 abortion pill and fetal-tissue research. The fourth issue on which the candidates disagreed had Isakson opposing the abolition of the Legal Services Corporation.

Isakson campaign manager Heath Garrett (1996) sounded like a number of Democratic candidates had in 1994 (Bullock and Grant 1995) when he charged the Coalition with biased selection of issues for inclusion. According to Garrett, of the 103 items contained in the questionnaire that the Coalition sent to candidates, Isakson agreed with the religious group on 97, yet four of six issues in disagreement made their way into the runoff voter guide. The extent of the anti-Isakson effort led Bill Shipp, dean of the state's political journalists, to conclude that "the Christian Coalition crusade and Day's followers seem more intent on defeating Isakson than electing Millner" (Shipp 1996).

The slope for Shafer exceeded that for Millner, which was surprising because, while the voter guides highlighted four issues on which the gubernatorial candidates disagreed, the ten issues on which candidates for secretary of state were compared reported no differences between Shafer and Smith. Some other cue must have advantaged Shafer. His stronger performance in counties with concentrations of evangelicals may have been due to endorsements from the pulpit, or conservatives reluctant to support women candidates may have turned against Smith because of her gender. A knowledgeable GOP operative noted that "the Christian Coalition was decisive in this runoff; there was a strong behind-the-scenes anti-Willou effort."

Table 4.2 also hints at possible tensions between evangelicals and traditional GOP supporters. Isakson and Smith, the chief threats to Christian conservative ambitions, showed great primary strength in counties loyal to the GOP in the past. Table 4.2 shows that in the runoff, the candidates favored by the Christian Right did significantly worse in loyal GOP counties. (Since only two candidates compete in runoffs, results for Isakson would have the same values as for Millner except that the slopes would be reversed; the same transformation would occur if Smith were substituted for Shafer.) Democratic campaign operatives generally believed that Isakson and Smith would have been stronger candidates in November, in part because they would have rallied more enthusiastic support from party sources.

Abortion and Nomination Outcomes

Did Isakson lose because he deviated from hard-line opposition to abortions? Key personnel from both the Isakson and the Millner campaigns interviewed in preparing this chapter agreed that Isakson benefited from his abortion stand.[4] He had consistently trailed badly in the polls and had yet to find an issue with which to cut into Millner's formidable lead. Instead of overtaking Millner, it appeared that Isakson might actually slip behind Day and finish out of the running for a slot in the runoff. The scion of the motel chain was hammering Millner with television ads claiming that Day was "the only true conservative." The Millner camp believes that had Isakson not "gone soft" on abortion, the front-runner might have won a majority in the primary, thereby avoiding a costly and combative runoff. Not only did Isakson block Millner's move toward a majority, he narrowed the gap in the runoff to 18,000 votes.

While Isakson's position on abortion failed to win a majority, it is not conclusive proof that a moderate stand on this contentious issue dooms Republican candidates to defeat. Four years earlier, Paul Coverdell, the successful GOP nominee who went on to defeat incumbent Wyche Fowler for a U.S. Senate seat, had a stand on abortion not unlike Isakson's, although he did not buy $100,000 worth of television ads to publicize his stand. Moreover, at the same time that Isakson was finishing second in the GOP primary, a pro-choice candidate won the Republican nomination in Georgia's suburban Fourth Congressional District, defeating two opponents.

Millner's pollster, political scientist Whit Ayres, reported that Georgia Republicans divided fairly evenly between pro-choice and pro-life adherents. Ayres, however, noted that "the key is not the numbers but the intensity. In the Republican Party, the intensity is all on the pro-life side" (Baxter 1996).

General Election

As in much of the rest of the nation, Georgia's election ushered in few changes, as GOP gains decelerated from the 1992 and 1994 rates. At the congressional level, GOP momentum stalled because Republicans had won everything readily accessible to them; Democrats were restricted to three districts held by African Americans. In statewide contests, Republican hopes to fill Sam Nunn's seat came up 30,000 votes short, as 81,000 white votes were siphoned off by a Libertarian candidate. If supporters of the Libertarian had divided between Millner and Cleland at the same rate as the rest of the white electorate, Millner would have still come up 9,000 votes short.[5] If, however, Libertarian supporters were more predisposed to vote Republican than the rest of the white electorate, Millner might have eked out a win.

Incumbents—one of them a Republican—held on to the two public service commission seats, and the incumbent retained the post of secretary of state. The only major incumbent not to win in Georgia, Bill Clinton, fell 27,000 votes short, about the same margin by which he had carried the state in 1992.

Abortion did not become an issue in the Senate general election. One of Millner's top lieutenants speculated that Democrat Max Cleland, hoping not to mobilize the Christian Right, steered clear of the issue. Although abortion was not a hot topic, preferences on the issue split the electorate; Millner was supported by almost two-thirds of those who wanted few or no abortions, and Cleland won two-thirds of voters who would make abortion legal in all cases.

The exit polls of general election voters asked white respondents whether they considered themselves to be part of the "religious right." Just over 20 percent of Georgia's voters responded in the affirmative, and these participants provided stronger support for Republican nominees than did other whites. Dole received votes from 80 percent of the religious right component, with Perot, who got 8 percent of these voters, doing almost as well among this component as did the sitting president. Among other white voters, Dole trailed Clinton by a margin of 56 to 37 percent. Similar patterns emerged in the Senate contest, with Millner besting Cleland among white, religious-right voters 75 to 22 percent but doing little better with other white voters than Dole did, losing to Cleland 56 to 39 percent.

We turn now to multivariate models to determine whether the presence of concentrations of evangelicals augmented GOP vote shares in the five statewide contests. Has the Christian Right become so integral to the GOP that its influence is subsumed by partisanship? Variables in table 4.3 are identical to those used in table 4.2 to examine results of the GOP primary and runoff, with one exception. Because Georgia's cities generally vote Democratic in general elections, suburbanization rather than urbanization is included in table 4.3.[6]

Table 4.3 shows past partisanship related strongly to the 1996 results. There is no surprise here. Concentrations of evangelicals did not contribute to greater support for Republicans, except for Bob Dole. The table further shows the fundamentalist variable to be positively associated with support for Ross Perot and opposition to Bill Clinton. Evangelical slopes for Republicans seeking statewide offices were small, as were slopes for their Democratic opponents (not shown).[7] Except for Millner, Republicans ran better in suburbia than other parts of the state, and three of them performed better in north than south Georgia.

The larger slope in the presidential than the senatorial election is surprising in light of what seemed to be the priorities of the Christian Right. According to Jerry Keen (1996), head of Georgia's Christian Coalition, "The Senate race has really taken the political spotlight more so from our people than the presidential race." Georgians believed Bob Dole to be less committed than Millner to a pro-family agenda.

Several explanations can be suggested for the evangelical slope's achieving statistical significance in the presidential contest. One is that the voter guides

Table 4.3
Support for Major Candidates in General Election, 1996

	a	Evangelical	Suburban	Region	Party	Adj. R^2	F
			President				
Dole	.025	.085***	.027*	-.000	.798***	.77	136.1***
		(3.28)†	(2.50)	(-.022)	(15.32)		
Perot	.027	.098***	-.001	-.000	.006	.35	22.1***
		(8.27)	(-.245)	(-.133)	(.242)		
Clinton	.948	-.184***	-.028*	-.001	-.811***	.79	145.2***
		(6.49)	(-2.35)	(-.171)	(-14.35)		
			U.S. Senate				
Millner	.059	.032	-.013*	.037**	.831***	.75	118.0***
		(1.09)	(-1.67)	(4.62)	(18.57)		
			Secretary of State				
Shafer	.027	-.046	.003	.028**	.801***	.70	91.1***
		(-1.42)	(.332)	(3.08)	(16.04)		
			Public Service Commission (Barber Post)				
Collins	.097	-.008	.049***	.018*	.663***	.73	108.4***
		(-.287)	(4.48)	(2.26)	(12.64)		
			Public Service Commission (Durden Post)				
Durden	.114	.005	.031**	-.005	.779***	.79	143.3***
		(.197)	(3.18)	(-.733)	(16.80)		

†T-tests in parentheses
*$p > .05$ **$p > .01$ ***$p > .001$

provided a starker contrast between Clinton and Dole, as the candidates disagreed on each of eight issues in the guides. In contrast, the guides presented positions on five issues for candidates for secretary of state, and only abortion elicited disagreement, although on a second, school vouchers, the Democrat was shown to be undecided while the Republican had pledged support. Candidates for the Senate were scored on six issues and disagreed on abortion on demand. On the other five, the Democrat declined to respond to the Christian Coalition survey item. The guides did not review the candidates for the public service commission because of lack of space (Gibbs 1997).

A second potential explanation is that local factors assumed greater importance in state contests than in balloting for president and overrode unique cues to Christian social conservatives. Of the major party nominees for the four state offices, all except the GOP nominee for secretary of state had previously held or run for statewide office. In the course of these activities, they developed ties with groups and individuals that may have muted the effects of Christian conservatives. For example, women found Millner less attractive than did men, so according to exit polls, he got 65 percent support among white men compared with 54 percent among white women. The campaign manager for the Democratic secretary of state nominee says that their polls also showed a gender gap (Mayfield 1997). Obviously, had Millner narrowed the gender gap, he would now be the state's junior senator. A Millner staffer fretted, "I don't know if God himself could have made an ad for Guy that would make women vote for him."

A third possibility is that Christian social conservatives have become so assimilated into the core of GOP voters in statewide elections that, unlike in 1994 (Bullock and Grant 1996), they no longer made an additional contribution of support to Georgia candidates. Some GOP activists interviewed for this chapter had speculated that concentrations of Christian social conservatives would no longer be related to support for GOP candidates because of the integration of the Christian Right into the GOP. Table 4.3 indicates the accuracy of those projections. In the words of a key Millner campaigner, "The Christian Coalition is now pretty much part of the mainstream." If that statement is accurate, the Christian Right has come a long way from the 1988 presidential primary, when it was seen as a fringe group (cf. Kellstedt et al. 1994).

A fourth possible explanation is that the voter guides, a major avenue for disseminating information about candidates to Christian conservatives, may have had less impact. Several political activists of both parties claimed that not as many copies of the guides got into the hands of the faithful in 1996 as two years earlier and that the publication had less impact because its novelty had worn off. The Coalition's Jack Gibbs (1997) denies these claims. He acknowledges that the national office's delay in mailing the primary guides kept some of the 350,000 from being passed out. He believes that 400,000 copies of the 650,000 printed for the runoff and most of the 1.3 million prepared for the general election were distributed. "We had more churches in more communities involved and got more copies into the hands of voters than ever before," Gibbs claims. Certainly not every copy got into the hands of a GOP primary voter, but some copies may have been shared by multiple Republicans.

Conclusions

Christian conservatives succeeded in nominating candidates with whom they agreed in the two high-profile primary contests. Their preferred candidate won nomination for secretary of state, and the Christian Right succeeded in turning back the bid of Isakson, who became anathema after embracing a woman's right to a choice on abortion. While having their way in the GOP primary, the favorites of the Christian Right came up short in the general election. Millner's shortfall was a tantalizing 30,000 votes, while Shafer fell to interim secretary of state Lewis Massey by a 54-to-43 percent margin, with the remainder corralled by a Libertarian.

Monday-morning quarterbacks had warned throughout the primary season that Millner was a weaker general election candidate than Isakson. No one can replay the election substituting Isakson for Millner, but the Cleland camp had been reported to favor having Millner as their opponent (Shipp 1996), and Isakson had good personal relations with a number of Democrats who disliked Cleland. To a degree, 1996 repeated 1992, when antiabortion candidates— including one who ran pictures of aborted fetuses in television ads—won GOP nominations in three Georgia congressional districts, only to fall in November.

Elections in 1998, when the state's constitutional officers run for election, may confront the Christian Right with a test if ideological purity crashes into electoral pragmatism. Is it better to nominate a candidate with correct views on the abortion issue if the price is alienation of so many white women that a Democrat who has little sympathy for a number of issues dear to Christian conservatives wins office? Key leaders among conservative congregations claim that they are becoming more pragmatic (Keen 1996; Gartland 1996). If the Christian Right scales back the emphasis on abortion and assigns greater significance to family values that are put into practice as tax cuts, welfare reform to encourage working, cracking down on the distribution of pornography, and school vouchers, it may increasingly not just secure the GOP nomination but actually win office. The downside is that if leaders opt for pragmatism, they risk alienating some members whom Guth and Green (1989) have found to be particularly prone to see compromise as betrayal.

Prospects for accommodation seem slight if the Christian Right follows the tack of Jim Glanton, husband of a state senator and head of the Christian Coalition chapter on Atlanta's south side. He warns ominously of the relationship between religious conservatives and the GOP: "They can't live without us. The moderates . . . are not going to make it without us" (Alexander 1996a). Moderates might retort that "Christian conservatives cannot make it without the moderates."

Notes

We appreciate the candor of the individuals whom we interviewed in preparing this chapter. A number of those helpful people were promised anonymity and are not identified.

1. The Voter News Service exit poll for the presidential election reported 21 percent of white Georgia voters to be part of the religious right, while the results of this exit poll for the U.S. Senate contest found 22 percent of the whites answering that they were members of the religious right. For both contests, 75 percent of the whites said they were not members of the religious right.

2. Georgia voters do not register by party. At the primary, a voter can ask for either party's ballot.

3. Denominations included in our measure are Southern Baptist; Presbyterian Church of America; Reformed Presbyterian; Assembly of God; Christian and Missionary Alliance; Church of God of Anderson, Ind.; Church of God of Cleveland, Tenn.; Pentecostal Church of God; Church of the Nazarene; Lutheran, Missouri Synod; Foursquare Gospel; independent churches (both charismatic and noncharismatic); and Wesleyan.

4. Not all participants from the Millner campaign saw Isakson benefiting from his abortion stand. The dissenter argues that because it had been six years since Isakson ran statewide, he had latitude to define himself, and had he adopted a more conservative abortion position, he could have overtaken Millner. Catching Millner would have required a spurt of support that Isakson had not managed up until the time of his abortion announcement.

5. Exit poll results show Cleland getting 37 percent of the white vote.

6. Suburban counties are those in metropolitan areas, excluding counties containing all or part of a central city, i.e., Atlanta, Athens, Augusta, Albany, Savannah, Macon, or Columbus.

7. Since Libertarian candidates competed for each of these posts, the absolute values of slopes for Democrats are not the same as for Republicans.

References

Alexander, Kathey. 1996a. "Christians Now Insiders in State GOP." *Atlanta Journal-Constitution* (10 February): C1.

———. 1996b. "Isakson Gambles by Pushing Abortion-Rights Stance in Ads." *Atlanta Journal* (13 June): B2.

———. 1996c. "Religious Group Rates Millner High." *Atlanta Journal* (29 July): B1.

Baxter, Tom. 1996. "Stirring Up Georgia Abortion Debate Puts Isakson in National GOP Spotlight." *Atlanta Journal* (13 June): B2.

Bradley, Martin B., Norman Green Jr., Dale E. Jones, Mac Lynn, and Lou McNeil. 1990. *Churches and Church Membership in the United States.* Atlanta: Glenmary Research Center.

Bullock, Charles S., III. 1997. "Partisan Changes in the Southern Congressional Delegation." Paper presented at the Hoover Institution Symposium on Congressional Elections in the Post–World War II Era: Continuity and Change, Stanford University, Stanford, Calif.

————. Forthcoming. "1996 Presidential Primaries: Short and Sweet." In *The 1996 Presidential Election in the South,* ed. Laurence W. Moreland and Robert P. Steed. Westport, Conn.: Praeger.

Bullock, Charles S., III, and John Christopher Grant. 1995. "Georgia: The Christian Right and Grass Roots Power." Chap. 3 in *God at the Grass Roots: The Christian Right in the 1994 Elections,* ed. Mark J. Rozell and Clyde Wilcox. Lanham, Md.: Rowman & Littlefield.

————. 1996. "Evangelical Christians and the 1994 Georgia Elections." Paper presented at the Symposium on Southern Politics, the Citadel, Charleston, S.C.

Foskett, Ken. 1996. "Religious Conservatives Figure Big in Tuesday's Vote." *Atlanta Journal* (8 July): B3.

Garrett, Heath. 1996. Telephone interview by senior author, 23 December.

Gartland, Pat. 1996. Telephone interview by senior author, 27 December.

Gibbs, Jack. 1996. Telephone interview by senior author, 23 December.

————. 1997. Telephone interview by senior author, 28 January.

Guth, James L., and John C. Green. 1989. "God and the GOP: Religion among Republican Activists." Pp. 223–41 in *Religion and Political Behavior in the United States,* ed. Ted G. Jelen. New York: Praeger.

Keen, Jerry. 1996. Interview by David Molpus, *Morning Edition*, National Public Radio, 14 October.

Kellstedt, Lyman A., John C. Green, James L. Guth, and Corwin E. Smidt. 1994. "Religious Voting Blocs in the 1992 Election: The Year of the Evangelical?" *Sociology of Religion* 55 (3): 307–26.

Mayfield, Shannon. 1997. Telephone interview by senior author, 29 January.

Pettys, Dick. 1996. "Christian Activists Gaining Influence in Political Arena." *Athens Banner-Herald* (June 30): 12A.

Shipp, Bill. 1996. "Abortion Issue Eclipses GOP Senate Runoff." *Athens Banner-Herald* (21 July): 5D.

5

North Carolina: Jesse's Last Stand? The Christian Right in the Elections

Ray Swisher and Christian Smith

The 1996 elections were a crucial testing ground for the influence of the Christian Right in North Carolina. Several high-profile races, most notably the senatorial rematch between longtime incumbent Jesse Helms and Harvey Gantt, drew national attention from the Christian Coalition and an army of "shadow campaign" organizations opposed to Helms and the Christian Coalition. A Federal Election Commission lawsuit against alleged illegal backing by the Christian Coalition of Helms in the 1990 elections highlighted the significance of this race. The gubernatorial race also featured a "born-again" Christian with strong backing from the Christian Coalition, Robin Hayes, against incumbent Democrat Jim Hunt. Finally, two hotly contested House of Representatives races pitted Christian Coalition–backed incumbents against Democratic challengers.

On the surface it appears that the Christian Right's success was mixed. Helms won reelection quite easily, while Robin Hayes and both incumbent representatives, Heineman and Funderburk, were losers. Americans United for Separation of Church and State, a national organization dedicated to combating groups such as the Christian Coalition, cites these races as evidence that the Christian Right's influence is on the downturn (Banisky 1996). Complicating matters is the perception that Jesse Helms would have beaten Gantt regardless of whether the Christian Right supported him. Further, both losing incumbents in the U.S. House races carried enormous personal baggage into the elections, having been involved in controversies that greatly reduced their electability. The role of the Christian Right in the Hunt-Hayes gubernatorial race is similarly equivocal, with the Christian Right having played a large part in nominating the more conservative Hayes over moderate Republican Charles Vinroot, ultimately to lose to a moderate Democrat, Jim Hunt. Is Hayes's nomination an indicator of the Christian Right's growing influence, or is it another sign that purists within the Christian Right are undermining the Republican Party's ability to elect more pragmatic candidates?

We seek to examine these issues through an analysis of statewide surveys administered prior to the 1990 and 1996 Helms-Gantt races, exit poll data from the 1996 elections, and analysis of media coverage of the races, including the opinions of key leaders of organizations of the Christian Right and organizations formed in opposition.

The Major Players in 1996

Before we analyze individual races, a brief description of the major religious and political players is in order. Most obvious is the North Carolina Christian Coalition, with fifty chapters and an estimated 160,000 members statewide (Christensen 1996d). The Coalition distributed more than 1.5 million voter guides throughout North Carolina in 1996 (Kotch 1996).

Liberal religious groups have formed as well, including North Carolina branches of the Interfaith Alliance, Evangelicals for Social Action, and Call to Renewal (Shimron 1996b). To counter the efforts of the Christian Coalition, the Interfaith Alliance mailed letters to churches asking them not to display or distribute Coalition voting guides, and the group distributed voting guides of its own. The Alliance also called for candidates to sign a "civility pledge" promising to campaign ethically and not to claim a monopoly on religious virtue (Nowell 1996).

Many nonreligious political organizations made their presence felt in North Carolina as well. The Helms race in particular, but also the two House of Representatives races, generated a network of oppositional shadow campaigns. A short list of those groups includes the gay rights Human Rights Campaign, Sierra Club, National Abortion Rights Action League, National Organization for Women, National Education Association, AFL-CIO, NAACP, and the environmentalist Clean Up Congress (Kotch 1996).

The importance of the 1996 races was evidenced also by visits to North Carolina by several national leaders in an effort to get out the vote. Jerry Falwell came as part of his National Committee for the Restoration of the Judeo-Christian Ethic's "God Save America" campaign, urging local pastors to get involved in voter registration (Banks 1997). Speaking with Falwell to a Raleigh-area pastors' policy briefing were Senator Jesse Helms, House Speaker Newt Gingrich, and Representative David Funderburk. Jim Wallis, leader of the more moderate evangelical group Call to Renewal, and the Reverend Gardner Taylor, a civil rights activist speaking for the Interfaith Alliance, visited North Carolina as well (Neff and Shimron 1996).

Helms and Gantt in 1990 and 1996

Jesse Helms *is* North Carolina politics, having served as senator for the last twenty-four years and never having lost a political contest. He is known nationally and, through his chairmanship on the Senate Foreign Relations Committee, internationally for his far-right conservatism. He has vocally opposed federal funding of abortion, gay and lesbian rights legislation, funding for the arts, and the Martin Luther King Jr. federal holiday (Christensen 1996c). Harvey Gantt, an African American and former mayor of Charlotte, was the hope of liberals nationwide. Gantt has a long history of civil rights involvement, having been the first black student admitted to Clemson University, just months after James Meredith's admission to the University of Mississippi provoked rioting. Gantt was also arrested for participating in the first lunch-counter sit-in in Charleston, South Carolina. Within the Democratic Party today, however, Gantt is somewhat of a moderate (Christensen 1996b).

Both candidates appeared to move toward the center in 1996, trying to appeal to the growing numbers of moderate voters. Helms softened his position on abortion by recognizing those within the Republican Party with views on abortion different from his own. Centrism was evident also in Gantt's emphasis on welfare reform and getting tougher on criminals. Gantt charged Helms with opposition to Medicare and Medicaid programs for the elderly, while Helms ran ads charging Gantt with advocating higher taxes, opposing the death penalty, and supporting homosexual marriages (Christensen 1996e).

Both Helms and Gantt are Southern Baptists. Upon winning the 1996 election, Helms proclaimed, "I am about as Baptist as you can get" (Nowell 1996). Gantt, described by others as "deeply religious," sings in the church choir and teaches adult Sunday school classes. Referring to Helms, Gantt said, "Sometimes I don't see a lot of compassion . . . that is one of the characteristics of Jesus Christ, who we all claim as our personal savior" (quoted in Christensen 1996b).

Helms was strongly backed by the Christian Coalition—so much so that a recent Federal Election Commission lawsuit alleges that the Coalition illegally supported Helms in the 1990 election against Gantt. The suit charges that the Coalition violated the ban on endorsing candidates through its efforts on phone banks, distribution of partisan voting guides, and Republican-targeted get-out-the-vote drives. It also alleges that the Coalition illegally coordinated with the candidates' campaign organizations (Rosen 1996a).

The Helms-Gantt races of 1990 and 1996 provide a natural quasi gauge of the changing influence of the Christian Right in North Carolina politics. The Carolina Poll, a statewide public opinion survey administered twice a year by the University of North Carolina at Chapel Hill School of Journalism, offers a unique data source to test the changing relationship between religion and politics. Carolina Polls in the fall of 1990 and fall of 1996 asked respondents: "If the election for Senator were held today, would you vote for Jesse Helms, the Republican, or Harvey Gantt, the Democrat?" The order of alternatives was reversed in half of the surveys to minimize question-wording biases. The surveys also included identical items tapping rates of church attendance, as well as a variety of political and socioeconomic control variables.

Although it is impossible to measure directly the impact of the Christian Right, we estimate the role of the movement by examining the strength of the effects of church attendance on support for Helms in each of the elections, controlling for other relevant variables. Given the tendency to vote "straight tickets" along party lines, we included dummy variables for Republican and Democratic Party affiliations; self-described independents or those without any party affiliation are the excluded category. Because of the differing races of the candidates, we include a control for nonwhite. The data set did not allow finer racial or ethnic distinctions. Other control variables included income, age, years of school completed, female, and whether the respondent lived in a metropolitan county.

Logistic regression models of supporting Helms are estimated separately for each election. Results appear in the first two columns of table 5.1. Not surprisingly, party affiliation, race, and gender were most predictive in both years. The third column of coefficients, labeled "Pooled," presents results for both years combined. For both years combined, Republicans were 3.92 times and Democrats 0.32 times as likely to support Helms as were respondents who identified as independents or no party affiliation. Nonwhites were 0.17 times as likely as whites, and women 0.51 times as likely as men, to support Helms, all other factors held constant.

Most important for present purposes is that the role of religion changed from 1990 to 1996. In 1990, people who said they attend church weekly or more often were 1.62 times as likely to support Jesse Helms as were less frequent attenders, all else held constant. Church attendance was insignificant in the 1996 election. To test whether the difference between 1990 and 1996 is statistically significant, we pooled the two data sets, creating a dummy variable for the 1996 election and an interaction term of the 1996 election and church attendance. The interaction term is negative and significant, indicating a real decline in the role of religion in predicting intention to vote for Helms. Religiosity was not an important predictor of vote choice in 1996. This result persists even when we estimate the equation for whites only.

Of course, our measure of religiosity fails to differentiate the Christian Right from all religious people, including religious liberals. Unfortunately, measurements of denominations or broad religious movements (e.g., evangeli-

Table 5.1
Odds Ratios of Support for Jesse Helms in the 1990 and 1996
North Carolina Senatorial Elections

Variables	1990	1996	Pooled
Republican	2.86***	4.86***	3.92***
Democrat	0.30***	0.30***	0.32***
Income	1.02	0.98	0.99
Age	1.01	1.01*	1.01*
Education	0.95	0.90*	0.93**
Nonwhite	0.16***	0.18***	0.17***
Female	0.56**	0.49***	0.51***
Urban	0.83	0.96	0.91
Church Attendance	1.73*	0.84	1.74*
1996 Election			1.31*
Church Attendance x 1996 Election			0.51*
N	494	603	1007
χ^2	161.88	205.92	364.47

Note: The question asked was "If the election for senator were held today, would you vote for Jesse Helms, the Republican, or Harvey Gantt, the Democrat?" The order of choices was reversed for half of the sample.
†$p < 0.10$ *$p < 0.05$ **$p < 0.01$ ***$p < 0.001$

cal, fundamentalist, mainline, etc.) to which people belonged were not available. Yet the fact that we are dealing with North Carolina, a state in which Christians tend to be strongly conservative, and are using a fairly stringent measure of religiosity (i.e., church attendance "every week" or "more than once a week") should mitigate this limitation. To further test the internal validity of the church attendance measure, we created a scale of moral conservatism from items tapping attitudes toward abortion, homosexuality, and premarital sex. Inclusion of this scale in the 1990 model (items not available in 1996) eliminates the effect of church attendance on voting for Helms, indicating that church attendance in North Carolina is highly correlated with attitudes consistent with Christian Right identification. (The bivariate correlation is 0.20.)

Jesse Helms coasted to his fifth term as senator in a fairly uneventful election. He is now seventy-five years old, and this will likely be his last term. The chances that he would have lost to any opponent appear to be slim. We do not wish to overstate our findings. Party identification, race, and gender were the dominating factors in both the 1990 and the 1996 elections. Yet in 1990, when Helms was perceived to be more beatable, religion also played a significant role in predicting his support. In 1996, by contrast, religion played very little role at all. This suggests that the Christian Right was not a critical factor in the 1996 North Carolina Senate race.

The Republican Gubernatorial Primary

The Christian Right played perhaps its greatest role in the Republican primaries for governor. The two leading candidates for the nomination were moderate former Republican mayor of Charlotte Charles Vinroot and the more conservative North Carolina state representative Robin Hayes. On most of the issues that a governor could influence, they largely agreed. They were both for reductions in government spending, school voucher programs, and local government control over welfare programs.

The candidates differed in their positions on abortion. Vinroot described himself as antiabortion but said, "I will not impose my religious views on any woman in this room" (Mitchell 1996). Robin Hayes criticized Vinroot's support of Planned Parenthood during his tenure as mayor of Charlotte. Vinroot's claim that he didn't know Planned Parenthood performed abortions rallied conservative Christians behind Hayes. Hayes, in contrast, advocated a ban on abortions and as state representative recommended slashing state abortion funds. Also as state representative, Hayes backed successful legislation promoting abstinence education in public schools and limiting discussions of other birth control methods to the failure rates of condoms (Wagner 1996b).

Both candidates were avowed Christians, though their self-descriptions identified Hayes more clearly as a conservative Christian. Vinroot described himself as a "Christian conservative," while Hayes preferred the evangelical term "born-again" Christian (Mitchell 1996). The Christian Coalition backed Hayes, as evidenced in the half-million primary voting guides they distributed statewide (Cochran 1996a) and in the efforts of local political activists (Christensen 1996a). More moderate and historically powerful Republicans backed Vinroot, viewing Hayes as too conservative to defeat Hunt in a general election. A low 21.5 percent turnout in the primary also worked in Hayes's favor. Hayes captured 50 percent of the vote, defeating Vinroot, who polled 46 percent. Sim Delapp, head of the North Carolina Christian Coalition, clearly thought his group made a difference, saying, "It was a joy to see the issues we espouse at the forefront of the campaign . . . and to see that people of faith had some say in the outcome. A lot of candidates were coming our way this time, and that hasn't always been the case" (quoted in Cochran 1996a).

The Gubernatorial Election

The governor's race pitted three-term incumbent Jim Hunt against Christian Coalition–backed Robin Hayes. The main issue in the campaign was education. Hunt called for raising teacher pay levels and expanding his early-childhood "Smart Start" program, while Hayes pointed to North Carolina's forty-eighth ranking on SAT scores as an indicator of Hunt's poor education record (Wagner 1996c).

The salience of religion in the 1996 race is revealed by the rhetoric of the candidates, particularly that of Jim Hunt. Hunt referred to his Smart Start program as helping children "become all that God wants them to be." Similarly, when discussing environmental issues, Hunt said, "God sculpted these mountains. It is our responsibility to take care of them" (quoted in Wagner 1996c). Hunt also worked to involve churches and religious groups in social service and other government programs. As part of his welfare reform plan, "Work First," Hunt urged churches to adopt families in an effort to help them escape welfare. Hayes was similarly unafraid to invoke religion in his political addresses. In one speech, Hayes said that he "wrestled with the Lord" in deciding whether to run for governor (quoted in Wagner 1996a).

Hunt won the election handily with 56 percent of the vote, the largest margin of victory since 1980 (Wagner 1996a). Although Hayes captured most conservative voters, he did not draw them in nearly as well as did Helms. Exit poll data (see table 5.2) indicates Hayes garnered only 66 percent of conservative voters, compared to Helms's 80 percent. Similarly, Hayes did not do as well as Helms among white "Christian Right" voters, taking only 59 percent compared to Helms's 77 percent. Most damaging was that only 29 percent of moderate voters supported Hayes, compared to 42 percent favoring Helms.

Some analysts have argued that Hayes's primary win split the Republican Party, alienating more moderate members, especially women (Wireback 1996). Hayes captured 75 percent of Republicans and only 34 percent of women voters, compared to Jesse Helms's 86 percent and 46 percent, respectively. Perhaps most telling is that Hayes garnered support from only 41 percent of Protestants, and only 47 percent of white Protestant voters. It appears that highly conservative candidates such as Hayes are unable to bridge the gap between conservative and more mainline or moderate Christian groups. At the national level, the Coalition has been making efforts to support candidates and issues that cross party and religious-tradition boundaries. Polling data presented here, however, indicate that the North Carolina Christian Coalition's backing of Hayes may have been counterproductive, a continuation of the ineffective "purist" strategy of past state-level elections (Wilcox 1994).

Table 5.2
Exit Polls, 1996 Senate and Governor's Races (percent of vote)

Categories	Senate Race		Governor's Race	
	Helms (R)	Gantt (D)	Hayes (R)	Hunt (D)
Male	56	43	45	54
Female	46	53	34	65
White	62	38	46	54
Black	8	91	9	89
Democrat	21	78	12	88
Republican	86	13	75	24
Independent/other	53	46	36	61
Liberal	16	83	14	85
Moderate	42	57	29	70
Conservative	80	19	66	33
Protestant	54	45	41	58
Catholic	55	44	42	57
Other Christian	53	47	42	57
White Protestant	63	36	47	52
White Catholic	59	40	48	51
White religious right	77	23	59	41
White not religious right	40	59	31	67

Source: Compiled exit polls from http://www.politicsnow.com website. Categories above are as presented on the website.

The House of Representatives Races

Two House of Representatives races were critical tests of the Christian Right's influence in North Carolina. Both involved conservative Republican incumbents with ties to the Christian Right. Both of those candidates ultimately lost.

In the Fourth District, incumbent Fred Heineman faced Democrat David Price, whom he had somewhat surprisingly defeated in 1994. Price had held the seat for the previous four terms. Price's loss in 1994 was seen as an upset, given the demographics of the Fourth District, which encompasses most of Raleigh, the "displaced northerners" suburb of Cary, and Chapel Hill, home of the University of North Carolina, which Jesse Helms had described on more than one occasion as a liberal "zoo." Among registered voters, the district is dominated by Democrats almost 2 to 1. A low voter turnout by African Americans and a strong turnout by conservative white voters elected Heineman in 1994 (Dew and Neff 1996). In addition to the disadvantage of district demographics, Heineman faced a potential backlash against the perception that he was out of touch with ordinary people, having recently described himself as lower middle class, despite earning almost $200,000 a year, and middle-class Americans as those earning $300,000 to $750,000 (Dew and Neff 1996).

The race between incumbent David Funderburk and Democratic challenger Bob Etheridge was equally heated. The Second District is more diverse, yet it is dominated by rural tobacco interests and traditionalist Democrats known as "Jessecrats," who, though registered Democrats, support Jesse Helms and frequently vote Republican. Funderburk is a longtime understudy of Helms, and his voting record reflects this connection (Rosen 1996b). Etheridge also has ties to tobacco country, having been a tobacco farmer all his life, and has a strong public record of experience as county commissioner, state legislator, and superintendent of public schools. Most in Etheridge's favor was the controversy surrounding a Funderburk motor vehicle violation in late 1995. Funderburk was charged with lying to a police officer following an accident that involved him and his wife. There was some uncertainty over exactly who was driving, and Funderburk also admitted that rather than calling 911 to get help for injured parties in the other car, he telephoned his lawyer (Dew and Neff 1996).

Funderburk and Heineman were card-carrying Republicans, advocating smaller government, tax cuts, and elimination of the budget deficit. Both opposed abortion and were strongly supported by the North Carolina Christian Coalition. Voter guides distributed by the Coalition clearly favored the incumbents. Yet both lost by sizable margins. Price defeated Heineman 54.4 percent to 43.8 percent; Etheridge defeated Funderburk 52.5 percent to 45.7 percent. Given their personal controversies, it is difficult to know to what extent their losses reflect on the influence of the Christian Right and to what extent on their own unelectability. What is clear is that the Coalition chose to back candidates who were politically vulnerable and that its support was insufficient to help them retain their seats.

Conclusions

On the whole, the Christian Right did not fare well in the 1996 North Carolina elections. Though Jesse Helms returns for a fifth term as senator, religion did not play a large role in his reelection. Perhaps this is because the real battle was fought and won by Helms in 1990; much less attention was paid to the 1996 race, whose outcome was more of a foregone conclusion. Perhaps it is also a result of heightened scrutiny stemming from the Federal Election Commission lawsuit against the Christian Coalition charging illegal support for Helms in the 1990 race.

The Christian Right's lack of effectiveness is more easily seen in other

North Carolina races. In the gubernatorial race, conservative Christians pushed the quite conservative candidate Robin Hayes through the primaries, only to be beaten soundly in the general election. As we have seen, Hayes received very little support from Christians outside the Christian Right and did not fare as well as other Republican candidates among conservatives, moderates, and Republican voters. Similarly, the Coalition backed politically vulnerable candidates, to no avail, in two highly visible House of Representatives races.

With this in mind, we conclude that the North Carolina Christian Coalition seems not to have learned from previous elections. The more moderate and pragmatic strategies of the "fourth wave of the evangelical tide" appear not yet to have washed ashore in North Carolina (Moen 1995). These failures in North Carolina no doubt contributed to Jerry Falwell's recent nationwide appraisal that "the so-called religious right . . . fell asleep against the switch" in the 1996 elections (Banks 1997).

References

Banisky, Sandy. 1996. "Christian Coalition Claims Victory Satisfied." *Baltimore Sun* (19 November): A2.

Banks, Adelle. 1997. "Religious Right 'Asleep' in '96?" *Durham Herald Sun* (15 February): C1.

Christensen, Rob. 1996a. "Durham Republican Seeks Right Balance between Politics, Religion." *Raleigh News and Observer* (19 August): A3.

———. 1996b. "Gantt: Fueled by Persistence, Faith." *Raleigh News and Observer* (25 October): A1.

———. 1996c. "Helms: A Political Trailblazer." *Raleigh News and Observer* (24 October): A1.

———. 1996d. "Jesse's People: Who Loves Helms?" *Raleigh News and Observer* (6 October): A1.

———. 1996e. "Senator Handed Fifth Term." *Raleigh News and Observer* (6 November): A1.

Cochran, John. 1996a. "Conservatism on the Rise, Race Shows." *Greensboro News and Record* (9 May): A1.

———. 1996b. "GOP's Hayes to Face Hunt." *Greensboro News and Record* (8 May): A1.

Dew, Joe, and Joseph Neff. 1996. "Party Strategists Eager to Claim Control of Triangle House Seats." *Raleigh News and Observer* (16 September): A1.

Heath, Jena. 1996. "Get-Out-Vote Efforts in High Gear." *Raleigh News and Observer* (4 November): A1.

Kotch, Noah. 1996. "'Shadows' Fall on the Campaign Trail." *Raleigh News and Observer* (5 August): A1.

Mitchell, Kirsten B. 1996. "Thunder on the Right." *Wilmington Morning Star–News* (21 April): A1.

Moen, Matthew C. 1995. "The Fourth Wave of the Evangelical Tide: Religious Conservatives in the Aftermath of the 1994 Elections." *Contentions: Debates in Society, Culture, and Science* 5(1): 19–38.

Neff, Joseph, and Yonat Shimron. 1996. "Falwell Rallies Triangle Faithful." *Raleigh News and Observer* (29 October): A1.

Nowell, Paul. 1996. "Baptists Reflect on Values in Politics." *Raleigh News and Observer* (17 November): B9.

Rosen, James. 1996a. "Federal Suit Filed against Christian Coalition." *Raleigh News and Observer* (31 July): A3.

———. 1996b. "Poles Apart in Backgrounds and Beliefs, Funderburk Still a Fiery Conservative." *Raleigh News and Observer* (3 October): A1.

Shimron, Yonat. 1996a. "'Call to Renewal' Founder Urges a 'Politics of Transformation.'" *Raleigh News and Observer* (28 October): B1.

———. 1996b. "For Some Voters, Faith Is the Main Issue at the Polls." *Raleigh News and Observer* (2 November): A1.

Wagner, John. 1996a. "Governor Strolls to Fourth Term." *Raleigh News and Observer* (6 November): A1.

———. 1996b. "Hayes Stresses Economic, Moral Beliefs." *Raleigh News and Observer* (17 October): A1.

———. 1996c. "Hunt Wants Action from Churches." *Raleigh News and Observer* (7 September): A3.

Wilcox, Clyde. 1994. "Premillennialists at the Millennium: Some Reflections on the Christian Right in the Twenty-first Century." *Sociology of Religion* 55(3): 243–61.

Wireback, Taft. 1996. "How Divisive Is Abortion in the GOP?" *Greensboro News and Record* (23 September): B1.

6

Florida: Losing by Winning? The Odyssey of the Christian Right

Kenneth D. Wald and Richard K. Scher

Floridians went to bed on election night in 1996 confident that the state had gone decisively Democratic in a presidential election for the first time in twenty years and awoke Wednesday morning to find that they had entrusted governance of the state to the Christian Coalition. Though widely reported, neither of these impressions was particularly accurate. The Democratic victory was remarkably limited. Although they carried the presidential vote and held three seemingly vulnerable congressional districts, Democrats still lost enough seats in both houses of the Florida legislature to fall to minority status for the first time since Reconstruction. The impression that the Christian Coalition was the driving force in the new Republican legislative majority, a claim widely trumpeted in the press, owed more to hyperbole than sober analysis. Nonetheless, the odd conjunction of these impressions presents a puzzle that the present chapter tries to solve. How can a social movement that has performed so modestly in the statewide electoral arena have reached a stage where it is regarded as a major player in state politics?

The answer, which we will develop at length, is that it hasn't. Despite its putative successes, the Christian Right remains a contender rather than a powerful force in Florida politics. Where the movement has won victories, it has done so by disguising its role and downplaying its influence. When it has attempted to move out of the shadows to assert a larger influence, it has been checked and deflected by other political forces. Although the results of the 1996 elections enhanced the conditions favorable to Christian Right impact on the policy process, it also raised the movement's public profile and stimulated countervailing forces that are likely to forestall far-reaching policy change.

The chapter begins with a discussion of the factors that constitute limiting conditions on Christian Right influence in Florida. The combination of political culture and unfavorable demography makes the Christian Right appear to be a narrow movement with appeal limited to a distinctive subset of the population. In the subsequent section, we explore what happens when the movement attempts to move beyond this core constituency to stake a broad claim on public policy. The focus is both on the efforts of the movement during the 1996 campaign and on the countervailing political factors that have checked its ability to convert local victories into larger political changes. While Christian activists have been more than willing to excoriate their liberal opponents, they may find it much harder to cope with the growing opposition much closer to home—among their erstwhile Republican allies.

The Context

In 1916, Sidney J. Catts, onetime Baptist preacher from Alabama and renegade Democrat, ran for governor on the Prohibition ticket. It was a period in Florida when anti-Catholic sentiment and nativism played prominent roles in state politics. Catts exploited both currents to the fullest. Running his campaign from a Model T Ford, Catts went from town to town in then heavily rural north Florida, claiming that Cardinal James Gibbons of Baltimore, the most powerful leader of American Catholicism, had spent the staggering sum of $180,000 in church funds to ensure his defeat. To emphasize the reality of the "Catholic menace" in Florida, Catts had his campaign manager, one Jerry Carter, dress up as a Catholic priest and make virulently anti-Catts speeches in the rural hinterlands. Catts also wore a gun on each hip, as he claimed Apalachicola Catholics had threatened his life. The emotional rhetoric of Catts, coupled with campaign efforts by Tom Watson and the Guardians of Liberty (another nativist, anti-Catholic set of forces in the campaign), carried Catts into office (Colburn and Scher 1980).

This vignette of Florida political history is suggestive because it is so atypical. During the twentieth century, no other gubernatorial campaigns—and very few for other offices—encompassed any religious dimension. Indeed, they were decidedly secular. Few advocates of either racial segregation or integration, the predominant electoral issue in state politics during the 1950s and 1960s, treated the issue as a holy crusade. The man who best embodied the "New South" in Florida, Governor Reubin Askew, avoided the path followed by his Georgia soulmate and contemporary, Jimmy Carter. Though noted for his pietistic manner and deep religious convictions, Askew studiously avoided any religious message or themes in his campaigns or his administration.

Even amid the subsequent upsurge in religiously based political action during the 1980s and 1990s, few statewide candidates profited from practicing confessional politics. His enthusiastic embrace of the pro-life movement was a major factor in the resounding 1990 reelection defeat of Republican governor Bob Martinez, and subsequent aspirants for the Republican nomination who have been closely identified with the antiabortion movement have fared poorly. A study of the Christian Right in the 1994 midterm elections found little evidence of statewide strength (Wald 1995). The decision by the unsuccessful Republican gubernatorial nominee to name an outspoken conservative Christian activist as his running mate appears to have energized a coalition of social liberals that produced huge Democratic margins in most populous urban counties. Identification with the Christian Right was often an electoral kiss of death for local school board candidates. When the Christian Right won, it did so in local settings, on a narrow set of nonpartisan "moral" issues, and by keeping its own role secret.

Advocates of a moralistic political style in Florida, past and present, face a significant hurdle in the form of the state's political culture. The concept of political culture, well known to political scientists, refers to the underlying set of attitudes and beliefs people have toward politics and government and is thought to set the outer limits of political and governmental activity. Florida, as many scholars from V. O. Key (1949) forward have pointed out, falls on the extreme, individualistic end of the political culture spectrum. Key's characterization of the state's culture as "every man for himself" was echoed years later by Kirkpatrick Sale's description of a "cowboy culture" that emphasizes rugged individualism and competitiveness (Sale 1976). The sense of collective purpose or common enterprise is poorly developed in such an environment. This helps to explain why a moralistic style of politics does not play well in Florida.[1] Political cultures that emphasize religious or quasi-religious elements, or at least those in which such elements play a role, imply some degree of community or collective consciousness. The very nature of a religious community requires a certain degree of like-mindedness among members and adherents. But traditionally in Florida the lack of this element has made it difficult to inject religiosity into politics.

This distinctive culture, which puts up a strong barrier against groups seeking to use government to achieve normative goals, rests on Florida's singular social profile. Well before the massive waves of twentieth-century migration that gave the state such a cosmopolitan sociological character, Florida diverged markedly from southern regional patterns. Sparsely populated and without a fully developed slave economy in the antebellum period, Florida was spared the crushing burdens of poverty, tenant-farm agriculture, low levels of education, and rigid post-Reconstruction racial and social codes characteristic of other Deep South states. After the end of World War I, as the Florida population began to grow rapidly through several waves of migration, the state was quickly transformed from a rural backwater similar to southern Georgia and

Alabama to a dynamic "megastate" with a religiously and ethnically diverse population clustered in large cities (Pierce 1972).

As a consequence, Florida is culturally the least "Southern" of the states below the Mason-Dixon line. In a region known for ethnic homogeneity, evangelical Christianity, and the dominance of rural culture, Florida stands out for its cultural diversity, religious pluralism, and urban/metropolitan character. The degree to which Florida diverges from regional norms is evident in table 6.1 which compares the Sunshine State to its closest neighbor, Georgia. Florida is more populous and urbanized than Georgia and includes an appreciably larger share of Hispanics—mostly Cubans but with generous concentrations of immigrants from the Caribbean and Central and South America. The level of formal religious affiliation is much lower in Florida and exhibits a strikingly different profile. Whereas Southern Baptists make up a large plurality of the church-affiliated in Georgia and have eight times the combined membership of Catholics and Jews, they are only the second largest religious tradition in Florida and are outnumbered nearly 2 to 1 by Catholics and Jews.

This relatively unfavorable demography helps to explain why the Christian Right—a movement whose greatest appeal is to white evangelical Protestants—seems to have made fewer inroads in Florida politics than in many other Southern states. In Florida's 1996 presidential primary election, 32 percent of Republican voters told pollsters that they considered themselves part of "the religious right" while 64 percent rejected the label. That figure is significant but closer to the pattern of midwestern states like Michigan and Ohio than to southern states like Georgia, where voters divided more evenly at 38 percent

Table 6.1
Demographic Comparison of Florida and Georgia

	Florida	Georgia
Population	14.2 million	7.1 million
Population in urban areas (%)	85	63
Population of Hispanic origin (%)	14	0
Level of religious affiliation (%)	44	58
Religious composition (%)		
Southern Baptist	21	42
Roman Catholic	28	6
Jewish	10	2

Source: Population data taken from U.S. Bureau of the Census, *Statistical Abstract of the United States, 1995* (Washington, D.C.: Government Printing Office, 1995), tables 35, 38, 44. Religious composition data taken from Martin B. Bradley et al., *Churches and Church Membership in the United States, 1990* (Atlanta: Glenmary Research Center, 1992).

versus 59 percent on the same question.[2] In the general election, self-described "religious right" voters constituted 19 percent of the Florida electorate, a smaller share by far than in any other Southern or border state.[3] By the same token, Florida's large and growing Republican congressional delegation contains half as many denominational evangelicals (just two) as Episcopalians or Roman Catholics. To put that figure in context, Georgia's Republican congressional delegation, though half the size of Florida's, contains the same number of evangelical Protestants.[4]

These figures matter because they reveal the limited electoral base of the Christian Right in Florida. Like the Christian Right nationally, the Florida movement has struggled to place itself in the mainstream of conservative and Republican politics. Disavowing "God talk" and religious particularism, it has presented itself in resolutely secular terms. Protesting claims that it was a narrow religious interest group, the leader of Florida's Christian Coalition insisted that his organization stood for such mainstream goals as "safer streets, lower taxes, less government, stronger families, schools responsive to the needs of parents and the protection of innocent human life" (Dowless 1997). Despite such claims, the Christian Right remains in Florida, as it has been elsewhere, a minority movement with a center of gravity in the subculture of white evangelical Protestantism and an issue base still firmly anchored in moral traditionalism.

The limited appeal of the movement is evident from statewide surveys of public opinion. Among registered voters polled in November 1996, the Christian Coalition, the most prominent of the Christian Right organizations, ranked in the bottom tier of institutions assessed by Florida voters using a "feeling thermometer."[5] With an average rating of just 49 on a scale of 0 to 100, the organization ranked well below the military, police, conservatives, environmentalists, and the political parties. Much to its dismay, we are certain, the Coalition shared the company of such disdained objects of public consciousness as welfare recipients, gays, the pro-gun lobby, feminists, and big business. Analysis of earlier surveys in table 6.2 reveals the distinctive social configuration of movement supporters. Looking across three samples of registered voters, white non-Hispanic registered voters, and Republican primary voters, we find few consistent demographic patterns save for evidence that Florida Hispanics, primarily Cubans with a strong Republican tilt, are appreciably cooler toward the movement than Anglos in general or Republicans in particular.[6] Public support for the Christian Coalition in Florida rests on the same constellation of religious traits and social attitudes that has distinguished mass support for social conservatism elsewhere (Wilcox 1992). The only religious group to rate the Christian Coalition above the midpoint of the feeling thermometer in all three samples is white Protestants who

Table 6.2
Feeling Thermometer Scores for Christian Coalition (0–100)

	All Registered Voters (N = 597)	Non-Hispanic Registered Voters (N = 488)	Republican Primary Voters (N= 602)
Demographic Variables			
Race			
White non-Hispanic	40	40	47
Black	57	—	—
Hispanic	30**	—	42**
Years of schooling			
0–12	40	40	49
13–16	42	41	47
17 or more	32*	33	43
Sex			
Female	43	42	47
Male	37*	37	47
Religious/Attitudinal Variables			
Religious tradition			
White evangelical/born-again			
Protestant	53	53	62
White mainline Protestant	36	36	35
Roman Catholic	41	41	44
Black Protestant	58	—	—
Jewish	15	16	28
Not affiliated	21***	21***	32***
Abortion label			
Pro-choice	30	29	35
Pro-life	58***	58***	61***
Abortion attitude	NA	NA	
Never legal			70
Rape/incest/medical danger only			54
Only during first trimester			37
Always by personal choice			34***
Principal national problem	NA	NA	
Mentioned a social issue			40
Did not mention social issue			50***

Table 6.2—*Continued*

	All Registered Voters (N = 597)	Non-Hispanic Registered Voters (N = 488)	Republican Primary Voters (N= 602)
Political Variables			
Partisan identification			
Strong Democrat	33	28	—
Weak Democrat	32	33	—
Independent Democrat	37	32	—
Independent	31	32	—
Independent Republican	44	45	41
Weak Republican	44	43	40
Strong Republican	53***	54***	51***
Republican presidential primary vote	NA	NA	
Economic conservative			43
Social conservative			67***

Source: Florida Voter Poll. First two columns are from a November 1995 survey of registered voters. The last column is from a March 1996 survey of registered Republicans who reported voting in the presidential primary.
Levels of significance are based on an analysis of variance: *$p \le .05$ **$p \le .01$ ***$p \le .001$

call themselves evangelicals and/or born-again Christians. The movement has much less appeal among white mainline Protestants or Roman Catholics (who together outnumber white evangelicals by 2 to 1) and is very negatively assessed by Jews and those who are not affiliated with a religious group. Those who embrace the "pro-life" label, only a third of registered voters in Florida, give the Christian Coalition twice the average rating of the two-thirds who adopt a pro-choice position. The movement is not popular among Democrats and independents, and even among Republicans it does well only among those who evince social conservatism in their issue priorities or choice of a presidential nominee.

To describe the Christian Right as the organizational weapon of a distinctive minority, one theme of this chapter, is not to deny its political potential. Virtually all interest groups represent distinct minorities, but many nonetheless wield considerable statewide influence. Noting that the Christian Right rests on a narrow popular base does, however, suggest that those outside its orbit may possess means to limit its political reach. These possibilities and limitations will become clearer when we examine the efforts of the movement in 1996.

The Christian Right as an Electoral Force in 1996

The Christian conservative movement has mobilized its electoral resources by combining old-fashioned political organizing with modern, high-tech voter targeting. As one analyst recently put it, the Christian Coalition has become an electoral force "by working along the fringes of public consciousness, quietly helping elect conservative Republicans with a mixture of prayer, grass-roots fund raising and misinformation about their more liberal opponents" (Judd 1996). The Coalition is the largest and best-known organization within the movement, but it has not had the playing field entirely to itself. In some communities local affiliates of the American Family Association were actively involved, and in a few other places indigenous organizations without formal ties to national groups appear to have been active. Whatever the organizational differences, these groups appear to have followed a common strategy in the 1996 election.

As noted in the study of the 1994 election (Wald 1995), the Florida Christian Right has for some years been actively engaged in electoral politics, especially at the local level. In 1996, the movement extended its focus more systematically to two electoral levels, the presidential and the state legislative. The two venues produced vastly different outcomes.

In the Florida presidential race, the Christian Right was a marginal and largely unsuccessful player. Part of the problem for the Florida movement, as for the national Christian Right, was the lack of a suitable standard-bearer. When such promising social conservatives as Dan Quayle, William Bennett, and Newt Gingrich elected to stay on the sidelines, the agenda of the Christian Right passed into the hands of Pat Buchanan and such marginal contenders as Alan Keyes and Robert Dornan. Although these candidates drew disproportionately from Republican voters with Christian Right sympathies (Dunkelberger 1996), they constituted no serious threat to Bob Dole, who swept both an early straw poll of Republican activists and the presidential primary in March. The Florida delegation to the national convention was economically conservative but preponderantly libertarian on social issues (Hollis 1996a). Even the grudging support of Christian Right activists did not enable Dole to carry Florida in November. His loss, the first by a Republican presidential nominee in Florida since 1976, was due partly to the Social Security concerns of the state's large retiree population and to significant defections among the Cubans of South Florida, a normally cohesive Republican voting bloc. While the surprising Democratic breakthrough among Cubans was attributed to President Clinton's skillful cooptation of the anti-Castro campaign, it subsequently emerged that many Cubans were deeply alarmed by the anti-immigrant sentiment and moralism of Republican social conservatives. Had Dole given more attention to social issues, as he was urged to do by Christian Right leaders, he might have energized one base constituency at the expense of the Cubans and others who worried about the rise of cultural conservatism in the state party (Hollis 1996c). That is a scenario that we shall observe at the state legislative level as well, albeit after the election.

The relative failure of religious conservatives in the presidential contest contrasted with their seemingly impressive showing in selected contests for the state house of representatives. The seeds of this effort actually go back to 1994 when conservative Christian activists targeted two races in the western Panhandle (Congressional District 1 and state house of representatives district 1). In districts long represented by conservative Democrats, religious conservatives were instrumental in nominating Republican social conservatives who defeated strong Democratic candidates in November. Buoyed by these successes, the movement expanded these tactics to other parts of the state in 1996.

Because most Florida congressional seats and state senate districts are deemed "safe" for incumbents, most of the focus of Christian activists was on races for the state house of representatives. This choice also reflected a strategic understanding of electoral realities. House districts are small enough, Christian activists recognized, to enable socially conservative voters and allies to hold the balance of power. But not all state house races were given equal attention. The Coalition especially focused on three kinds of races: the reelection contests of sympathetic incumbents (virtually exclusively Republicans), challenges to potentially vulnerable Democrats, and open seats. They were aided in this last connection by the fact that some thirteen incumbent Democrats had chosen not to seek reelection in 1996; as the balance of power between Democrats and Republicans in the state house was very much in doubt, those races were targeted in an effort to help Republicans attain a numerical majority in the Florida House of Representatives.

These districts were also targeted because the balance of social forces played to the strength of Christian Right candidates. Many, but not all, of the favored Republican incumbents represented districts in what is called the I-4 corridor, a strip of Florida running roughly northeast to southwest through the center of the state from Daytona Beach through Orlando to the Tampa Bay area. It is the "newest" part of Florida, characterized by rapid growth and suburban sprawl (as opposed to urban decay), places populated by middle-class whites and relatively few minority groups, and areas where fundamentalist churches have been able to establish deep roots—precisely the environment that has proved hospitable to Christian Rightt political activity aimed at national office (Green, Guth, and Hill 1993). Not surprisingly, some of the Coalition's most fervent allies in the state house come from this I-4 corridor: new house speaker Dan Webster (Ocoee), Bob Brooks (Winter Park), Lee

Constantine (Altamonte Springs), Tom Feeney (Oviedo), and Bob Sparks (Casselberry), among others.[7]

Fully aware of the legal and financial constraints that federal laws place on political activity by nonprofit groups, the Christian Coalition and its allies did not overtly endorse or oppose candidates for election. Instead, the religious groups operated in the 1996 election indirectly and obliquely. Their major political device was the distribution of some 2.3 million *'96 Christian Coalition Voter Guides,* which became very controversial. The guides were produced regionally, so they could highlight elections of local interest. The guides listed individual races and candidates, along with a carefully selected grouping of "issues" and the positions held or allegedly held by the candidates. They were distributed to voters just before the election, often from churches. Similar guides were issued by affiliates of the American Family Association and other Christian Right organizations.

It was the selection of issues and characterization of candidate positions that created the most controversy. Only issues of concern to the Coalition were included—for example, school choice, prayer in the schools, abortion on demand, no-fault divorce, and so forth. Other issues—including those that might have figured heavily in local races but that were not a part of the Coalition's agenda—were ignored. The guides included an assessment of the candidates' positions, in some instances making inferences from recorded votes by incumbents. Furthermore, rather than select a constant set of issues across House districts, a technique that would have revealed when Democrats' positions were close to those of Republican candidates, the selection of issues was tailored to maximize the differences between the party nominees in each district and to portray the Republican as the guardian of traditional values.

In a number of instances, the guides seriously distorted these positions. For example, in state house district 6, in the Panhandle, the guide listed Democratic incumbent Scott Clemons as requiring employers to "pay for health benefits for abortions." In fact, Clemons had never voted for any such measure but rather voted in such a way that a state-subsidized health care plan was neutral on the subject of whether state-supported health care plans should pay any portion of the costs of abortions (Judd 1996).

This distortion of candidate positions—especially of Democrats' views— appeared to become quite common. In quite a number of instances, Democrats declined to answer the questionnaire prepared by the Coalition, on the grounds that the characterization of responses was unfair. As a retiring conservative Democrat put it, the guides were "a sham. They're not interested in issues. They're interested in Republicans. It's all cooked" (Nurse 1996). Other observers noted much the same thing. Susan Glickman of People for the American Way stated that the guides were "marching orders" to religious conservatives and added that "Many times they are not honest about their agenda. They misstate candidates' positions. . . . They're playing fast and loose with the facts" (Judd 1996).

Even when Democrats declined to complete its questionnaire, the Coalition listed them anyway, generally using the letters "DNR" (for "did not respond") next to the issue item. These letters were prominently displayed in the guide.

Just as the guides appeared to be designed to put Democrats in an unfavorable light (as far as the Coalition agenda was concerned), so did they appear to make Republicans the favored candidates. In no instance did the guides actually list an endorsement, as such a step would have undermined the legal status of the Christian Coalition as an educational institution. Nonetheless, through selection of issues and careful delineation of candidate positions on them, even the most unsophisticated voter could readily determine which candidate the Coalition actually favored. Moreover, there was nothing to prevent individual members and sympathizers from contributing to, working on behalf of, endorsing, and voting for favored candidates. There is evidence that the Coalition in fact did encourage its members and sympathizers to engage in exactly this kind of activity. Some of the encouragement, moreover, came from the pulpits of churches affiliated with, or sympathetic to, the Coalition agenda. For example, some seventy-five thousand voter guides were distributed to voters in Polk County alone on the Sunday before the November election. Polk County lies directly along the I-4 corridor.

The Christian Coalition's use of voter guides during electoral campaigns is not new in either Florida or southern politics. Groups of all political persuasions, from environmental and feminist groups to business organizations to those on the right of the political spectrum, have often put out ratings sheets or other indicators of candidate positions. What is particularly important, even unique, about the Christian Coalition's use of the voter guide, in contrast to other groups', is its impact on Florida's political agenda. Not only have voters noted it, but so have candidates and the media; indeed, during the 1996 election, the media gave considerable coverage to the guide's ratings, and in some cases candidates who did not score high in Coalition ratings tried to cover themselves by shifting positions, if only slightly. The Coalition's ability to influence the political dynamic of the state through the voter guides finds a parallel in the guides used by the White Citizens Councils of the 1950s, which affected public discussion of school desegregation and other racial issues (Bartley 1969; Scher 1997).

How effective were these efforts in November? We have already noted the way the Christian Coalition specifically targeted certain seats, especially when it perceived Democrats as potentially vulnerable. Did Coalition activity make the marginal difference between victory and defeat in these cases? Sophisticated data are lacking to make such an assertion authoritatively, but anecdotal evidence suggests that it did. Vernon Peebles, for example, a seemingly invulnerable seven-term Democrat from Punta Gorda, was portrayed by a voter guide as a supporter of "new age religious practices (yoga) in school without parental permission" (Judd 1996). In fact, Peebles had merely voted on a procedural amendment, but the Coalition distorted the meaning of the vote, flooded Peebles's district with voter guides, and helped elect a conservative Republican opponent to replace him.

The Coalition was not always successful in either electing its candidates of choice or defeating those it felt were out of step with its pro-family Christian agenda; for example, Democratic incumbent Scott Clemons, whose vote on health care was noted earlier, won anyway. Nonetheless, the consensus among those who watched the November election carefully was that in those races that the Coalition specifically targeted and where it mobilized voters on behalf of, or in opposition to, certain candidates, it was a powerful force and may well have spelled the difference between victory and defeat in a considerable number of state house of representatives and local races.

After the Election: The Emergence of the Christian Coalition in the State Legislature

The role of groups like the Christian Coalition in state legislative elections was largely overlooked by commentators during the campaign. Thus it came as a considerable shock to many observers when the Christian Coalition was identified publicly as a powerful, if not dominant, force in the newly elected Florida House of Representatives, an organization that was "ready to start calling the shots" in Tallahassee (States News Service 1996). The group was cited for the manner in which it had gained a foothold through the legislative leadership.

The new speaker of the Florida house, Dan Webster, an intensely religious Baptist who strongly advocates the pro-family agenda favored by religious conservatives, is a close ally of the Coalition. First elected to the legislature in 1980, when Republicans were a lonely band largely ignored by Democrats, Webster slowly and assiduously worked his way into a position of party leadership. By the 1994 session, when Republicans had almost reached parity with Democrats, Webster was minority leader and a powerful player in legislative deliberations. When Republicans became a numerical majority following the 1996 elections, Webster was the obvious choice to become speaker.[8] He was confirmed as speaker late in the fall, after facing token opposition from a small group of Cuban Republicans from South Florida, who were nervous about

Webster's religious agenda, and some residual support for an urban Republican from Jacksonville.

Although there was some thinking that Webster, a mild-mannered individual, might not push a Coalition agenda hard during his first year, his actions immediately after his elevation to the speaker's office suggested otherwise. Perhaps his most controversial move as far as demonstrating his commitment to the Coalition agenda is concerned has been the creation of "policy councils." These are composed of groups of close allies, all of whom are Republicans and virtually all of whom are closely associated with the Christian Coalition or its close allies, the American Family Association and the Family Action Council (Berger 1996). In a remarkable and unprecedented centralization of power, Webster has given these councils the authority to direct all legislative activity prior to floor consideration and even to determine whether bills get to the floor for full house debate. Given the makeup and predisposition of these councils, it is difficult to imagine significant legislation not acceptable to the Coalition or its allies having much success (Hollis and Judd 1996).

Yet it is also true that the Coalition itself appears to be taking a fairly low profile in its initial legislative session. It has adopted the strategy of allowing Webster and his allies to carry its agenda, rather than overtly doing so itself. Webster and a group of Coalition supporters used to be members of the so-called God Squad, an informal group of largely Republican house members who met regularly for breakfast to pray and talk politics, including discussing issues and legislation important to the Coalition. The God Squad has apparently been disbanded, probably because it is no longer needed; its former members now run the house of representatives. It has been replaced, however, by the Traditional Family Caucus, a more institutionalized version of the God Squad. Chaired by Representative Bob Brooks of Winter Park (a wealthy suburb of Orlando, on the I-4 corridor), it met to discuss its upcoming agenda before the start of the legislative session in March. Attendees included former God Squad members, a smattering of Democratic sympathizers, one or two state senators, and John Dowless of the Florida Christian Coalition.

No one expects either the Traditional Family Caucus or the Christian Coalition to push its agenda hard during the 1997 session. Knowledgeable observers express the view that the Coalition and its allies will take a "wait and see" attitude and perhaps raise their profile during 1998, when another election cycle looms. Nonetheless, the close ties between the Coalition, speaker Webster, and the formal and informal leadership in the house suggest that the Coalition and its agenda will loom large, even if from a discreet distance, during 1997.

To augment the power inherent in control over the house leadership, religious conservatives can also take advantage of the conservatizing climate within the state legislature. As a barometer of trends, consider the annual legislative report card issued by the Christian Coalition. The 1996 legislative scorecard ranked legislators on the basis of some ten bills that included such core items of the Christian Right as school prayer, home schooling, charter schools, and approval of parental spanking. What is especially noticeable about the Coalition rankings is the rapid rise in scores among Democrats. In 1993, house Democrats rated only 9 percent; by 1996, their score was 44 percent. In the senate, Democratic support moved less dramatically, from 42 percent to 49 percent. Republican support also jumped up, although it was always high. In the house it reached 87 percent in 1996, and 83 percent in the senate. Overall, the house rankings went from 47 percent in 1993 to 65 percent in 1996, while in the senate the numbers moved from 57 percent to 66 percent (Griffin 1995, 1996).

The rankings undoubtedly reflect more than just Coalition influence. Florida has become a more conservative state in the past five years; issues such as school choice and charter schools are no longer the exclusive property of the Christian Coalition but are very much in vogue even among previously liberal politicos. Nonetheless, it is the publicizing influence of Coalition ratings that causes some concern among politicians, especially Democrats in marginal seats. Given what they perceive to be the electoral power of the Coalition and its allies, especially the Coalition's willingness to distort the meaning of votes and oversimplify positions on voter guides, they see what can happen should the Coalition choose to target them in their next election. Thus, the impact of Coalition ratings has combined with a rightward shift in Florida politics generally to produce occasional Democratic votes in the legislature supportive of Coalition positions.

Assessing Influence

Despite conditions so conducive to Christian Right influence, it is crucial to recognize just how many obstacles still stand in the way of the movement's high-priority items. It is useful to distinguish between "the usual suspects"—the predictable opponents of Christian conservatism—and its adversaries within the Republican Party.

The Christian Right, Republican and conservative in orientation, will face opposition from those who usually resist Republican and conservative initiatives. In Florida, the first line of defense consists of a Democratic governor and Democratic legislators. In the previous term, in the face of rural representatives from his own party, Governor Lawton Chiles was willing to veto a school prayer amendment tacked onto a bill raising graduation standards. Chiles and the urban Democrats in both houses can similarly be counted on to resist many of the initiatives sponsored by the Christian Coalition during the next legislative session. With a razor-thin majority of sixty-one facing fifty-nine Democrats, House Republicans will find it difficult to pass controversial legislation over determined Democratic opposition. Beyond the partisan challenge, the Christian Right also faces potent opposition from such traditionally liberal interest groups as public school teachers, big-city mayors, trade unionists, African Americans, Jews, Catholics, social services professionals, gays and lesbians, child advocates, and others who have no love for the movement's agenda. Such groups have noted the role of the Christian Coalition in the new leadership group and are likely to monitor its actions closely. When the school prayer amendment was on the governor's desk earlier in the year, its opponents managed to flood the executive office with letters, calls, faxes, and telegrams urging a veto. The opponents still have these tools at their disposal.

The more immediate challenge for the movement is to master opposition from its natural ally and beneficiary, the Republican Party. Republicans are not of one mind about the benefits of association with cultural conservatism. We noted earlier that championing the pro-life cause may well have destroyed the career of the state's second Republican governor in 1990 and selecting a strong antiabortion running mate appears to have damaged the party's gubernatorial nominee in 1994. In both cases, the uncompromising pro-choice position alienated Republican women whose votes were necessary to carry the state and gave liberal Democrats a theme to rally their base. These lessons have not been lost on many Republicans who represent state senate districts, larger and more socially diverse than state house districts, and who recognize the gender gap as a powerful threat to their hopes for statewide dominance.

As was true in the U.S. Congress when Republicans first took control in 1995, Christian Right activists may well find the senate somewhat less hospitable than the house to its more controversial agenda items. From 1994 to 1996, the senate was led by Jim Scott from Fort Lauderdale. An urban Republican, a fiscal conservative sensitive to the requirements of public services, Scott was a pragmatic, nondoctrinaire Republican who eschewed controversy and confrontation. While he did not oppose all of the issues on the Coalition agenda, neither did he make any particular effort to foster or support them. The new senate president, Toni Jennings, an urban Republican from Orlando, is cut from much the same cloth. Although representing part of the I-4 corridor, she has not shown any special predisposition to support the Coalition's agenda any more strongly than did Scott. An Episcopalian, Jennings has a background in public education. She is also very closely allied to big-business interests, especially Associated Industries, arguably one of the half dozen most powerful lobbying groups in the state. Big business to this date has not shown any particular interest in the Christian Coalition agenda. While this could change, the political interests of Associated Industries and its allies lie much more in the area of economic development, a strong business climate, and a favorable tax system than anything in which the Christian Coalition is involved.

This is not to say that Christian Right interests will not succeed in the senate. However, because the political climate of the senate differs from that of the house, the Christian Coalition and allied forces will have to make a much stronger case in the senate before its measures are adopted. In a sense, the senate will take a much more skeptical, moderate, "show me" approach than the house. Traditionally a more conservative branch, the Florida Senate may well now be the more moderate body, at least as far as Christian Coalition interests are concerned.

The Christian Right and Florida Republicans

Beyond senate Republicans, the movement faces a significant challenge from Republican activists who want to retain the state party's traditional reputation as a nondoctrinaire, conservative version of the Democratic Party. The Christian Coalition's effort to push the Republican Party, indeed the state as a whole, sharply to the right has activated vocal opposition from powerful elements within the state Republican Party organization (Chepak 1995). So-called country club Republicans, predominantly mainline Protestants found heavily in southwest Florida from Sarasota County on down, have shown relatively little interest in the religious agenda of the Coalition. The same could be said of the large numbers of retired military personnel and families congregated in the Pasco-Hernando-Sumter–Citrus County region.

To confirm these impressions, there is some evidence from intraparty nomination contests that Christian Right activists find it easiest to win primaries where Republicanism is weak and disorganized and face a more difficult task in centers of Republican strength with "winnable" legislative seats. In a central Broward County district well outside the core Republican concentration in central Florida, a district that usually votes Democratic, a former Christian Coalition spokesman who campaigned on his opposition to abortion and gay rights won a clear Republican primary victory over a better-financed candidate who focused on crime control (Benjamin 1996). Only about 10 percent of registered voters turned out for the Republican primary, a sign of the general hopelessness of the Republican cause in the district, and the Christian Right nominee was trounced by the Democratic incumbent in the general election. By contrast, a nominee with similar credentials had a much harder time in the primary in a house district at the western end of the I-4 Republican corridor. Rhonda Storms, a Baptist Sunday school teacher active in both the Christian Coalition and the local Family Action Council, was endorsed by the influential leader of the American Family Association in Hillsborough County. Her record of picketing abortion clinics and campaigning actively to rescind gay rights prompted the county Republican chairwoman to warn about "extremists" and the "super right" taking over the party organization (Talev 1996). In the end, the Christian Right activist lost a runoff primary to a Republican lawyer, an Episcopalian who held conservative social values but generally rejected the use of government coercion on behalf of traditional values. He held the normally Republican seat in November. This mirrors the national tendency of the Christian Right to take control in states where Republicanism has been weak but face much stiffer resistance where the party has traditionally been a competitive electoral force.

If the Christian Right has encountered hostility from traditional Republicans, it has also faced opposition from some of the party's newest recruits. The Cubans in Miami, a growing influence within the party, are deeply concerned about certain nativist impulses that they read into the Coalition and remain skeptical of the close tie the Coalition wants to establish between religion and government activity. Several Cuban state representatives organized an abortive revolt against Daniel Webster's speakership late in 1996, citing his social agenda as a matter of concern. The divergence between Cubans and Christian conservatives also shows up in the Florida Republican congressional delegation. The two Cuban American representatives have scored twenty to thirty points below their Republican colleagues on a national Christian Coalition voting index. The concern reflects not only the religious differences between Catholicism and evangelical Protestantism, a factor that produces few common political priorities, but also the reality that Cuban Republicans often represent urban districts with residents who rely on high levels of government service. Despite their Republicanism, a loyalty molded largely in the realm of foreign policy, Cuban state legislators have been in the forefront of efforts to raise minimum wages, expand public education, and other liberal initiatives.

In short, the relationship between the Christian Right and state Republicans remains uneasy, as it has in many states since the movement first emerged as an electoral power. Thus, Florida Republicans need to decide how to relate to the Christian Coalition and how much of its agenda to adopt without driving at least some important segments of the party away, if not to the Democrats then into the independent column. It may well be that the Christian Coalition needs the Republican Party more than the Republicans need it. Nonetheless, there are enough Christian Rightists in the party, with a documented record of electoral activity and support of Republican candidates and causes, that the party cannot afford to ignore or wish away the movement. Right now, it is fair to say, there are two very different camps within the big tent of the Florida Republican Party, each very wary of the other.

There is a useful historical parallel that can shed light on what could happen to the Florida Republican Party if this dilemma is not soon and satisfactorily resolved. In the late 1960s and early 1970s, the Republican Party (then on the rise) was badly split between two competing factions, each representing very different versions of state Republicanism (Mandel 1968; Cohen 1976; Baker 1977; Colburn and Scher 1980). The differences were not so much ideological/religious, as they are now, as sociological/geopolitical. Nonetheless, the split grew ever more fractious and was not fully resolved until well into the 1980s. Many analysts of Florida politics thought that if this split had not occurred, or had not lasted so long, the Republican Party would have achieved a position of political preeminence much earlier than it did (Scher 1997). In fact, the party's fortunes waned badly for years because of it.

Something similar could well happen to the modern Florida Republican Party if Christian conservatives and mainline Republicans fail to create an effective working relationship. It is not possible as of this writing to tell when, or if, this will come about. But unless and until it does, both the party and the Christian Right may find that they have missed an opportunity to increase their statewide political strength.

The Christian Right continues to confront the dilemma that it encountered in 1994 (Wald 1995). The movement does best when it operates at the local level, focusing on narrow issues and minimizing its own role. Such a strategy limits the ability of the Christian Right to influence decision making at the state level. Yet when the movement opts for a higher profile by contesting state offices and demanding a place at the table, it activates the resistance of both Republicans and Democrats. Every electoral gain stimulates greater scrutiny and mobilizes opposition. That dilemma is inherent to a minority movement whose core policy positions do not enjoy consensus support among the electorate.

Notes

We are grateful to Maureen C. Tartaglione for her outstanding research assistance and to Jim Kane of the Florida Voter Poll for providing us with his statewide surveys. We also want to thank Steve Bosquet, Mark Hollis, and Alan Judd for sharing their impressions with us in telephone interviews.

1. Note that this description, as well as our use of terms such as "moralistic," differs from the Elazar (1984) formulation. We use the term "moralistic" to identify a style of political culture that Elazar labeled "traditionalistic." Unlike Elazar, who classifies Florida as a compound of traditionalism and individualism, we see the individualistic strand as the primary component.

2. These figures from exit polls of Republican primary voters conducted by the Voter News Service were reported in the *New York Times* on 6 March 1996, p. B7 (Georgia), and 21 March 1996, p. A14 (Michigan and Ohio).

3. The general election figures, also produced by the Voter News Service, were downloaded from the "Politics Now" website: http://politicsnow.com.

4. Information on the religious affiliation of congressional representatives was obtained from the *Almanac of American Politics* at http://politicsusa.com/Politics USA/resources/almanac/.

5. These data were generously supplied by Jim Kane of the Florida Voter Poll in Fort Lauderdale. The telephone surveys of self-reported registered voters utilized a random digit dialing protocol. Samples are weighted to conform to the partisan distribution of registered voters in Florida. All analysis and interpretations are the responsibility of the authors.

6. We found no large or consistent differences in attitudes to the Christian Coalition based on age or income.

7. Each of these legislators scored a perfect 100 on the Christian Coalition's annual report card (Griffin 1996). However, not all of the Coalition's house allies were Republicans. State representatives Bud Bronson of Kissimmee (part of the I-4 corridor) and Randy Mackey of Lake City in north Florida also scored high on the Coalition report card. Mackey is the house legislator whose principal claim to fame is his annual introduction of prayer-in-the-schools legislation, an important Coalition goal; in 1996 the bill actually passed, although it was vetoed by Governor Lawton Chiles. In spite of these Democratic allies, however, the Coalition for the most part felt Democrats were fair game, and it targeted them in areas of the state beyond the I-4 corridor. Democrats Vernon Peebles of Punta Gorda (in far southwest Florida) and Helen Spivey of Crystal River (west of Ocala on the Gulf Coast) were defeated, in significant part because of Coalition efforts.

8. The speaker of the Florida House of Representatives is one of the most powerful players in state politics. The individual occupying the position has at least as much power as the president of the senate and arguably in some instances (especially on fiscal affairs) can rival the governor. See Morris 1996.

References

Baker, Gregory Lee. 1977. "Intraparty Factionalism: The Florida Republican Party." Master's thesis, University of Florida.

Bartley, Numan. 1969. *The Rise of Massive Resistance*. Baton Rouge: Louisiana State University Press.

Benjamin, Jody. 1996. "$250 Goes Long Way for Boyle." *Sun Sentinel* (4 September): B5.

Berger, Daniel. 1996. "Boundaries Blur between Religious Right Groups." *Tampa Tribune* (14 October).

Chepak, Rob. "Riding the Tide: Religious Right Buoyed Up in Florida." *Tampa Tribune* (30 July): 1.

Cohen, Paul. 1976. "Two Groups of Republican Voters." Florida Poll, *Gainesville Sun* (18 January): B1

Colburn, David R., and Richard K. Scher. 1980. *Florida's Gubernatorial Politics in the Twentieth Century.* Tallahassee: University Presses of Florida.

Dowless, John. 1997. Letter to the Editor. *Gainesville Sun* (11 January): 6a.

Dunkelberger, Lloyd. 1996. "Christian Conservatives in Florida Flock to Buchanan." *Gainesville Sun* (27 February): 1a.

Elazar, Daniel. 1984. *American Federalism: A View from the States.* New York: Harper & Row.

Green, John C., James L. Guth, and Kevin Hill. 1993. "Faith and Election: The Christian Right in Congressional Campaigns, 1978–1988." *Journal of Politics* 55: 80–91.

Griffin, Mike. 1995. "Christian Coalition Puts State Legislators to the Test." *Orlando Sentinel* (3 September): G6.

———. 1996. "Coalition Rates Legislators." *Orlando Sentinel* (8 September): G5.

Hollis, Mark. 1996a. "Florida's GOP Urges Tolerance on Abortion." *Gainesville Sun* (18 July): 1a, 8a.

———. 1996b. "State Delegates Foresee Dole Win." *Gainesville Sun* (12 August): 5a.

———. 1996c. "Two Sides of GOP Vie for Dole's Soul." *Gainesville Sun* (11 August): 1a, 8a.

Hollis, Mark, and Alan Judd. 1996. "A Right Turn in Tallahassee." *Gainesville Sun* (18 December), 1a, 6a.

Judd, Alan. 1996. "Religious Group's Influence Grows." *Gainesville Sun* (22 December): A1.

Mandel, Stuart. 1968. "The Republican Party in Florida." Master's thesis, Florida State University.

Morris, Allan. 1996. *The Florida Handbook.* 25th ed. Tallahassee: Peninsular.

Nurse, Doug. 1996. "Democrats Rap Poll by Coalition." *Tampa Tribune* (5 November).

Pierce, Neal R. 1972. *The Megastates of America.* New York: Norton.

Sale, Kirkpatrick. 1975. *Power Shift.* New York: Vintage.

Scher, Richard K. 1997. *Politics in the New South.* 2d ed. Armonk, N.Y.: M. E. Sharpe.

States News Service. 1996. "Christian Coalition Gains Clout." *States News Briefs* (23 December): 1.

Talev, Margaret. 1996. "Christianity Plays Role in Runoff Race." *Tampa Tribune* (28 September): 1–2.

Wald, Kenneth D. 1995. "Florida: Running Globally and Winning Locally." Chap. 2 in *God at the Grass Roots,* ed. Mark J. Rozell and Clyde Wilcox. Lanham, Md.: Rowman & Littlefield.

Wilcox, Clyde. 1992. *God's Warriors: The Christian Right in Twentieth-Century America.* Baltimore: Johns Hopkins University Press.

7

Virginia: When the Music Stops, Choose Your Faction

Mark J. Rozell and Clyde Wilcox

In 1990 Republican senator John Warner was such a strong candidate for reelection that the Democratic Party chose not to field a candidate to oppose him. His reelection made him the first Republican in Virginia history to win statewide three times. Yet Warner did not get a free ride to a fourth term in 1996. He faced, first, a serious challenge for renomination—serious enough that he had hinted of leaving the GOP to run as an independent—and, second, a historically well-financed Democratic opponent in the general election. Despite repeated predictions of Warner's political demise, the senior senator easily won renomination and then succeeded in his quest for a fourth term.

Warner's falling-out with the leadership and activist base of the GOP in the 1990s tells much about the internal party struggle between the moderates and economic conservatives on the one side and the Christian social conservatives on the other. For the former group, Warner represents the mainstream of the GOP electorate in the state. For the latter, he is a disloyal party leader and a member of the GOP elite who caused the defeat of party nominees in 1993 and 1994. Moreover, Christian Coalition director Ralph Reed arued that Warner did not have the slightest clue what it means to live a middle-class life with at least three children and shop at Wal-Mart to save money (Reed 1994).

Warner had become anathema to the Christian Right in Virginia despite a voting record that earned him consistent high grades in Christian Coalition ratings. Christian conservatives were upset with Warner for having refused to back former Moral Majority leader Michael Farris for lieutenant governor in 1993 and Oliver North, another Christian Right favorite, for the Senate in 1994. To the Christian Right activists and leaders, Warner had violated an unwritten GOP pact: that the Christian Right would stay loyal to the GOP and work for moderate party nominees as long as the moderates stayed loyal and backed Christian conservatives nominated by the party. Christian Right members said that Warner was among those Republicans who wanted the support of the Christian Right but would never reciprocate. Warner said that he merely considered North unfit to hold public office and Farris not qualified to be a heartbeat from the governorship (Warner 1994).

Both Farris and North blamed Warner for their defeat, and their view was widely shared by Christian conservatives in the GOP. As a result, our survey of Republican convention delegates in 1993 and 1994 showed that Republicans from the Christian Right faction were quite hostile to Warner, with many rating him at zero degrees on a feeling thermometer. Indeed, a surprising number of Christian conservatives penciled in derogatory comments about Warner, most often comparing him to warm buckets of various whale effusions.

Many Christian Right leaders and activists attributed Farris's and North's defeats solely to Warner, and they pledged revenge in 1996. Yet North decided not to run again in 1996, preferring to spend his time hosting a lucrative talk-radio show. Farris too decided not to challenge the senator, despite having spent time promoting a possible challenge and distributing "Is It 1996 Yet?" bumper stickers. That left former Reagan administration Office of Management and Budget director James C. Miller III to challenge Warner as the candidate of the Christian Right.

Miller's failed challenge and Warner's eventual reelection tell much about the possibilities and limits of Christian Right activism in the GOP. Before analyzing the GOP contest and the general election campaign, it is important to establish their context.

The Context

In his seminal *Southern Politics in State and Nation* in 1949, V. O. Key Jr. described Virginia as a "political museum piece." He wrote that "of all the American states, Virginia can lay claim to the most thorough control by an oligarchy" (Key 1949, 19). At the time, the Democratic political machine of Harry F. Byrd dominated Virginia politics. Byrd served as governor from 1926 to 1930 and as a U.S. senator from 1933 until he retired in 1965. He assembled his machine from the county courthouse organizations of the landed gentry, who preferred stability over economic growth and were fiercely committed to racial segregation (Barone and Ujifusa 1993).

The Byrd machine succeeded by restricting participation. Long after the demise of the organization, the state holds its gubernatorial and other statewide elections in odd-numbered years. This has long meant that organized interests can exert disproportionate influence in the general election.

Another remnant of the Byrd machine is the system of no formal party registration. This restriction suited the Byrd machine's objectives during the era of single-party dominance of state politics. Today it means that in those rare cases in which a party nominates a candidate for statewide election by primary, all registered voters may participate.

In most cases, Republicans nominate their candidates in large, statewide conventions that allow almost any citizen to participate who is willing to pledge to support the party nominees and pay a registration fee. These conventions select the candidates and pass the planks of the party platform. As the Republican Party has grown, so has attendance at these conventions. For example, in 1994 more than fourteen thousand Virginians participated as delegates to the convention that nominated Oliver North for the U.S. Senate.

In the second half of the twentieth century, the GOP has held an open primary nomination for statewide election only twice: the gubernatorial nomination of 1989 and the senatorial nomination of 1996. The difference in nominating process has a profound impact on party nominations.

The party nominating conventions favor candidates backed by organized interests; most recently this has meant the Christian Right and the pro-life movement. Ralph Reed said that "the caucus-convention nominating process in the [Virginia] Republican Party is unusual in that it does tend to give [our] grassroots activists a greater voice than they have in primaries" (Reed 1994).

The evidence for GOP primaries is less clear only because of the limited number of cases. In 1989, the GOP gubernatorial primary favored the most conservative candidate, who won with under 37 percent of the low-turnout vote in a three-way race. In 1996 the primary heavily favored the more moderate candidate in a two-way contest.

The evidence is nonetheless clear that Christian Right influence on Republican nomination politics has hurt the party in general elections. The urban corridor that includes the Washington, D.C., suburbs has a majority of the state's population, and the northern Virginia suburbs are distinctive in their affluence, their relatively low levels of religious involvement, their social liberalism, and their many Republican voters. Many of these Republican voters are unwilling to support candidates backed by the Christian Right and have defected in large numbers in recent elections to moderate Democrats and even an independent candidate.

Virginia is a heavily Protestant state, full of Baptist and Methodist churches. Surveys show that nearly half of the state's residents profess an affiliation with an evangelical denomination and that more than 10 percent identify as fundamentalists. More than 40 percent of likely voters indicate that they believe that the Bible is literally true. The northern Virginia area has a sizable number of Catholics and even non-Judeo-Christian immigrants. John Green reports that

"Virginia is one of the most cosmopolitan and diverse of the southern states, which are the most religious overall" (Green 1995). During the 1970s and early 1980s, Virginia was home to the Moral Majority, a Christian Right organization based in the Bible Baptist Fellowship that was centered mainly in the fundamentalist right. The Reverend Jerry Falwell, former head of the Moral Majority, lives in Lynchburg, and his huge congregation is a major institution in that region of the state. In the 1990s, Virginia is home to the Christian Coalition, an organization that grew out of Pat Robertson's failed 1988 presidential campaign. Although that campaign appealed mainly to charismatics and Pentecostals, the Christian Coalition has sought to build bridges to other religious groups.

Not surprisingly, then, the Christian Right has long exerted influence on Virginia politics. In 1978, conservative Christians attended the state Democratic convention to support G. Conoly Phillips, a Virginia Beach car dealer who said that God had called him to run for the U.S. Senate. Phillips expressed surprise that the call had even specified the Democratic Party, for he would have preferred to run as an independent. Campaign mentor Pat Robertson, the son of a former Democratic U.S. senator, also urged that choice. Phillips lost the nomination, although his strong support surprised many observers. A smaller number of Christian conservatives participated in the GOP nominating convention, backing the eventual nominee, former state party chair Richard Obenshain. Obenshain died in a plane crash, and the party committee eventually selected John Warner as the nominee. Warner went on to win a historically close race for the Senate.

The Republican realignment took on metaphysical overtones in the 1980s, as the Christian Right moved into the GOP. In 1981 the Moral Majority helped to mobilize some seven hundred delegates to the state GOP nominating convention, primarily to support lieutenant governor candidate Guy Farley, a former Byrd Democrat turned born-again Republican. Farley lost a bitter nomination fight in which opponents characterized him as a Christian Right extremist. Nonetheless, the GOP fielded a conservative ticket led by Attorney General J. Marshall Coleman, and Falwell embraced the Republican nominees. Falwell's open endorsement and activities on behalf of the GOP ticket became a focal point of contention in the campaign. Despite his large following among social conservatives, polls showed that Falwell was the most unpopular figure in state politics, and Democrats, led by moderate gubernatorial candidate Charles S. Robb, succeeded in linking Republican nominees to Falwell and the Christian Right. Republicans lost all three statewide offices, and this campaign inaugurated the Democrats' use of Christian Right support for the GOP as a wedge issue.

In 1985, Christian conservatives mobilized behind the gubernatorial candidacy of Wyatt B. Durette, a pro-life advocate who opposed abortion even in cases of rape and incest. Durette advocated a constitutional amendment to ban all abortions. He also advocated organized nondenominational prayer recited aloud in schools and a constitutional amendment to permit those prayers (Cox 1985). Partially in response to pressure from his own backers, late in the campaign Durette said that he favored the mandatory teaching of creationism in the public schools. Once again, Falwell endorsed the GOP ticket, and again a moderate Democrat, Gerald Baliles, succeeded in portraying Durette as a pawn of the Christian Right. Once again, all three GOP candidates for state office handily lost. In 1988, Pat Robertson's presidential campaign did poorly in the state primary but well in the local and congressional caucuses that selected delegates to the national convention. Because the state party central committee is selected out of those caucuses and the resultant state convention, Christian conservatives gained a strong foothold in the party apparatus.

In 1989, the GOP experimented with a party primary, its first since 1949. Coleman ran as the most conservative candidate on abortion and won the gubernatorial nomination in a close three-way contest. The Supreme Court handed down the *Webster* decision after the primary, and because that decision allowed states to enact some abortion restrictions and consequently energized pro-choice activists, Coleman scrambled toward the middle on abortion in a general election race that centered on that issue (Cook, Jelen, and Wilcox 1994). Large numbers of moderate Republicans defected to support Democratic nominee L. Douglas Wilder, who became the nation's first elected black governor.

By 1993, Christian conservatives had a strong foothold in the party. The state GOP chair, Patrick McSweeney, had won office by appealing to the Christian Right, and our survey of the state central committee showed that about one-third of its members were strong supporters of Christian Right organizations and issues (Rozell and Wilcox 1996). A number of organizations, including the Christian Coalition, Concerned Women for America, and the Family Foundation (associated with Focus on the Family) were active in Virginia politics, and their members were primarily Republicans. But in 1993 it was the Christian home-schoolers who dominated Republican politics.

The 1993 convention nominated Michael Farris for lieutenant governor. Farris, a former Washington State Moral Majority executive director and a former attorney for Concerned Women for America, currently heads a legal defense organization for home-schooling families. Farris's supporters were new to GOP politics, but they flooded the nominating convention. Farris won nomination easily against a pro-choice moderate woman and longtime GOP activist, Bobbie Kilberg.

At the top of the ticket was former U.S. representative George Allen, who appealed to Christian activists with promises to push hard for parental notification on abortion, support for charter schools, and rollbacks in the state's Family Life Education program. Yet unlike Republican nominees in earlier contests, Allen did not stress his socially conservative views. In fact, he portrayed himself as a moderate on abortion, favoring only limited restrictions on the procedure. He emphasized instead his promises to cut taxes and abolish parole. Unlike the 1980s campaigns when Christian Right leaders made uncompromising demands on GOP candidates as a condition for support, these leaders in 1993 decided to play smart and back a gubernatorial candidate who was not a purist on the social issues but who was clearly a better choice from their perspective than the pro-choice Democratic nominee, Mary Sue Terry. Allen won in a landslide, as did GOP attorney general candidate James Gilmore, who also was supported by, but not a part of, the Christian Right

Farris, however, lost, running an extraordinary 12 percentage points behind the top of his ticket. Don Beyer, his Democratic opponent, characterized Farris as a Christian Right extremist who would ban books from public schools and whose ideas were dangerously out of the mainstream. Farris was a prolific writer and public speaker, and a number of passages from his writings and published statements gave Beyer ample and credible ammunition.

Robertson and the Christian Coalition were actually more supportive of Allen and Gilmore than of Farris. According to a good many accounts, Robertson considered Farris potentially damaging to the Christian Coalition's goal of becoming an organization with a reputation for taking reasonable stands on issues and party politics (Rozell and Wilcox 1996).

Allen benefited from the comparison to Farris. Voters could compare Allen and Farris and conclude that Allen was far more moderate. Farris mobilized a large number of social conservatives who then also voted for the rest of the GOP ticket. Terry failed in her attempts to get the public to accept that Allen, too, was a Christian Right extremist, although, according to Allen's own tracking polls, his momentum temporarily slowed once in the campaign: when Terry ran ads linking Allen to Robertson and Falwell. Warner refused to back Farris, although he campaigned on behalf of the rest of the GOP ticket. In 1994 Warner again broke with the party and refused to support the Senate nomination of Oliver North. But there was one important difference: Warner merely refused to endorse Farris, whereas the senator openly opposed North and recruited a moderate Republican to run as an independent. Ironically, Marshall Coleman, the candidate of moderate Republicans in 1994, had run as a Christian conservative in an earlier bid for the governorship.

Warner's actions in 1993 and 1994 set the stage for his renomination battle in 1996. Social conservatives pledged to challenge Warner and to replace him with a more reliable conservative. Party centrists hailed Warner's actions as rare displays of political courage and pledged to work for his renomination. And there were disturbing signs of political vulnerability for Warner. In both January and October of 1995, Mason-Dixon polls of likely primary voters showed that Warner and challenger Jim Miller were statistically tied (Lee 1995; Baker 1996c). Until mid-April 1996, it remained unclear whether Warner would be able to run for reelection in a primary, and it remained undoubtedly clear that, given his alienation from party leaders and activists, in a convention nomination he would lose.

The 1996 Republican Nomination

> "Old guard vs. new. Country-clubbers vs. Christian soldiers. Economic conservatives vs. social conservatives." (Baker and Hsu 1996c, describing the Warner-Miller race)

After North's defeat, state party chair McSweeney vowed that Warner would be "dealt with." He spoke of going to Capitol Hill to try to persuade GOP leaders to deny the senator the chairmanship of the Rules Committee. The state GOP chair even considered challenging Warner himself for renomination. Ultimately McSweeney decided instead to challenge Warner's decision to run for renomination in an open primary.

A provision of a Virginia law allows the incumbent candidate running for renomination to request an open primary. Warner knew that an open primary was his only hope of winning. The Virginia GOP, led by McSweeney, challenged the constitutionality of the state law that gave Warner the right to choose his own method of renomination.

The state GOP charged that the law was an infringement on the party's constitutional right to select its own nominating process and its own candidate. The coplaintiff in the suit was Delegate Robert G. Marshall, a social conservative and director of the American Life League. The plaintiffs requested that if Warner indeed had the right to request a primary, then either (1) Democrats and independents should be barred from voting—difficult to imagine in Virginia, since there is no party registration; or (2) that voters should be required to sign a GOP loyalty oath. The federal judge threw out the lawsuit on 16 April 1996, guaranteeing Warner an open primary. It was the senator's most important victory. The federal judge who issued the opinion called McSweeney a "disgruntled maverick" who had tried to purge from the GOP those "impure of thought" (Baker and Hsu 1996b). A poll released the same week as the court decision showed Warner for the first time with a substantial lead over Miller (P. Baker 1996c).

Despite all of this good news for the senator, he could not take lightly the intraparty challenge. Miller had run for the GOP U.S. Senate nomination in 1994 and had come close to defeating Oliver North in the convention, despite having been heavily outspent by the Iran-contra figure. The Virginia GOP lacked a tradition of statewide primaries, having held just one since 1949. It was conceivable that Warner would lose even an open primary if Christian conservatives mobilized and moderate voters stayed home.

Indeed, conventional wisdom during the primary suggested that support from the Christian Right could deliver an upset victory to Miller. That was a reasonable conclusion to draw given Christian conservatives' widespread anger with Warner and the fact that on almost every issue, Miller staked out the most conservative position. On abortion, for example, Miller opposed the procedure even in cases of rape or incest. A *Washington Post* profile summarized the feelings of many in the GOP toward Warner: "The hatred for Warner among the rank-and-file party activists is raw and unrelenting." The Republican National Committee member from Virginia, Morton Blackwell, stated, "If we renominate the incumbent we ought to take up a collection and erect . . . a statue of Benedict Arnold" (Baker and Hsu 1996g). Miller had the support not only of the state party chair and national committee member but also of former governor Mills Godwin, and he selected Farris as a campaign chairman. Farris maintained that he could easily deliver tens of thousands of Christian Right votes to Miller in a primary.

Yet our survey of the 1994 Virginia GOP convention delegates revealed that Miller could not automatically count on the support of the Christian Right. Even though Miller ran to the right of North, those delegates who supported the former Reagan budget director were much closer to the GOP establishment than to grassroots movement conservatives. Miller's delegates were more moderate than North's and had longer affiliations with the GOP and higher levels of income and education. Miller's delegates overwhelmingly stated that their major motivation for supporting him was negative: opposition to North and lack of any other option. By contrast, North's supporters stated a positive motivation: their admiration for North, who many believed was a national hero. Although he was supported mostly by the anti-North moderates, Miller tried to appeal to North's conservative base. The delegate survey makes it clear that despite Miller's extreme conservative stands, he had very little success at attracting delegates from the far right (Rozell and Wilcox 1996). Moreover, since Miller had been the vehicle for party moderates who sought to deny the nomination to North in 1994, he was an unusual choice to embody Christian conservative hostility to Warner.

These findings are bolstered by a *Washington Post* computer analysis of campaign disclosure reports. The analysis showed that only 23 percent of

Miller's 1994 donors contributed to his 1996 campaign and 18 percent defected to support Warner. Even more discouraging, Miller received support from only 3 percent of North's seven thousand contributors from 1994 (Baker and Hsu 1996e).

Consequently, Miller, the candidate of the moderates who ran with John Warner's support and assistance in 1994, had to appeal in 1996 to the same grassroots conservative activists who had earlier rejected him and in many cases even despised him for daring to challenge North. Throughout the primary campaign, it became evident that Miller could not excite the conservative grass roots the way that North had in 1994. This failure was not due to a lack of effort on his part or on the part of leading organizations. Miller campaigned tirelessly throughout rural Virginia, moving from town to town in a pickup truck. The Christian Coalition ran radio advertisements on his behalf and distributed voter guides that clearly favored him. Americans for Limited Terms spent about $350,000 to run radio ads and send out mass mailings intended to help Miller, who supported term limits for members of Congress.

Senator Warner had the support of established party figures (e.g., George Bush, Colin Powell, Dan Quayle, and Bob Dole) and a large fund-raising advantage that he used to great effect by running frequent television advertisements. In the final two weeks of the campaign alone, Warner spent over $600,000 on television ads in the northern Virginia market (Baker and Hsu 1996g). Ten days prior to the primary, the state GOP held its convention in Salem. In a straw poll of the three thousand delegates, Miller beat Warner by a 3-1 margin. Christian conservatives were a dominant force at the event, which featured a battle between the party factions for state party chair and Republican National Committee (RNC) member. The social conservatives easily won both votes, beating back a moderate challenge to Blackwell for RNC member and electing a social conservative to replace outgoing party chair McSweeney. According to the *Washington Post,* at this party event, "the antipathy among convention-goers toward Warner was palpable and even ugly" (Baker and Hsu 1996a, A19).

The most dramatic moment of the convention came when Oliver North addressed the delegates and urged them to get behind Miller's candidacy. He asked that each delegate pledge $20 to Miller's campaign and actively work to identify, and urge similar help from, every 1994 North supporter. North mailed a plea to 16,500 supporters asking for their assistance for Miller's campaign.

Although on the surface this endorsement seemed destined finally to energize the conservative base for Miller, on closer inspection North did severe damage to the cause. As North's 1994 campaign manager, Mark Goodin, correctly predicted: "Now they [the opposition] have a demon involved in the race. . . . It could backfire" (Baker and Hsu 1996f, B7).

Just days before the primary, a Mason-Dixon poll revealed the dynamics of the race: Warner held a large lead among likely voters, one-half of whom were Democrats and independents. Among Republican likely voters, Warner and Miller were statistically tied.

Leading Democrats urged party members to sit out the Warner-Miller primary, preferring to run against Miller rather than a popular incumbent. Warner ran ads saying "not voting is a vote for Miller"—a clear pitch to non-Republicans. Perhaps very telling about the impact of Warner's actions against North in 1994, the chair of the Democratic caucus in the state senate openly defied his party's leadership and voted in the GOP primary for Warner. State senator Ed Hauck made no secret of the fact that he believed that Warner deserved to be thanked even by Democrats for opposing North (P. Baker 1996b).

Warner soundly defeated Miller, taking 66 percent of the popular vote. Although there were no exit polls and it is impossible to determine exactly how many non-Republicans participated, there is some telling evidence of Warner's broad-based appeal. For example, turnout was very strong for Warner in traditionally Democratic-leaning urban areas. Although turnout statewide was 15.9 percent, the turnout was significantly stronger in the Democratic strongholds of northern Virginia, including Fairfax City (21.5 percent), Falls Church (26.1 percent), Arlington County (18.9 percent), and Alexandria (17.3 percent). Results provided by the Virginia State Board of Elections show that in those four jurisdictions, Warner took 68 percent, 77 percent, 75 percent, and 78 percent of the vote, respectively. Clearly Warner had benefited from non-Republican support that most likely could be attributed to his opposition to North and to his estrangement from the Christian Right movement. On election day, the *Washington Post* interviewed dozens of voters at polling sites throughout the state and heard many statements of support for Warner from non-Republicans who praised his actions against North.

In the eyes of most observers of the state political scene, with such a resounding renomination win, Warner was virtually assured of reelection. Miller's loss continued the Christian Right's series of statewide electoral disappointments; bids to elect Farris and North also failed. Once again it appeared that voters even in this conservative state are uncomfortable with candidates who either are from the Christian Right or are very closely aligned with the movement. Perhaps the most apt comment after the primary came from former state GOP spokesman Mike Salster, who said that the Christian Right had been "spoiling for this fight for three years [since Farris's defeat], with their yellow and blue 'Is it 96 yet?' bumper stickers. Now they have found their base, and it is 34 percent, not 50.1 percent" (D. Baker 1996).

Most of the Christian Right leadership announced that they would support Warner as the rightful GOP nominee. A conspicuous exception was state party chair McSweeney, who persisted in opposing Warner and made the case the day after the primary that perhaps a defeat of Senator Warner in the general election would be better for the party in the long run. He reasoned unpersuasively that Warner had personally cost the GOP two statewide races (Farris and North) and that maintaining that one seat for the GOP in the U.S. Senate was not worth such a price (WNVT-TV 1996).

Given the depth of anger toward Warner among Christian Right activists, there was a real concern in his campaign that many GOP voters would not turn out in the general election. Some activists even spoke of a "grudge vote" against the senator in the general election, and still others agreed with McSweeney's reasoning that losing the Senate seat to the Democrats might be preferable to Warner's reelection.

In addition to continuing acrimony within the GOP, the senator had to prepare for his first serious general election campaign since his election to the Senate in 1978. The Democrats had nominated their former state party chair, Mark Warner (no relation to the senator), a man with a personal fortune of over $100 million and a willingness to spend heavily on his campaign.

The General Election Campaign

Mark Warner followed much of the Democratic Party script nationally in campaigning against the incumbent. In the first candidate debate, the Democratic nominee blasted Senator Warner as a far-right Republican who opposed abortion rights and voted "94.7 percent of the time" with House Speaker Newt Gingrich. But the senator's response—that he was an independent-minded Republican who broke with GOP conservatives at much political cost—evidenced the enormity of the task ahead for the challenger (Senate debate 1996). How could anyone credibly claim that the man who refused to back one Christian Right party nominee and openly opposed another was a far-right extremist, a Newt Gingrich clone? To most voters, Senator Warner was a politically courageous moderate, not an ideologue. To further bolster his reputation for independence, the senator openly refused to support presidential nominee Bob Dole's campaign centerpiece, a 15 percent across-the-board tax cut.

Yet the challenger persisted with this tack, and to some extent he succeeded in convincing a good many voters that the senator really was not a Republican moderate. By spending over $10 million of his immense personal fortune largely on television ads, Mark Warner was able to convince the electorate that the senator had a very conservative voting record. That was key to the Democrat's bringing home the base party vote, much of which had gone to the Republican incumbent in the 11 June primary. The Democrat was helped somewhat by the senator's own renomination battle, in which he openly touted a 100 percent rating in 1995 from the Christian Coalition and ran ads saying that he was "fighting for common sense, conservative principles." And some organized liberal interests, such as the National Abortion Rights Action League (NARAL), aided the challenger's efforts. NARAL in fact targeted Virginia as one of four states in which it focused its energies in Senate campaigns (Gearan 1996).

The senator nonetheless had an untarnished reputation for integrity, another huge obstacle for the challenger to overcome. Yet that reputation suffered as the result of a serious ethical breach by a political consulting firm hired by John Warner. One of the senator's negative ads was intended to convey that his challenger was an ideological liberal with close ties to President Clinton (who remained unpopular in the state). The ad showed a picture of the challenger shaking hands with President Clinton and standing next to former Democratic governor L. Douglas Wilder. In truth, it was a picture of Mark Warner's head placed on Senator Charles Robb's body with computer imaging technology.

Although the senator apologized and immediately fired the consulting firm, this unethical tactic gave an opening to the Democratic campaign once again to challenge John Warner's exalted image. Later in the campaign, a campaign aide to the senator complained that a candidate debate sponsored by the NAACP was a "nigger-rigged event," and once again political damage was done to Senator Warner, who fired the individual immediately upon hearing of the remark. By the end of the campaign the senator was defending both his voting record in Congress and his ethics, neither of which had ever been a point of contention for Virginia voters.

Clearly created out of frustration, one of the senator's ads referred to Mark Warner's attacks as "dirty, reckless, dangerous and stupid." Although this line had been lifted (with attribution) from a newspaper editorial, the statement appeared to many to be beyond the boundary of reasonable political discourse. Four days before the election, the senator angrily denounced his challenger's heavy spending on negative ads as "not the Virginia way" and lamented the arrival of the day when "we put our candidacies up for sale on the stock exchange for the highest bidders" (Warner 1996).

Despite some campaign pratfalls and the onslaught of Democratic spending to defeat him, the senator secured the endorsement of all eighteen newspapers in the state that had made endorsements, including such reliably liberal editorial sources as the *Washington Post,* the *Norfolk Virginian-Pilot,* and the *Fredericksburg Free-Lance Star.* The senator won reelection with 53 percent of the vote, a much closer contest than anyone had predicted.

The exit polling data revealed that Christian conservatives did not sit out this election after all and that they overwhelmingly supported the senator's reelection. Fully 21 percent of the electorate were white self-described "religious right voters," and they supported the senator by over a 3-1 margin. The Christian Right accounted for nearly 30 percent of the senator's overall vote total (CNN/Time 1996).

The Christian Right in 1996

John Warner's reelection, while not an entirely happy outcome for the Christian Right, was from its standpoint clearly better than his defeat at the hands of a pro-choice Democratic challenger. The Christian Right did all that it could to try to defeat the senator in the GOP primary and then ultimately supported him in the general election.

The most telling example was the activity of the Christian Coalition. Although a January 1996 Christian Coalition scorecard gave the Senator a 100 percent voting record for 1995, during the GOP primary in June 1996 the group's voter guide gave him a 20 percent rating (Miller received 100 percent). But after the primary a new Coalition guide gave the senator an 83 percent rating! The organization cleverly selected issues on which to base its ratings according to the campaign and the group's preferred outcome. But for some congressional races, the Coalition kept the issues the same for both the primary and the general election. As the *Norfolk Virginian-Pilot* editorialized: "The tailoring of ballots shows how voting records can be selectively cited to reach a preordained conclusion in political campaigns. It is also evidence that the Coalition's claim to nonpartisanship is largely a charade" (*Norfolk Virginian-Pilot* 1996).

In August, a state Democratic senator requested that the attorney general's office investigate whether the Christian Coalition's political activities had violated state election laws. Much like the FEC case against the Coalition, this request focused on the organization's claim that it is nonpartisan. The attorney general's office, headed by the 1997 Republican gubernatorial nominee, James Gilmore, turned down the request, fueling charges of political motivations. Gilmore had won office in 1993 with substantial financial backing from Pat Robertson, and the televangelist had attended a Gilmore fund-raiser in 1996 (Associated Press 1996a).

In the one open congressional seat, the Fifth District in the rural southwest, a conservative Democrat soundly defeated a Christian Right Republican nominee. In the presidential campaign Bob Dole won Virginia with 47.1 percent to Clinton's 45.1 percent. That was the best presidential showing by a Democrat since Jimmy Carter lost the state to President Ford in 1976 by only 1 percent. Yet in a sense Clinton scored a victory by making competitive a state that was normally reliably Republican in presidential campaigns and forcing Dole to expend campaign resources on a state the GOP nominee should have won easily (McNair 1996; Nakashima 1996).

An Associated Press survey of the Virginia delegates to the Republican National Convention showed the continued strength of the Christian Right in the state party. Of the fifty-two delegates, forty-eight responded to the survey. Of those, twenty-one said that they considered themselves a part of the Christian social conservative movement, nineteen said no, and eight chose "no answer." Among those who chose "no answer" were delegates Pat Robertson and Ralph Reed (O'Dell 1996). The delegation also included Farris, former National Right to Life spokesperson Kay Coles James, antiabortion leader Anne Kincaid, and Family Foundation (of the Focus on the Family) head Walter Barbee.

The Christian Right achieved most of its success in 1996 through the continued support of the Allen administration. Until 1997, Virginia was the only state to refuse to accept federal education dollars through the Goals 2000 program. Christian Right groups lobbied hard for the governor to turn down the federal funds because of their belief that the money would force localities to accept nationally mandated values and standards and would therefore undermine educational choice. The governor launched a $300,000 "traditional values"–based series of advertisements to extol the importance of fatherhood. Called the "Virginia Fatherhood Campaign," the initiative was an outgrowth of the gubernatorial Commission on Citizen Empowerment. The governor supported initiatives in the state legislature to mandate parental notification on abortion for underaged girls and to establish a new criminal category of "feticide" to declare the act of killing a fetus a murder. The former measure passed the general assembly in 1997, and the latter went down to defeat.

Despite their disappointment at not being able to defeat Warner in the primary, the Christian Right actually benefited from his victory in the general election. Despite all the anger the social conservatives feel toward Warner for what they consider his disloyalty, the fact remains that he is a reliable vote in the U.S. Senate for many of the Christian Right's policy positions.

The results of the 1996 elections in Virginia and the Allen administration's agenda lead us to conclude, as we did after the 1994 elections (Rozell and Wilcox 1995), that the Christian Right fares best when it backs mainstream conservative candidates who have a realistic chance of winning. In Virginia, when newly mobilized activists have supplied the margin of victory for Christian Right candidates seeking the GOP nomination for state office (e.g., Farris, North), the party has fared poorly. When the GOP has backed mainstream conservatives who support much of the agenda of the Christian Right but are not members of that movement or closely aligned with it, the party has fared well (e.g., Allen, Gilmore, Warner). Perhaps the great irony of the 1996 Senate election result for the Christian Right is this: Had the Christian Right's leaders prevailed in their effort to defeat John Warner in the primary, it is almost certain that the Senate seat would have gone to a pro-choice Democrat. The failure to beat Warner in the primary ensured his reelection and gave the Christian Right a very friendly vote in the Senate for the next six years.

References

Associated Press. 1996a. "Gilmore Nixes Virginia Probe into Coalition Work." *Fairfax Journal* (15 August): A5.

———. 1996b. "It's Official: John Won." *Fairfax Journal* (26 November): A6.

———. 1996c. "Virginia to Pass Up U.S. Money." *Fairfax Journal* (25 November): A10.

Baker, Donald P. 1996. "With Warner's Victory, GOP's Right Wing Clipped for Third Time." *Washington Post* (12 June): A8.

Baker, Peter. 1996a. "Degrees of Difference Separate Warner, Miller in GOP Contest." *Washington Post* (13 May): D1, 5.

———. 1996b. "Democrats Miffed by Vote for J. Warner." *Washington Post* (4 July): Virginia 1, 3.

———. 1996c. "Sen. Warner's Rising Lead Falls Short of Majority, Poll Finds." *Washington Post* (18 April): B5.

———. 1996d. "Warner Openly Woos Non-Republicans." *Washington Post* (23 May): C1, 5.

Baker, Peter, and Spencer S. Hsu. 1996a. "North Seeks Revenge in Senate Race." *Washington Post* (2 June): A1, 19.

———. 1996b. "Sen. Warner Wins: Open Primary Upheld." *Washington Post* (17 April): D3.

———. 1996c. "They're United on GOP, Divided on Its Direction." *Washington Post* (9 June): A1, 13.

———. 1996d. "Warner Crushes Milller in GOP Primary." *Washington Post* (12 June): A1, 8.

———. 1996e. "Warner, Miller Are Counting on Rural Virginia Appeal." *Washington Post* (10 June): D1, 3.

———. 1996f. "Warner's Ads Pull No Punches as He Tries to Get Independents in His Corner." *Washington Post* (7 June): B1, 7.

———. 1996g. "Warner's Moderation, Usually an Asset, Is under Seige." *Washington Post* (6 June): Virginia 1, 7.

Barone, Michael, and Grant Ujifusa, 1993. "Virginia." Pp. 1301–6 in *The Almanac of American Politics 1994*. Washington, D.C.: National Journal.

CNN/Time. 1996. "Virginia Senate Exit Poll Results." www.allpolitics.com (6 November).

Cook, Elizabeth Adell, Ted G. Jelen, and Clyde Wilcox. 1994. "Issue Voting in Gubernatorial Elections: Abortion in Post-*Webster* Politics." *Journal of Politics* 56: 187–99.

Cox, Charles. 1985. "Baliles, Durette Dramatize Differences." *Richmond Times-Dispatch* (3 November): C2, 6.

Farris, Michael P. 1994. Interview by author, Purcellville, Va., 12 August.

Gearan, Anne. 1996. "Mark Warner Blasts Senator's Votes on Abortion," *Fairfax Journal* (17 October): A3.

Green, John C. 1995. Telephone interview by author, 17 January.

Hsu, Spencer S. 1996a. "Divided on Main Street." *Washington Post* (19 May): B1, 5.

————. 1996b. "Fetal Homicide Measure Fails in Virginia House." *Washington Post* (5 March): B4.

————. 1996c. "Mark Warner Toughens Talk in Campaign Shift." *Washington Post* (28 August): D1, 6.

————. 1996d. "Senate Contest in Virginia Becomes Race to Center." *Washington Post* (25 August): B1, 4.

Key, V. O., Jr. 1949. *Southern Politics in State and Nation*. New York: Knopf.

Lee, Elizabeth. 1995. "Warner Tops Va. Poll." *Fairfax Journal* (24 January): A1, 8.

McNair, Jean. 1996. "Virginia Clings to Center of Road." *Fairfax Journal* (8 November): A11.

Nakashima, Ellen. 1996. "Virginia Becomes a Battle in Presidential War." *Washington Post* (21 October): B1, 5.

Norfolk Virginian-Pilot. "Good Warner, Bad Warner, Same Warner: Inconsistent Coalition." Editorial (6 November): A26.

O'Dell, Larry. 1996. Telephone interview by author, 26 July.

Redmon, Jeremy, and Robert White. 1996. "Dems Hope Gains Noticed." *Fairfax Journal* (31 July): A1, 6.

Reed, Ralph. 1994. Interview by author, Washington, D.C., 29 September.

Rozell, Mark J., and Clyde Wilcox. 1995. "Virginia: God, Guns and Oliver North." Chap. 6 in *God at the Grass Roots: The Christian Right in the 1994 Elections*, ed. Mark J. Rozell and Clyde Wilcox. Lanham, Md.: Rowman & Littlefield.

————. 1996. *Second Coming: The New Christian Right in Virginia Politics*. Baltimore: Johns Hopkins University Press.

Senate Debate. 1996. Hot Springs, Va. (2 July): Sponsored by Virginia Bar Association. Moderated by author.

Warner, John. 1994. Interview by author, Washington, D.C. (22 July).

————. 1996. Interview by author, Falls Church, Va. (1 November).

WNVT-TV. 1996. "Capitol Connection." Falls Church, Va. (6 November). Author appearance with Patrick McSweeney.

8

Michigan: Veering to the Left?

Corwin E. Smidt and James M. Penning

During the summer of 1996, conventional assessments of the campaign for president viewed the major industrial states of the Midwest, specifically Michigan, Illinois, and Ohio, as important "battleground" states. By the end of the campaign, however, there was little drama; Dole hardly challenged President Clinton in these crucial states. And with the election returning a Democrat to the White House and Republicans to control of Congress, the election was generally interpreted nationally as an election that solidified the status quo. Despite such appearances of continuity, important changes occurred in Michigan between the 1994 and 1996 elections.

The purpose of this chapter is to analyze the 1996 election in Michigan, particularly in terms of assessing what role, if any, groups that might be associated with the term "Christian Right" played. A variety of Christian Right groups have organized and become politically active in Michigan over the past several decades, generally working on behalf of conservative GOP candidates. What factors have contributed to their rise? How active have they been? And what impact have they had on Michigan politics? In order to answer these questions, we begin by examining the geopolitical and historical context of the 1996 election. We then discuss the emergence of Christian Right groups within Michigan politics, their historical evolution, and their organizational structure. We conclude by examining the 1996 election and assessing the impact of the Christian Right on election outcomes within the state.

The Political Context

The Partisan Context

During the early years of this century, Michigan could be accurately classified as a one-party Republican state. But the Great Depression stimulated a

115

revival of the Democratic Party in Michigan that transformed the state into a partisan battleground.[1]

Michigan's two major parties are rooted in differing patterns of social class, race, ideology, and region. The contrasts are stark and meaningful; the parties don't like each other very much and find it difficult to locate common ground. Michigan's GOP finds its primary bases of support among small business-persons, farmers, and suburban professionals. It also receives substantial support from conservative Protestants and traditional middle-class "WASPs." In contrast, the core of the Michigan Democratic Party is organized labor, particularly the powerful United Auto Workers union and the Michigan Education Association. The party also receives considerable support from university liberals; working-class, Roman Catholic "ethnics" (particularly Irish and Polish ethnics); and African Americans. As one would expect, the Michigan Democratic Party is ideologically to the left of the GOP.

A variety of Christian Right groups have been formed in recent years, and they have become increasingly active, particularly in the Republican Party. In 1988, for example, supporters of the Reverend Pat Robertson threw the Michigan GOP into a state of chaos with their aggressive efforts on his behalf. The chief intraparty split was between the Christian Right supporters of Robertson and the more moderate supporters of George Bush. At least twenty-six of Michigan's counties produced competing conventions controlled by the warring factions, with each voting to send its own slate of delegates to the state convention. The state Republican convention also split into two groups—a regular convention dominated by Bush delegates, and a "rump" convention dominated by Robertson's supporters (Penning 1994, 329). The resulting ill will has taken a long time to dissipate. According to one recent study, Michigan's GOP state organization still exhibits a "substantial" level of Christian Right strength within its ranks (Persinos 1994, 22).

The Geopolitical Context

To a greater extent than most other states, Michigan "is driven by the politics of place" (Browne and Verberg 1995, 270). GOP support tends to be concentrated in the more prosperous agricultural regions, in the small and medium-sized cities of west Michigan (Grand Rapids, Holland, Kalamazoo), and in the suburban ring of counties (e.g., Oakland and Macomb Counties) surrounding the city of Detroit. The Democratic Party finds its greatest support in Wayne County (Detroit), in the cities of the I-75 corridor (Ann Arbor, Saginaw, Pontiac, Flint, Bay City), and in the economically depressed Upper Peninsula. While Michigan is divided into eighty-three counties, roughly three-quarters of all the votes cast within the state are cast within the seventeen most populous counties.

Generally, one or two counties serve as the major anchor(s) of a particular con-gressional district, though not every populous county falls fully or neatly with-in one of the state's sixteen congressional districts.

The Christian Right

The decade of the 1980s helped to set the stage for the proliferation and growth of many political organizations with ties to conservative Christians. Three factors in particular should be noted: (1) the impact of the Reagan rev-olution, (2) the candidacy of Pat Robertson, and (3) the changing political agenda. While the Reagan administration did not implement many of the pol-icy objectives of conservative Christians, one important legacy was that power began to shift back to state governments. Accordingly, Christian Right leaders began to view organizational decentralization as the key to political success. Not only was it desirable to create organizations built from the precincts upward, but organizations needed to be given considerable local autonomy.

According to Ralph Reed, national director of the Christian Coalition, Robertson's presidential campaign in 1988 served as "the political crucible" for the proliferation of many of these local Christian Right groups (Reed 1994, 193). Whether or not this is true nationally, Robertson's presidential candidacy did have an important impact on Christian Right activity in Michigan. Some of the organizations that arose in the wake of the Robertson candidacy have direct ties to his presidential campaign; others have little direct relationship but arose in the political climate that existed following his statewide efforts. Of the four major statewide Christian Right organizations described below, three originat-ed with or after Robertson's candidacy.

A third reason for the growing success of Christian Right organizations is their development of a broader political agenda. Initially, the abortion issue dominated the agenda of conservative Christians. But as the political context changed, more issues were included. Euthanasia, the rights of homosexuals, pornography, sex education in schools, charter and home schools, and gam-bling have become issues of concern to the "pro-family" movement. Finally, the Christian Right is also beginning to speak to various economic issues, particularly issues related to taxation. With such a proliferation of issues, Christian Right organizations have been able to develop unique functions and particular issue "niches." For example, while some organizations focus primarily on issues related to abortion and euthanasia, others address policy issues related to the family or "traditional values" such as the teaching of creationism.

Right-to-Life of Michigan

Begun in the late 1960s, Right-to-Life of Michigan (RTLM) received a major boost as it prepared for a 1972 state referendum that would have legalized abortion for the first twenty weeks of pregnancy. Although the referendum was defeated, the Supreme Court's ruling the following year in *Roe v. Wade* made the referendum moot.

Headquartered in the Grand Rapids area, RTLM is nonsectarian, and the organization itself makes no effort to assess the religious affiliation of its membership. In fact, other organizations with a distinct religious base, such as Baptists for Life, operate alongside RTLM. RTLM is organized into fourteen relatively autonomous regional affiliates. Each affiliate elects one representative to the state board of directors; twenty additional voting representatives are selected on an at-large basis. RTLM has a strong base of support in Kent and Ottawa Counties in the west side of the state, Grand Traverse County in northern lower Michigan, Bay County in the Saginaw Bay region, and Oakland and Macomb Counties on the southeast side of the state. Currently, RTLM has a membership of approximately 200,000 households in its data base, up 40,000 over the past two years, and a mailing list of approximately 600,000, an increase of approximately 100,000 since 1994.

Michigan Family Forum

Michigan Family Forum (MFF), headquartered in Lansing, was founded in April 1990 as a 501(c)3 organization.[2] Its executive director has been Randall Hekman, a former probate judge who resigned from the bench to head the organization. Hekman announced his resignation in mid-1996, and by the end of the year no new director had been appointed. While MFF associates closely with the national organization Focus on the Family, it is not legally or financially tied to the national organization, which was founded and is led by psychologist James Dobson, whose radio program, *Focus on the Family,* is aired on over 1,450 radio stations throughout the country (Moen 1992, 61). Headquartered in Colorado Springs, Focus is a parachurch organization dedicated to fostering traditional family values based on biblical teachings. Focus is loosely associated with the Family Research Council in Washington, D.C., headed by former Reagan staffer Gary Bauer, and produces a monthly political publication, *Citizen,* that has more than a quarter of a million subscribers (Steinfels 1990).

MFF was organized to function as a "family policy council" to address issues related to the family within the state of Michigan. Approximately thirty such state organizations currently exist around the country, each functioning independently. MFF seeks to provide information to government leaders and the general public on "critical family issues of the day." To that end, it offers the following services: (1) Info Paks—materials that contain research, essays, and articles on various issues related to families, (2) LegiService—a newsletter that provides in-depth analysis of eight to twelve important state bills each month as well as voting records of state legislators on two or three selected key legislative votes on family issues over the past month, (3) voter guides—publications each election year to assist citizens in ascertaining where candidates for state and national office stand on family issues; and (4) research publications—documents based upon the efforts of the Research and Public Policy Division of the Michigan Family Forum.[3]

Citizens for Traditional Values

Headquartered in Lansing, Citizens for Traditional Values (CTV) traces its roots, in part, to Robertson's presidential bid in 1988. Organized in 1986 as the Michigan Committee for Freedom, the organization quickly became involved in Robertson's presidential bid. However, after Robertson's efforts faded and as the Robertson campaign incurred huge debts, the Robertson organization withdrew its national people from the organization. At that time the board of directors of the Michigan Committee for Freedom invited James Muffett to become its executive director. Muffett, who had been involved in the Robertson campaign in Vermont, assumed the post in 1988 and took on the task of eliminating a debt of $200,000 incurred by the organization in the Robertson effort. Muffett's initial effort was to eliminate the debt and to develop a distinct niche for the organization.

In 1990, the organization filed as a 501(c)4 organization,[4] and in 1991 it changed its name to Citizens for Traditional Values. In seeking to develop a distinct niche, CTV chose not to become a "mass based" membership organization with a "high profile." Rather, in the words of James Muffett, CTV chose to adopt "a servant" rather than a "confrontational" mode. To that end, CTV decided not to affiliate with any national organization (such as the then-emerging Christian Coalition). Instead, it decided to remain an independent organization that focused on state, rather than federal, campaigns. In 1993, it created the Foundation for Traditional Values, a 501(c)3 entity that serves as the educational wing of the organization. Thus, CTV sees itself as a "broad-based" organization in that it (1) engages in both educational and campaign activities through endorsements, PAC contributions, and voter mobilization efforts; and (2) addresses a range of issues, rather than a single issue or narrow range of issues (unlike, e.g., RTLM).

The first statewide election in which it mounted a major effort was in

1992. The 1992 election proved to be critically important, as Republicans gained control of the state senate and were able to obtain an even split in the house. CTV used its limited resources strategically. The group sent a questionnaire to 110 candidates for public office in order to ascertain whether their issue positions merited the support of the organization and, after analyzing the responses, concluded that 64 candidates were worthy of support. However, CTV decided to focus only on the 17 most competitive races. Within those seventeen districts, CTV conducted voter registration drives in churches, distributed candidate information (approximately ten thousand to twenty thousand voter guides per district), and organized voter turnout efforts, primarily through "phonathons" targeted to particular churches. Of the 17 races targeted by CTV, 3 were decided by fewer than 120 votes. CTV continued this strategy in 1994 and 1996. However, in 1996 an emphasis was also placed on getting out the vote. CTV produced pamphlets entitled "From the Pews to the Polls" that sought to mobilize congregants in different churches to serve as coordinators in their local churches to get their members to the polls.

Christian Coalition of Michigan

Though it also traces its history, in part, to the Michigan Committee for Freedom, Christian Coalition of Michigan (CCM) was officially created as a 501(c)4 organization in 1991. According to Ralph Reed, national director of the Christian Coalition, the organization was built with a "*Field of Dreams* strategy: build it and they will come" (Reed 1994, 197). The CCM is an affiliate of the Christian Coalition but remains a separate legal entity. This independence permits a relatively flexible relationship between the national and the state headquarters.

As a (c)4 organization, the CCM cannot endorse candidates, and contributions to the organization are not tax deductible; its activities must be primarily educational in nature. Thus, the CCM has given considerable effort to developing and distributing voter guides for election campaigns. The first CCM guide appeared in the 1992 election. As the CCM had no paid staff at the time, the guide was prepared and distributed totally on a voluntary basis.

In August 1994, Glen Clark was hired as state CCM director and helped oversee the publication and distribution of its second voter guide, as well as engineer its recent move to an office in Birmingham, a suburb of Detroit. While the CCM claims to be statewide in nature, for organizational and strategic reasons it has focused primarily on areas close to its headquarters. No other major organizations geared to conservative Christians are headquartered in that region of the state, and both Macomb and Oakland Counties, which are contiguous with Wayne County (Detroit), are major population centers with many relatively competitive electoral districts.

The CCM presently is organized primarily on a county basis but is moving toward a structure that will include city and township chapters. Up to this point, the CCM has focused on federal rather than state races, but it hopes in the future to provide voter guides for state legislative races as well. The CCM presently boasts fifty-five thousand "contributors"—people who have contributed either time or money.

The 1996 Election

The GOP Presidential and Senatorial Primaries

While Bill Clinton faced virtually no opposition in his bid for renomination, the GOP nomination process was wide open, at least in early 1996. However, by the time Michigan held its 19 March presidential primary, the field had narrowed considerably. Such early hopefuls as Richard Lugar, Phil Gramm, and Lamar Alexander had dropped out, convinced that they had no realistic chance of winning the Republican nomination. Thus, the primary race in Michigan essentially boiled down to a contest between front-runner Bob Dole and Pat Buchanan. Since Michigan's GOP uses a proportional primary system to select national convention delegates, Buchanan found good reason to remain in the race, even though he was trailing Dole in the polls. Alan Keyes also stayed in the race but with so little money and support that he had no realistic hope of garnering any delegates.

During the primary campaign, Buchanan, aided by his state field coordinator, Tom McMillan, a member of the Christian Coalition (Hornbeck 1996b, 2), gave considerable attention to courting members of the Christian Right and received enthusiastic support from many members of the movement. The *Detroit News* (Hornbeck et al. 1996, 1–3), for example, described an address Pat Buchanan made to a Christian Coalition "God and Country" rally in Clawson. According to the *News,* "An estimated 1,000 Christians stood in their pews at Zion Evangelistic Temple, cheering, 'Go Pat go!'" At the same rally, national Christian Coalition leader Ralph Reed elicited "amens" from the audience, asserting that "We have not yet won the political battle, but we have won the moral argument. . . . What we say to the liberal, pro-choice agenda is 'you have failed and now it's our turn.' And that's what this election is about." According to Reed, "There is a cultural war going on for the soul of this country. . . . The issue is about making this God's country again."

Although the CCM does not officially endorse candidates, Buchanan's strong pro-life stand and his active solicitation of Christian Right support paid political dividends. CCM leaders, including executive director Glenn Clark, pledged to vote for Buchanan (Hornbeck et al. 1996, 2). On the other hand, most of the state's veteran GOP political leaders backed Bob Dole. Among the prominent Dole endorsers were former Michigan Republican chairman David Doyle, Oakland County Executive Brooks Patterson, Speaker of the House Paul Hillegonds, Senate Majority Leader Dick Posthumus, and Secretary of State Candice Miller. The only major Michigan GOP leader refusing to endorse Dole was Governor John Engler, who, as chairman of the Republican Governors Association, preferred to remain officially neutral (Hornbeck 1996b, 1).

The 1996 GOP contest reminded some observers of the 1988 primary, when party outsider Pat Robertson battled establishment candidate George Bush. In 1996, Pat Buchanan played the role of outsider and was able to win considerable support from those who had backed Robertson in 1988. Bob Dole, on the other hand, played the classic insider role, working most closely with traditional party elites. This strategy certainly worked to Dole's financial advantage. By the end of 1995 Dole had raised $335,000 in Michigan, ten times the amount raised by Buchanan (Hornbeck 1996b). On the other hand, Dole's strategy was criticized as being "top heavy," with "too many heavy hitters and not enough utility players." Dole failed to translate his support among party leaders into an effective grassroots organization, a failure that may have cost him dearly in the general election. As Daniel Kreuger, chairman of the Ottawa County Republican Party, remarked during the primary campaign, "There's little conversation out in the field about Dole being the nominee" (Hornbeck 1996b, 2).

Dole's failure to generate widespread enthusiasm among GOP voters stemmed in part from his approach to the key issues of the campaign. While Dole gave lip service to hot-button social issues such as abortion and gay rights, his primary focus was on economic issues (Penning and Smidt 1997). "True believers" of the Christian Right found it difficult to energize themselves in support of a candidate who failed to share their enthusiasm for conservative social issues. Dole sorely missed that energy during the general election campaign.

The 1996 Dole-Buchanan contest never degenerated to the tragicomic levels of 1988, when Bush and Robertson staged separate conventions in the same building (Penning 1994, 329). However, the campaign did produce its share of conflict, especially in counties where Buchanan enjoyed considerable support. Particularly noteworthy was conflict in Macomb County, one of the state's largest and most politically significant counties. In early 1996, Macomb Republicans split into three warring factions. The first faction, consisting largely of members of the Christian Right, dominated the leadership of the county GOP organization and tended to support Buchanan. A second group, calling itself the Macomb Coalition of Republicans (MCOR), labeled its members as "true conservatives" and felt more comfortable with Dole's economic conservatism. The remaining members of the Macomb GOP refused to align themselves with either group. Divisions among the groups, however, were about personalities and power as much as about issues. Of particular concern to those seeking GOP unity was the simmering resentment of traditional party elites toward Christian Right newcomers. Complained MCOR chairman and former county party leader Dean Ausilio of Clinton Township, "We operated in a peaceful coalition a couple of years back. . . . The Christian Right muscled us out and took control of the party in 1991" (Saviske 1996, 1).

The 19 March primary found Dole winning handily, garnering approximately 51 percent of the Michigan GOP primary votes compared to 34 percent for Buchanan.[5] This translated into thirty-four convention delegates for Dole and twenty-three for Buchanan.[6] But just who were the core supporters of each candidate? Table 8.1 permits us to answer this question better. The table breaks down the GOP primary vote in three states—Michigan, Ohio, and Illinois—according to key social and political dimensions. The table reveals that in all three states, men made up a slightly higher percentage of the total GOP primary voters than did women, and non–college graduates made up a higher percentage than college graduates. Majorities in each state also proved to be moderate to slightly conservative ideologically, Republican, and not part of the Christian Right. Although there was no gender gap in Ohio or Illinois, in Michigan, Dole did better among women than among men, possibly because Buchanan's positions on such issues as the North American Free Trade Agreement and gun control resonated well with male "Reagan Democrats." In all three states, Buchanan, with his populist appeal, did better among those without college degrees than among voters with college degrees.

Dole tended to do better than Buchanan among voters in all ideological categories, although Buchanan was able to make notable inroads into Dole's margin among very conservative voters. Indeed, in Michigan, Buchanan actually enjoyed a slight majority among very conservative voters. In all three states, Dole received large majorities of the votes of Republican identifiers. However, he did somewhat less well among independents, particularly in Michigan, where Buchanan received a plurality of the votes of self-identified political independents. Finally, although Dole earned solid majorities among voters who were not part of the Christian Right in all three states, his margins of support were smaller among members of the religious right. Indeed, in Michigan, Buchanan received just as many religious right votes as did Dole.

Table 8.1
1996 Republican Presidential Primary Voters in Three Midwestern States

Voter	% of GOP Voters			Candidate Voted for (%)					
				MI		OH		IL	
Category	MI	OH	IL	Dole	Buch*	Dole	Buch	Dole	Buch
Men	53	55	51	48	38	66	22	65	25
Women	47	45	49	55	30	66	21	66	21
College grad	44	40	47	53	30	66	17	69	19
Not college grad	56	60	53	50	38	66	25	63	27
Liberal	12	11	11	47	33	70	17	66	20
Moderate	33	40	38	54	27	67	19	71	18
Somewhat conservative	34	31	35	57	34	72	18	68	21
Very conservative	19	17	15	39	51	50	37	47	44
Republican	62	79	70	60	30	70	19	72	19
Independent	28	18	24	39	43	52	32	53	30
Part of religious right	29	26	25	45	45	56	37	52	35
Not part of religious right	65	66	69	53	30	70	15	70	19

Source: New York Times, 21 March 1996, A14. Based on exit polls of Republican primary voters conducted by Voter News Service, an organization of ABC News, CBS News, CNN, NBC News, and the Associated Press.
*Buch = Buchanan

These results correspond to popular stereotypes portrayed in the media. While Dole dominated the Michigan primary election, Buchanan did reasonably well among men, those without college educations, very conservative voters, political independents, and members of the Christian Right. His supporters corresponded closely to the profile of 1988 Robertson voters—brash ideologues, more committed to their issues and their candidate than to the party (Penning 1994).

If the Dole-Buchanan contest for the GOP presidential nomination was a battle, the clash between Ronna Romney and Jim Nicholson for the right to challenge the Democratic incumbent, U.S. Senator Carl Levin, was a war. The *Detroit News* labeled the campaign leading up to the 6 August primary "a bitter race, the most expensive and arguably the most contentious in state history"

(Young 1996, 1). Romney, a radio talk-show host and daughter-in-law of former governor George Romney, had run for the GOP senatorial nomination two
years earlier, only to be defeated by current U.S. Senator Spencer Abraham.
That race, while unsuccessful, had given Romney considerable name recognition and valuable political experience.

Nicholson, a wealthy businessman from Grosse Pointe Farms, lacked Romney's experience and name recognition but benefited from his personal wealth.
Nicholson spent a total of $2.8 million on his campaign, half from his own
pocket. Approximately $300,000 of that money went into a television ad blitz
during the 1996 Atlanta Olympic games, a tactic of dubious value since voters
seemed more interested in the athletic than in the political contests (Young
1996, 2). Nicholson attempted to portray Romney as a "socialite" with little
knowledge of the issues who was trying to win on the basis of her famous name.

Romney, with a budget of only $1.5 million, was nevertheless able to wage
an aggressive campaign against Nicholson, accusing him of attempting to purchase the election through "checkbook politics." Romney also attacked
Nicholson for skipping six elections and called him a hypocrite for allowing
taxpayers to provide $81,000 annually to keep his mentally challenged brother
in a group home (Young 1996, 2).

Although early polls showed Romney with a lead of 20 points or more,
Nicholson's spending helped to narrow the gap so that Romney's winning
margin was only 4 percentage points statewide. Although Nicholson had
counted on the metropolitan Detroit area to carry him to victory, Romney actually enjoyed a slight edge in the Detroit area, taking 51.8 percent of the vote in
Macomb, Oakland, and Wayne Counties. Furthermore, Romney enjoyed a sizable advantage in the politically conservative west Michigan counties (Alle-
gan, Kent, and Ottawa), winning 61.8 percent of the vote (Luke and Golder
1996). Exit polls showed Romney, who enjoyed the endorsement of RTLM,
beating Nicholson 63 percent to 37 percent among pro-life voters. Moreover,
Romney reportedly won 61 percent of the 45 percent of GOP voters who identified themselves as born-again Christians (Young 1996, 1).

RTLM also played a major role in nominating candidates for other state
offices. In September, a minor race for the GOP nomination for a University of
Michigan Board of Regents seat turned into a battle over abortion, pitting pro-
choice activist Judy Frey of East Grand Rapids against pro-life candidate Mike
Bishop of Rochester. Bishop enlisted the support of Christian conservatives and
other GOP pro-lifers attending the state GOP convention in Lansing. On the other
hand, pro-life governor John Engler took the podium in support of Frey, declaring that "I apologize to no one for my pro-life credentials," but adding, "Judy has
earned this opportunity for her involvement in the party, which goes back many
years" (Golder 1996a, A1). A nasty floor fight ensued, with Bishop defeating

Frey by just 23 votes, 952-929. Complained Third District Chair Tom Shearer of Grand Rapids, "Single-issue orientation will destroy the base in the party among a broad spectrum of individuals and Republicans" (Golder 1996a, A1).

Nevertheless, some activists in the Christian Right contended that the 1996 Michigan primaries generated less political interest than did the elections of 1994, largely owing to the lack of competition at the top of the ticket. Thus, Daniel Jarvis, the coordinator of research and public policy for the MFF, indicated that his organization had distributed only 300,000 voter guides in the 1996 Michigan primary season, down from 500,000 in 1994. According to Jarvis, this decline reflected the fact that there was less demand for such guides in the 1996 primaries than there had been in the 1994 primaries.[7]

The General Election Campaign

Nationally, the 1996 election might be viewed as a status quo election. Although Bill Clinton handily won reelection as president, that success did not necessarily translate into Democratic Party success in other races. The GOP succeeded in retaining control of both houses of Congress and did reasonably well at the state and local levels as well. For example, although 5,989 state legislative seats were contested nationwide, the Democrats were able to make a relatively small net gain of only 100 seats (National Conference of State Legislatures 1996).

With some justification, Christian Right leaders claimed much of the credit for limiting the impact of Clinton's coattails. According to a nationwide survey conducted by Wirthlin Worldwide, "more than one out of four voters (29 percent) was a self-described, born-again Christian who frequently attends church. . . . This constituency voted overwhelmingly Republican (53 percent Dole to 36 percent Clinton)." In addition the leaders reported that "religious conservatives provided a positive [GOP] margin in both House and Senate races, acting as one of the most loyal and best-performing voter groups in the electorate" (Christian Coalition 1996, 1). *New York Times* exit polls revealed that the "white Christian Right" voted 73 percent to 27 percent for GOP candidates in House races (*New York Times* 1996, B3). Claimed Ralph Reed: "Conservative evangelicals were the firewall that prevented a Bob Dole defeat from mushrooming into a meltdown all the way down the ballot. . . . For the first time in 68 years, a Republican Congress has been reelected, and it would never have happened without conservative people of faith, who provided the margin of victory" (Christian Coalition 1996, 1).

Since Michigan is socially heterogeneous and politically competitive, one might have expected the state's 1996 election to exhibit the same status quo orientation as the national election. However, the 1996 general election actually proved to be encouraging for Michigan Democrats. Not only did Bill Clinton defeat Bob Dole (with 52 percent of the popular vote), but Democrat Carl Levin easily defeated Ronna Romney in the U.S. Senate race (with 58 percent of the popular vote). In addition, Democrats won ten of Michigan's sixteen congressional seats (picking up one seat) and regained control of the state house of representatives (with a 58-52 margin). The strength of the Democratic "tide" is illustrated by the party's success in winning races at the bottom of the statewide ticket, races in which voters depend heavily on partisan cues in making their voting decisions. Democratic candidates won virtually all of the bottom-of-ticket contests, including those for the state board of education and the various university governing boards.

What role, if any, did the Christian Right play in facilitating or limiting this Democratic success? One way to address this is to examine Michigan's largest and arguably most important religious denomination, the Catholic Church. The Catholic Church in Michigan is important, in part, because its members, while tending to be slightly Democratic in party identification, are nevertheless sufficiently independent to constitute a key swing vote. In addition, the Catholic Church is important both because of its large size and because of the distribution of its membership in some of the state's largest counties. For example, the Catholic percentage of the total population reaches double digits in virtually all of the state's seventeen most populous counties. In two of the largest counties, Macomb and Wayne, the Catholic proportion exceeds one-third. Furthermore, Catholics constitute over 20 percent of the total religious adherents in virtually all of the seventeen counties.

The potential importance of the Catholic Church in 1996 was enhanced by the salience of the abortion issue. President Clinton's vetoing of the congressional ban on partial-birth abortions prompted church leaders to ask parishioners to flood Congress with 25 million postcards nationwide, urging Congress to override the veto. In Michigan, the bishops conducted a massive postcard effort, particularly in the Archdiocese of Detroit, where 525,000 postcards were distributed in all 316 parishes (Lewis 1996, 1).

GOP candidates such as Ronna Romney were quick to recognize the importance of the abortion issue, moving to seek RTLM endorsement and to feature the issue in their campaign advertising. So too was the Christian Coalition. In 1995 Ralph Reed, head of the national Christian Coalition, helped form the Catholic Alliance, a division of the Christian Coalition dedicated to increasing the number of Catholic members. To Reed, the abortion issue offered perhaps the best way of bridging the gulf between Catholics and conservative evangelicals. Reed estimated that 16 percent of Christian Coalition supporters are Catholic nationwide and hoped to add an additional 250,000 supporters in 1996 (Stevens 1996, 1). According to Glenn Clark, former executive director of the MCC, the Michigan coalition "was a pilot program for the Catholic Alliance" because of the state's large and politically active Catholic population (Rust 1996, 1).

The Christian Coalition tried to facilitate the growth of the Catholic Alliance in Michigan by selecting metropolitan Detroit as the site of a major meeting between Coalition members and Michigan Catholics. As Ralph Reed explained: "I think the jump ball of the 1996 presidential election is the Catholic vote. . . . Whoever wins that will be the next president" (Stevens 1996, 1). Nevertheless, the Alliance never attracted widespread Catholic support in the state, in part because of opposition from the Catholic hierarchy. Complained Ned McGrath, director of communications for the Archdiocese of Detroit, the Catholic Alliance "never asked for permission to use the term, 'Catholic'" and "in no way represents" the archdiocese or Cardinal Adam Maida (Stevens 1996, 1). The Alliance has also struggled because the primary target of its appeals—younger Catholic boomers—are already Republicans, but Republicans who are more engaged by economic than by the sociomoral issues dear to the Christian Coalition. On the other hand, the boomers' parents are more attracted to such sociomoral issues. Unfortunately for the Alliance, these parents "remain within the Democratic fold because they are closer to the Democratic Party on all but a couple of the 'consistent life ethic' issues" (Appleby 1996, 21).

An examination of the two-party vote for president in Michigan's seventeen largest counties over the last three elections (see table 8.2) reveals a pattern of increasing Democratic Party success. Democrats were able to increase their share of the two-party presidential vote in virtually every county with each succeeding election and often achieved impressive increases in vote share over the six-year period. However, such increases were most pronounced in the four counties (Macomb, Oakland, St. Clair, and Wayne) with the highest Catholic percentage of total population.[8] While these aggregate totals tell us nothing about the voting behavior of individuals, they at least cast doubt on the likelihood that the Catholic Alliance made much difference in the outcome of the presidential election.

Indeed, there was probably little that Dole could have done to carry Michigan in 1996. He did try. Dole sought and received the postprimary endorsement of Michigan's popular Republican governor, John Engler (Hornbeck 1996a). In addition, Dole made numerous visits both to Detroit and to the Bible Belt counties of west Michigan, including holding an election-eve rally in Grand Rapids. But his every move was effectively countered by a Clinton visit or Clinton television advertisements. Moreover, Dole's campaign had expended all its funds in securing the nomination in the early months of the year. But, given that Clinton had no opposition in securing his nomination, he

Table 8.2
Percent of Democratic Vote of Total Two-Party Vote for President by County
(seventeen largest counties)

County	1988	1992	1996
Bay	57.7	61.8	63.4
Berrien	36.7	46.9	46.5
Calhoun	45.9	56.3	55.6
Genesee	59.7	68.7	68.3
Ingham	49.0	58.4	59.6
Jackson	39.2	48.2	49.6
Kalamazoo	44.0	53.4	52.9
Kent	35.8	41.7	41.5
Livingston	30.5	39.3	42.4
Macomb	39.1	46.9	55.7
Muskegon	46.3	57.8	61.8
Oakland	38.1	47.0	52.4
Ottawa	23.4	28.1	30.5
Saginaw	51.8	57.7	60.1
St. Clair	39.3	48.8	56.2
Washtenaw	52.9	63.9	64.6
Wayne	60.7	69.1	74.1

could delay spending the bulk of his public funding monies for the nomination campaign till late spring and the summer months, allowing Clinton's media ads to go basically unanswered and unchallenged for the five months prior to the GOP convention in late August. In fact, Clinton's coffers were so full that newspaper reports indicated that, in key west Michigan counties that are traditional GOP strongholds, Clinton's television advertising spending from March to October 1996 exceeded Dole's by a 3-to-1 margin (Golder 1996b).

Popular Democratic incumbent senator Carl Levin easily won reelection, doing just as well as he did in his 1990 quest for reelection. Like Levin's 1990 opponent, Bill Scheutte, Ronna Romney could not convince sufficient voters that it was "time for a change." Moreover, Romney was hampered by such a serious shortage of funds that toward the end of the campaign she was unable to purchase significant advertising time.

Not only were Democrats able to regain their U.S. Senate seat, they were also able to pick up one congressional seat, giving them ten of Michigan's sixteen seats. The Democratic gain occurred in the Eighth Congressional District (the

Lansing–Flint–Ann Arbor triangle) in a race that pitted incumbent Dick Chrysler, a member of the GOP freshman class of 1994, against political veteran Debbie Stabenow. Chrysler had benefited from the Republican tide in 1994 and now faced a difficult reelection bid in this competitive but slightly Democratic district. Both parties targeted the district, but the combination of a Democratic "year," extensive union political activity (particularly by the UAW), and a strong Democratic candidate helped the Democrats regain the seat after a two-year Republican hiatus. Organized labor was especially delighted with the outcome, since labor had made winning this congressional seat one of its highest priorities.

Table 8.3 reveals that, in general, the 1996 election returns for the congressional races more closely paralleled the 1992 than the 1994 congressional returns. As such, these patterns reflect the classic "surge and decline" phenomenon, whereby high-stimulus presidential elections are more likely to attract larger numbers of occasional voters, who are not as likely to vote in lower-stimulus, off-year elections. Thus, it is not surprising that, despite being further apart in time, the congressional returns in 1992 and 1996 were more sim-

Table 8.3
Percent Republican of Total Congressional Vote Cast by Congressional District

District	1996 Winner	1992	1994	1996
1	Stupak (D)	44	42	27
2	Hoekstra (R)	63	75	65
3	Ehlers (R)	61	74	69
4	Camp (R)	63	73	65
5	Barcia (D)	38	32	28
6	Upton (R)	62	73	68
7	Smith (R)	88†	65	55
8	Stabenow (D)*	46	52	44
9	Kildee (D)	45	47	39
10	Bonior (D)	44	38	44
11	Knollerberg (R)	58	68	61
12	Levin (D)	46	47	41
13	Rivers (D)	43	45	41
14	Conyers (D)	16	17	12
15	Kilpatrick (D)**	17	14	10
16	Dingell (D)	31	40	36

*Candidate had no Democratic opposition in election
**Partisan shift in congressional district
***Race had no incumbent candidate

ilar to one another than either year's returns were to 1994, a nonpresidential year. Consequently, Michigan did not so much "veer to the left" in 1996 as it "swerved to the right" in 1994.

Conclusion

One can draw several conclusions from this chapter. First, the Christian Right is alive and well in Michigan, with numerous groups playing notable political roles. Particularly important are the "big four" organizations—RTLM, MFF, CTV, and CCM. This proliferation of Christian Right groups has enabled them to develop distinct "marketing" niches. That does not mean that the organizations never cooperate with each other. But it does mean that they tend to draw their support from somewhat different segments of the population.

Not only have Christian Right groups proliferated, they have also developed increased political sophistication. Gone are the days when the Christian Right was dominated by fulminating preachers who lacked a long-term strategy for political success. Today's groups are in politics for the long haul. They are developing effective grassroots organizations and using the latest media technology to communicate their messages.

Second, the target constituencies to which these organizations appeal constitute a major component of the GOP coalition in Michigan. White evangelical Protestants provide the starting base for the GOP coalition, just as blacks do for the Democratic Party. And while white evangelical Protestants' loyalty to the GOP does not yet match blacks' loyalty to the Democratic Party, it is beginning to approximate it. Moreover, this lower level of loyalty is more than offset by the fact that white evangelical Protestants far outnumber blacks. Yet the GOP in Michigan cannot take white evangelical Protestant support for granted. Indeed, members of the Christian Right in Michigan failed to warm to Bob Dole, in part because he failed to stress their socially conservative agenda with sufficient zeal. Moreover, there is evidence of growing Christian Right disenchantment with the Republican Party (Penning and Smidt 1997). In a politically competitive state such as Michigan, the loss of even a small degree of Christian Right support could seriously harm the GOP. Perhaps that is one reason why certain Christian Right groups are seeking to broaden their base to include Catholics. Thus far, however, even conservative Catholic governor John Engler has been unable to persuade a majority of Catholics to support the GOP.

In the 1996 election, the Christian Right in Michigan failed to achieve its major objectives of victories for Bob Dole and Ronna Romney. Moreover, Christian Right groups were unable to prevent the loss of one GOP congressional seat and control of the state house of representatives. On the other hand, one could argue that in Michigan, as in the nation at large, the Christian Right helped to prevent a wholesale GOP rout. The Republican Party retained control of the state senate. And, in a Democratic year, the loss of only one congressional seat might be considered at least a moral victory.

Finally, the Christian Right is likely to continue to play an important role in Michigan politics. As Leege argues, its public agenda is cultural politics—a type of politics with considerable staying power (Leege 1992, 203). Yet the Christian Right in Michigan, as in the rest of the nation, faces a number of important problems that may well determine its degree of success or failure in future years. Most important, Christian Right groups must decide whether, and under what circumstances, to work both with each other and with political opponents. To the extent that it follows the leadership of Christian Coalition leader Ralph Reed and settles merely for a "seat at the table," it risks cooptation and the loss of support from true believers. On the other hand, if the Christian Right refuses to compromise, it risks political ineffectiveness and marginalization. The issue, then, is not whether the Christian Right in Michigan will survive; it is whether and how it will flourish.

Notes

1. For a discussion of the history of political parties in Michigan, see Smidt and Penning (1995).

2. The designation "501(c)3" relates to an Internal Revenue Service code describing corporations exempt from taxation. A 501(c)3 is a corporation, foundation, or organization in which "no part of the net earnings . . . inures to the benefit of any private shareholder or individual" and "no substantial part" of the organization's activities are directed "to influence legislation . . . and which does not participate in or intervene in (including publishing or distributing of statements) any political campaign on behalf of (or in opposition to) any candidate for public office." A 501(c)4 organization is one that is organized not for profit and "is operated exclusively for the promotion of social welfare . . . and the net earnings of which are devoted exlcusively to charitable, educational, or recreational purposes."

3. When asked whether the Michigan Family Forum's membership has been growing over the past two years, Daniel Jarvis, the forum's coordinator of research and public policy, indicated that the organization had not necessarily been growing in terms of numbers but that it had been growing more influential within the legislative process.

4. See note 2 above.

5. None of the other GOP candidates received more than 5 percent of the total primary vote; all but Keyes dropped out prior to the primary election.

6. As one would expect, Buchanan's delegates were strongly supportive of a conservative social agenda. Of his twenty-three delegates, twenty-two publicly identified

themselves as pro-life and nineteen identified themselves as Christians (*Detroit News* 1996).

7. This explanation seems plausible. Jarvis also indicated that the Michigan Family Forum distributed five hundred thousand voter guides in the 1996 general election in the state, the same number that had been distributed in the 1994 general election campaign.

8. These four all place among the top five counties in terms of Catholic percentage of the total population. The fifth county, Bay County, registered only a 6 percent increase in Democratic presidential vote share over the period, but it began the period with an exceedingly high 57.7 percent Democratic share.

References

Appleby, R. Scott. 1996. "Catholics and the Christian Right: An Uneasy Alliance." Paper presented at the Conference on the Christian Right in Comparative Perspective, Calvin College, Grand Rapids, Mich., 4–5 October.

Browne, William P., and Kenneth VerBurg. 1995. *Michigan Politics and Government.* Lincoln: University of Nebraska Press.

Christian Coalition. 1996. "Religious Conservative Firewall Protects Pro-Family Candidates." (16 November): http://www.cc.org/publications/ccnews1.htm/.

Detroit News. 1996. "A Look at the State's Buchanan Delegates." (26 May): http://www.detnews.com/menu/stories/49544.htm.

Golder, Ed. 1996a. "Frey Loses U-M Bid Despite Engler's Help." *Grand Rapids Press* (8 September): A1, A23.

_____. 1996b. "Politicians' Cash Makes for a Lot of Hot Airwaves." *Grand Rapids Press* (13 October): A1, A23.

Hornbeck, Mark. 1996a. "Engler Supports Dole's 'Tolerance' Abortion Plank." *Detroit News* (13 June): http://www.detnews.com/menu/stories/51953.htm.

_____. 1996b. "Ground Troops Battle for Votes." *Detroit News* (29 February): http://www.detnews.com/menu/stories/37892.htm.

Hornbeck, Mark, et al. 1996. "Fiery Buchanan Preaches to Converted in Clawson." *Detroit News* (17 March): http://www.detnews.com/menu/stories/40250.htm.

Kurtz, Karl. 1996. "American State Legislative Results." National Conference of State Legislatures, Denver: http://www.ncsl.org.statevote96/stvote96.htm.

Leege, David. 1992. "Coalitions, Cues, Strategic Politics, and the Staying Power of the Christian Right, or Why Political Scientists Ought to Pay Attention to Cultural Politics." *PS: Political Science & Politics* 25 (June): 198–204.

Lewis, Shawn D. 1996. "Postcard Tactic Blurs Line between Religion, Politics." *Detroit News* (28 June): http://www.detnews.com/menu/stories/53917.htm.

Luke, Peter, and Ed Golder. 1996. "West Michigan Rockets Romney." *Grand Rapids Press* (7 August): A7.

Moen, Matthew. 1992. *The Transformation of the Christian Right.* Tuscaloosa: University of Alabama Press.

National Conference of State Legislatures. 1996. "State Legislative Elections a Mixed Bag." (14 November): http://www.ncsl.org/statevote96/stvote96.htm.

New York Times. 1996. "Breakdown: Who Voted for Whom in the House." (7 November): B3.

Penning, James M. 1994. "Pat Robertson and the GOP: 1988 and Beyond." *Sociology of Religion* 55 (Fall): 327–44.

Penning, James M., and Corwin E. Smidt. 1997. "What Coalition?" *Christian Century* (15 January): 37–38.

Persinos, John. 1994. "Has the Christian Right Taken Over the Republican Party?" *Campaigns & Elections* 15 (September): 20–24.

Reed, Ralph. 1994. *Politically Incorrect: The Emerging Faith Factor in American Politics.* Dallas: Word Publishing.

Rust, Michael. 1996. "Quest for Unity Hits Bumps for Evangelicals, Catholics." *Detroit News* (11 February): http://www.detnews.com/menu/stories/33513.htm.

Savitskie, Jeffrey. 1996. "GOP Stands Divided in Macomb County." *Detroit News* (13 March): http://www.detnews.com/menu/stories/39712.htm.

Smidt, Corwin, and James M. Penning. 1995. "Michigan: Veering to the Right," Chap. 8 in *God at the Grass Roots: The Christian Right in the 1994 Elections,* ed. Mark J. Rozell and Clyde Wilcox. Lanham, Md.: Rowman & Littlefield.

Steinfels, Peter. 1990. "Dobson Counsels Way to Influence on Right." *Grand Rapids Press* (9 June).

Stevens, Carol. 1996. "Christian Coalition Will Try to Attract Catholics at Metro Detroit Meeting." *Detroit News* (14 March): http://www.detnews.com/menu/stories/39898.htm.

Young, Dale G. 1996. "Senate Race: Anti-Abortion Vote Helps Romney Win." *Detroit News* (7 August): http://www.detnews.com/menu/stories/59400.htm.

9

California: Between a Rock and a Hard Place

Joel Fetzer and J. Christopher Soper

It was apparent after the 1994 midterm elections that Christian conservatives were a significant electoral force in California despite the state's opposition to traditional social values (Soper 1995). The Christian Right had become a powerful faction within the state Republican Party, having gained control of the state party apparatus in 1993. In the 1994 midterm elections, moreover, one-quarter of all Republican voters described themselves as white evangelical Christians—the core supporters of the Christian Right. In that election, the leaders of the Christian Right pursued a pragmatic political strategy that accentuated the movement's ties to the party, and conservative Christian voters helped sweep Republicans, even socially moderate Republicans such as Governor Pete Wilson, into office. For better and worse, it was no longer possible to discuss the political fortunes of the Christian Right without talking about the success and failure of the GOP.

The year 1996 was not, however, a good one for the Republican Party or the Christian Right in California. The GOP presidential candidate, Bob Dole, all but conceded the state to Bill Clinton by the end of the summer, then changed course and invested heavily in California in the last month of the campaign. Yet he still ended up losing the state by 13 percentage points. The GOP also lost three seats of its House delegation to the Democrats, and in a particular blow to the Christian Right, two incumbent Republicans closely associated with the movement, Andrea Seastrand and Robert Dornan, lost their bids for reelection. Finally, after two years of historic bickering between the parties in the state legislature—there were four separate speakers of the state assembly in a little over a year—the Republican Party lost control of the assembly and the Democrats retained control of the senate.

The 1996 elections demonstrated the strengths and weaknesses of the Christian Right in California politics, how far the movement has come, and how far it has to go as it attempts to have both political and policy impact. The

135

Christian Right is a powerful group within the Republican Party and an electoral force in state politics. In the past two elections, the Christian Right leadership has minimized its social-issue conservatism and strengthened its ties to the Republican Party, but the Christian Right does not have much to show for its political pragmatism. The party has not proved to be an effective conduit for changing policy on social issues or for nominating candidates who are sympathetic to a Christian Right agenda. As it sets its sights on the midterm elections of 1998 and the presidential election of the year 2000, the movement finds itself between a rock and a hard place, between a political party that has not been all that accommodating to the movement and a state political culture that is even less sympathetic to the policy agenda of conservative Christians.

This chapter examines the influence of the Christian Right in California politics. First, we show how California's political culture and institutions provided strategic opportunities for the mobilization of the Christian Right in the late 1980s and early 1990s. California's weak party system favored Christian Right activism and enabled conservative Christians to gain control of the state Republican Party; once the Christian Right was in power, however, those structures limited the ability of conservative Christians to shape party policy and affect policy outcomes. Second, we evaluate the political strategy of the Christian Right leadership in the 1996 election and assess the influence of conservative Christian voters in several races. We conclude the chapter with a discussion of the prospects for the Christian Right in California politics.

The Background

Growing dissatisfaction with California's liberal social policies on abortion, gay rights, and religion in public schools led Christian conservatives to form organizations in the 1980s to promote their religious and political values. The religious convictions of conservative Christians provided them with clear priorities and policy stances as well as a well-integrated network of churches, television programs, and associations that made them relatively easy to mobilize. From a resource perspective, conservative Christians proved to be ideal for political activism as group leaders recruited members through sympathetic evangelical and fundamentalist churches (Gilbert 1993). The two most significant groups that formed were the Traditional Values Coalition (TVC) and the state chapter of the Christian Coalition.

The TVC claims a nationwide membership of 31,000 churches, but the movement is particularly strong in California, where its chairman and founder, the Reverend Lou Sheldon, has his headquarters. Sheldon founded the TVC in 1981, three years after he led efforts to retain the state's antisodomy law and to pass an initiative that would have prevented gay and lesbian people from teaching in public schools (Dunlap 1994). Both campaigns failed, but they propelled Sheldon to the forefront of the Christian Right movement. The Coalition remains particularly active on gay-rights issues at both the state and national levels; it produced and distributed the controversial videotape "Gay Rights/Special Rights: Inside the Homosexual Agenda," to which several members of Congress referred in debates on gay rights. In its mobilization and activism, the TVC is uncompromising and focused on a small number of moral issues. In an interview with one of us on 22 October 1996, Sheldon said that the five most important issues for the TVC are homosexuality, abortion, pornography, family values, and religious freedom (Sheldon 1996). This commitment is also apparent in the group's 1996 presidential voter guide, which compares the candidates' positions on eight issues, seven of which relate to public policy on homosexuality, abortion, and religion in the schools.

California was also one of the first states to have its own chapter of the Christian Coalition after Pat Robertson founded the organization in 1989. Most of the people who led the state office had worked for Robertson's presidential campaign in California, and they recruited group members through evangelical churches throughout the state. The Coalition established a network of grassroots support, grew rapidly, and became the most significant Christian Right organization within California. The group currently has close to one hundred thousand members (Perez 1996) and forty-three chapters in the state. Unlike Sheldon and the TVC, from its inception the Coalition pursued a more strategic and sophisticated approach to politics. Recognizing the limits of a conservative Christian political agenda in California, for example, the Christian Right supported dozens of "stealth" candidates for state and local races who had the backing of the Christian Right but minimized their formal ties to the movement. The Coalition also stressed a wider range of conservative issues than the TVC; half of the issues listed in the group's 1996 presidential voter guide were not issues of personal morality.

California's political institutions provided the ideal context for Christian Right mobilization. Since the Progressive reforms of the early twentieth century, California's political system has been open to the mobilization of outside pressure groups (Mayhew 1986; Gerston and Christenson 1991). Among the most important Progressive innovations that provided the opportunity for Christian Right activism were initiative and referendum campaigns, political primary elections, a ban on preprimary endorsements by the party, and no limit on the amount of money that an individual or political action committee (PAC) can give to candidates for state office. The Christian Right took advantage of the political opportunities at its disposal to extend its political influence within the state.

Led by the Christian Coalition, the Christian Right has focused most of its attention on electioneering and party mobilization. The group has registered voters, distributed millions of voter guides in churches throughout the state in primary and general elections, recruited candidates for public office, and provided them with the resources needed for their campaigns. The number of state and local candidates elected who were sympathetic to the Christian Right increased in the early 1990s. Christian conservatives also initiated several noteworthy primary battles within the GOP. A typical example was the 1992 Senate primary campaign that pitted the socially moderate John Seymour against the socially conservative William Dannemeyer. The Christian Coalition supported Dannemeyer, a seven-term congressman and outspoken opponent of abortion, but Seymour easily defeated him in the party primary.

The primary battles signified the tensions that existed between socially conservative and moderate factions within the Republican Party. Delegates to state party conventions had frequently fought resolutions on abortion, gay rights, and other issues of personal morality. The leaders of the Christian Coalition claim it is a nonpartisan organization, a claim Sheldon also makes about the Traditional Values Coalition. Both organizations were nevertheless instrumental in forging stronger links between the Christian Right and the Republican Party in the early 1990s (Perez 1996; Sheldon 1996). The Christian Coalition coordinated the effort of conservative Christians to take control of the state Republican Party as a way to increase their political influence. The weakness of California's party structures made it relatively easy for the Christian Right to wrest control of the GOP from party moderates who opposed this incursion into the party but were powerless to stop it. Christian conservatives committed both time and resources and turned out for party leadership elections to county and state committees to which few party members pay attention. By 1993 conservative Christians controlled thirty-eight of the fifty-eight county GOP central committees and were effectively in charge of the state Republican Party (Nollinger 1993).

The Christian Right also became active in state and local politics. In 1991, four wealthy businessmen with close ties to the Christian Right founded the Allied Business PAC to funnel money directly to candidates for state offices. Allied supports candidates for state office only; with no limit on the amount of money that a PAC can give to a candidate for a state position, it is easier, according to the group's executive director, Danielle Madison, "to have an impact on those races" (Lutterbeck 1995). Allied sought candidates who supported the group's fiscal and social conservative ideals. By 1992 Allied had become the largest PAC in the state, contributing more than $1 million to thirty-four candidates in state assembly and senate races. In 1993 one of the group's founders, Robert Hurrt, won a seat in the state senate. The group spent

$1.1 million in the 1994 elections, and Hurrt spent an additional $1.2 million of his own money on Allied-backed candidates, all of whom were Republicans. In 1994, candidates supported by Allied won twenty-six of the Republicans' forty-one seats in the assembly and seven of the sixteen seats in the state senate, and Hurrt was elected to the important post of leader of the senate Republicans after only two years in office (Morain and Ingram 1995).

The openness of California's policy ensured the Christian Right access to the political process, and the movement made much noise in California politics at the end of the 1980s and early 1990s. Access did not, however, translate directly into a policy impact for the Christian Right. As V. O. Key noted (Key 1964), there are three ways to assess a political party, or in this case a social movement: by looking at the party in the electorate, the party as organization, and the party in government. By 1993 the Christian Right had made great strides in the first two areas. Christian conservatives were a significant voice within the electorate; a 1993 poll categorized 21 percent of Californians as part of the religious right—people who were both religious and political conservatives (California Opinion Index 1993).[1] The Christian Coalition successfully mobilized conservative Christians into the Republican Party, and the movement gained control of the state party apparatus.

In terms of policy impact, however—Key's "party in government"—the Christian Right has less to show for its activism. If there has been any change within California on the issues of abortion and gay rights in the past decade, it has been in a more liberal direction. In addition, the Christian Right quickly discovered that it was far easier to gain "control" of a political party in California than it was to direct it in any meaningful way. Control of a weak political party did not, for example, mean the power to shape who gets nominated for elective office; no candidate closely affiliated with the Christian Right ever won a statewide political primary. Nor did the presence of conservative Christians in significant positions within the state Republican Party mean that politicians within the party would heed the directives of the party's ostensible leaders. Prominent Republicans in California, including the state's governor, Pete Wilson, publicly distanced themselves from the Christian Right and its socially conservative agenda in the early 1990s.

The Christian Right recognized by 1994 that California was not the ideal context in which to press a conservative moral agenda. More than half of Californians are secularists—people who are not religious or are not religiously active—and a large majority of secularists is liberal on the social issues of abortion and homosexual rights. California is also among the most pro-choice states in the union. In 1972, a year before the decision in *Roe v. Wade* that legalized abortion, Californians approved an amendment to the state constitution that specifically added the right of privacy to the other inalienable rights of individuals, and a large majority of state residents continues to oppose efforts to restrict a woman's access to abortion (Russo 1995).

In response to these challenges, the leadership of the Christian Right, particularly the Christian Coalition, became more pragmatic in its political orientation. In an effort to defuse tensions within the GOP, for example, the Christian Right downplayed its social-issue conservatism in the 1994 midterm elections. The 2.6 million voter guides distributed by the Christian Coalition for that election favorably portrayed Pete Wilson and Mike Huffington, the party's Senate nominee. Both candidates were pro-choice and pro–gay rights, however, and Wilson had a long history of disputes with Christian conservatives within the party. Wilson and Huffington made overtures to Christian Right voters, but neither candidate wavered in his pro-choice views. In that election, white, church-going evangelicals represented 17 percent of the electorate, and they voted for Wilson by a margin of 78 to 22 percent and for Huffington by a margin of 70 percent to 30 percent.

The moderation of the Christian Right can be read as a sign of the movement's political maturation; social movements often need to accommodate and compromise their goals in order to have a policy and political impact. On the other hand, the very idea of stealth candidates and accommodationist tactics demonstrates the inherent weakness of the Christian Right in California. The strategy suggests that candidates with close and open ties to the Christian Right cannot easily win elective office, particularly in statewide races. California's political culture places natural limits on the movement—forcing it to be more compromising than it might otherwise be—because a majority of state residents opposes the social-issue conservatism of the Christian Right. In a state that is ideologically hostile to its agenda, the Christian Right struggles to influence policy.

In politics nothing succeeds like success, and the dramatic victory of the Republican Party in the 1994 midterm elections buoyed the confidence of those within the Christian Right who had wanted to forge a closer link with the GOP. Not only had the Republicans gained control of the U.S. House for the first time in forty years, but the GOP also won a majority of seats within the California state assembly for the first time in twenty-five years. Republicans eventually even managed to elect Curt Pringle, whose views were congruent with those of conservative Christians, as speaker of the assembly. The Christian Right hoped it might use its influence within the state party to win policy concessions on social issues. For the most part, however, this did not happen, as Republicans in Sacramento focused most of their attention on welfare and educational reform, crime, and taxes rather than the moral issues of abortion and gay rights. Leading Republican lawmakers in the assembly did not want to test party solidarity on the issues of abortion and gay rights, which had internally divided the party in the past (Lesher 1996). When the state GOP assembly released its "Contract with California" in December of 1996, one year after gaining a majority in the state's lower house, it did not include any plank on abortion, gay rights, or religion in the schools. The Christian Coalition of California claimed the Republican contract "lacked many of the pro-family planks that would excite the pro-family base" (*Christian American* 1996).

Despite this setback, the leadership of the Christian Right within California continued its pragmatic course up to the 1996 elections. At the California Christian Coalition's Faith and Freedom Banquet that one of us attended on 28 September 1996, Sara Divito Hardman, the chair of the state office, pledged to deliver five million voter guides for the 1996 elections (Fetzer observation). This was almost double the number that the group had distributed in 1994 (Martinez 1996). As in 1994, the Coalition's voter guides consistently presented Republican candidates, even moderate ones, in as sympathetic a light as possible. Ralph Reed, the national Coalition's executive director, also spoke at the banquet and told the audience that the upcoming election was "one of the most important of our lifetimes" (Fetzer observation).

This accommodation certainly pleased party leaders who worried about the divisive effects of the Christian Right on the GOP, but even before the election there were signs that conservative Christians lacked enthusiasm for Bob Dole, the GOP's presidential nominee. As if to defuse those activists within the movement who must have wondered about the lack of emphasis on moral issues in the presidential race, Hardman wrote in an undated preelection letter to Coalition supporters: "Too often voters tend to decide whether or not to vote based on the race at the top of the ticket. We cannot afford to have Christians sitting at home on election day because they are not inspired by the presidential candidates." What remained to be seen was how well this pragmatism would play among movement followers if the Republican Party did not fare well in the 1996 elections.

The Christian Right and the 1996 Election

In 1996 California's evangelicals—the principal component of the Christian Right—turned out to vote in significant if reduced numbers. The *Los Angeles Times* 1996 Exit Poll[2] suggests that self-described "born-again or evangelical Christians" composed almost 7 percent of California's electorate (though not necessarily of the state's population), a much smaller proportion than in 1994 (Soper 1995).[3] Self-identified evangelicals[4] also made up a noticeable fraction of the GOP's electorate, constituting about 13 percent of the vote for Dole in the state and close to 12 percent of the vote for Republican candidates to the U.S. House of Representatives. If one looks at these data from a different angle, 71 percent of evangelicals in California voted for Dole, and 73 percent voted for Republican House candidates. Finally, evangelicals contributed more than 9 percent of the yes votes on Proposition 209, California's anti–affirmative action measure (or. in other terms, 67 percent of evangelicals voted yes).

Being an evangelical or "born-again" Protestant,[5] moreover, powerfully increased one's propensity to vote Republican and significantly boosted one's chances of voting to abolish affirmative action. These results hold even after statistically controlling for the effects of education, income, changing family finances, gender, race/ethnicity, and age (see table 9.1). The logistic regression coefficients reported in the first column of table 9.1, for example, suggest that a forty-year-old, white, nonevangelical Protestant woman who holds a bachelor's degree, receives a household income of $35,000 per year, and has experienced no change in her family's financial situation over the past four years would have a 37 percent probability of voting for Bob Dole. If this same person were evangelical, however, her likelihood of voting for the Republican presidential candidate would double to 74 percent. A similar dynamic applies to the congressional vote. Here our prototypical nonevangelical would have a 39 percent probability of voting for the Republican congressional candidate, but her evangelical counterpart would be 37 percentage points more likely to vote Republican.

In California, at least, this strong Republicanism among evangelical Christian voters does not appear to arise merely because they are predominantly white (78 percent), middle-class[6] (62 percent), and Protestant[7] (95 percent). Rather, the above analysis suggests that they tend to vote more Republican than even other middle-class, Protestant Anglos. Mobilization by groups such as the Christian Coalition and Traditional Values Coalition thus appears to be having an independent, pro-Republican effect on California's evangelicals.

The pro–Proposition 209 effect of being evangelical appears more modest (our previously specified nonevangelical voter has a 50 percent probability of voting yes, while her evangelical counterpart has a 66 percent chance) but still substantively and statistically significant. Though Christian Right organizations thus seem to have rallied the evangelical electorate in favor of Proposition 209 (see discussion below), they do not appear to have affected evangelicals' views on the *principle* of affirmative action.[8] A parallel analysis of attitudes toward affirmative action itself (as opposed to one's vote on Proposition 209) shows no statistically significant effect of being evangelical. And of the 70 percent of evangelical respondents who voted for Proposition 209, 28 percent also claimed to support "affirmative action programs designed to help women and minorities get better jobs and education."[9]

Table 9.1
Determinants of Presidential, Congressional, and Proposition 209 Vote

	GOP Pres. Vote	GOP Cong. Vote	Yes on Prop. 209
Independent Variables			
Education	-.039	-.074	-.158**
Income	.316**	.341**	.190**
Female	-.502*	-.596**	-.494*
Economic improvement	-.957**	-.897**	-.407**
African American	-2.184**	-2.504**	-1.563**
Latino	-1.129**	-1.211**	-1.611**
Asian	.232	-.344	-.830**
Native American	-.870	-.090	-.139
Other race	-.575	-.671*	-.919**
Under age 30	.024	.452**	.280**
Over age 64	.071	.115	.095
Evangelical	1.617**	1.583**	.690**
Ethnic evangelical	-1.164**	-1.086*	-.615
Jewish	-1.727**	-1.786**	-1.007**
Catholic	-.467**	-.580**	.025
Other religion	-1.668**	-1.418**	-.484**
Secularist	-1.599**	-1.388**	-.709**
Constant	1.396**	1.554**	1.546**
Model Statistics			
Sample size (N)	1959	1887	1883
% correctly predicted	73.4	72.7	67.8
χ^2	587.9[†]	571.3[†]	305.8[†]
Degrees of freedom	17	17	17
Pseudo R^2	.231	.232	.140

Note: Data from *Los Angeles Times* 1996 Exit Poll. Estimates obtained by dichotomous logistic regression. Pseudo R^2 calculated according to Aldrich and Nelson (1984). Range of nondummy independent variables: education (1–6), income (1–8), and economic improvement (1–3). Ethnic evangelical variable is an interaction term between evangelical religious identification and African American, Latino, Asian, American Indian, or other race race/ethnicity. Evangelicals not likely to have been Protestant (N = 8) excluded from the analysis. Cases with missing variables deleted listwise.
*p < .10, two-tailed test   **p < .05, two-tailed test   [†]p < .05, one-tailed test

Despite the substantial pro-Republican influence of California's evangelicals, the final results of the 1996 election proved very disappointing for the Christian Right. Not only did Dole lose badly in the state (receiving 38 percent of all votes cast as opposed to 51 percent for Clinton [*New York Times* 1996a]), but three Republican incumbents from California lost their House seats to Democratic challengers without any counterbalancing Republican gains (*New York Times* 1996b; *Orange County Register* 1996). Analysis of the *Los Angeles Times* Exit Poll, moreover, suggests that had all of California's evangelicals stayed home on election day, the results would have been even worse for the Christian Right (i.e., around 2 percentage points less for Dole and close to 3 percentage points less for California's Republican candidates for U.S. Congress). In both the California Senate and Assembly, meanwhile, control shifted to the Democrats. Commenting on the dismal results for the Christian Right in 1996, California Christian Coalition president Sarah Hardman questioned whether "we [groups such as her own] have lost the ability to read the public's mind" (Dart 1996).

But perhaps the most depressing results for California's Christian Right came from Santa Barbara and Garden Grove. In Santa Barbara's U.S. Congressional District 22, the socially "moderate" favorite of the Christian Right, Republican incumbent Andrea Seastrand, lost to Democratic challenger Walter Capps. In Orange County's District 46, meanwhile, the socially "extremist" darling of California's Christian Right, incumbent Robert Dornan, fell to relatively inexperienced Democrat Loretta Sanchez.

In many ways Andrea Seastrand made the perfect "New Guard" candidate for the Christian Right. While her press secretary, Will Bos, cautioned that she did not necessarily consider herself a member of the Christian Right (Bos 1996), both the Christian Coalition's congressional scorecard (1996a) and the Traditional Values Coalition's voter guide (1996) gave her the most positive ratings possible. Not "tainted" by a direct link to the Christian Right, Seastrand might be less likely to scare off social moderates. Yet her sterling voting record would nevertheless ensure that she would deliver on the Christian Right's policy agenda. Another advantage, in the view of Christian conservatives, was the stark ideological contrast between Seastrand and her Democratic challenger, Walter Capps, a religious-studies professor at the University of California–Santa Barbara. In opposition to Seastrand, Capps strongly supported legalized abortion, strict environmental protection, federal education programs, AIDS research, gays in the military, gun control, and abolition of the death penalty (Christian Coalition 1996b; Jacobs 1996; Sipchen 1996).

Yet even though Seastrand's press secretary told the first author that he expected conservative Christians to distribute many voter guides in the district and vote for her "en masse," on election day this freshman Republican representative lost to Capps by a margin of 43 percent to 49 percent (*New York Times* 1996b). Several factors might explain this otherwise surprising loss by a House incumbent. Republicans and Democrats are very closely balanced in this district, and in 1994 Seastrand beat Capps (her opponent in that election also) by less than 1 percent. Probably lured by Seastrand's narrow margin of victory in 1994 as well as by her social and environmental conservatism, several political activist groups also specifically targeted her district. The National Abortion Rights Action League distributed anti-Seastrand literature, sponsored pro-choice meetings in the area, and canvassed her constituents for months before the election. The AFL-CIO broadcast advertisements in her district that criticized her views on Medicare. The Sierra Club spent over $50,000 on an "educational campaign" attacking Seastrand's record on the environment. This effort in the Twenty-second Congressional District was the first time ever that the Sierra Club had conducted such an independent expenditure campaign (Sipchen 1996). And the Interfaith Alliance, a recently formed group of religious but politically liberal activists, published its only Southern California voter guide for the Twenty-second District, supporting Capps (Dart 1996).

If Andrea Seastrand represented the model "New Guard" candidate for the Christian Right, Robert Dornan fit the pattern for what model Christian Right candidates used to look like. A devout Catholic with strong public ties to the Christian Right, Dornan also received perfect scores from the Christian Coalition (1996a) and Traditional Values Coalition (1996). The Christian Right could not have asked for a more vocal or persistent opponent of abortion and gay rights, for instance. While such views historically had played well in Dornan's Orange County district—once a bastion of conservative white Republicans—elsewhere his views and rhetoric made the nine-term House member a pariah (*New York Times* 1996c; *Orange County Register* 1996; Warren 1996a).

In the words of a *New York Times* editorial (1996c) celebrating his defeat, Dornan "brought the subtlety of a blowtorch to national political discourse." Indeed, in his long political career he had publicly referred to various opponents as a "sneaky little dirtbag," a "sick, pompous little ass," a "disloyal, betraying little Jew," "lesbian spear-chuckers," and "coke-snorting, wife-swapping, baby-born-out-of-wedlock, radical Hollywood left." Dornan accused Representative Steve Gunderson (R-Wis.) of being a homosexual with a "revolving door on his closet" and once called then-House-colleague Thomas Downey (D-N.Y.) a "draft-dodging wimp" before grabbing him by the tie. But Dornan's most controversial rhetorical flourish—which earned him a one-day censure from Congress—probably came when he asserted during a 1995 speech on the floor of the House that President Clinton had treasonously given "aid and comfort to the enemy [in Vietnam]." Upon being asked to apologize, Dornan retorted, "Hell no! Hell no!" (Ayres 1996; Grimaldi and Elboghdady 1995; *Orange County Register* 1996; States News Service 1994; Warren 1996a).

Loretta Sanchez, his Democratic challenger in 1996, represented a marked contrast in style, experience, and policies to "B-1 Bob" Dornan. A Latina financial analyst from Anaheim, Sanchez seemed little given to rhetorical grenade throwing and could boast of no experience in elective office. In addition, she supported legalized abortion (including the controversial "partial-birth" abortion), gun control, sex and AIDS education, and gay rights (Ayres 1996; Warren 1996a, 1996b).

Despite Dornan's extensive political experience and the Christian Coalition's distribution of four hundred thousand voter guides in Orange County (Schindler 1997; Warren 1996c), the final vote tally showed that Sanchez had beaten the incumbent by only 984 votes. Three main causes apparently led to Dornan's demise. First, Dornan appears to have neglected his constituents at home by embarking on a fruitless bid for president in the spring of 1996 and by waiting too long to begin his reelection campaign in the district. Second, Dornan's perceived vulnerability led liberal donors to pour hundreds of thousands of dollars into Sanchez's coffers, giving her access to about as much campaign money as Dornan. Finally, over the years Congressional District 46 had been becoming more and more ethnically diverse, until by 1996 it contained roughly 50 percent Latinos and 15 percent Asians. At a certain point, the ratio of Anglo Republicans to Latino Democrats became too small for the increasingly unrepresentative Dornan to win reelection (Ayres 1996; *New York Times* 1996c; *Orange County Register* 1996; Warren 1996b, 1996c).[10]

The role of liberal organizations in the Dornan and Seastrand races underscores the fact that the mobilization of the Christian Right has spawned a countermobilization of liberal groups that has blunted the political impact of conservative Christians. To encourage liberal activism, the Sierra Club and the Interfaith Alliance emphasized the "extremist" agenda of the Christian Right and the right's contribution to the Republican Party, and this liberal tactic appears to have worked.

The Future Role of the Christian Right in California

The 1996 elections offer some troubling lessons for the Christian Right in California. The movement has become an important part of the electorate and a powerful faction within the state Republican Party, but the Christian Right's influence is offset by an even larger group of voters who are liberal on traditional social values. In response to this political limitation, the movement pursued a pragmatic strategy that accentuated its ties to the GOP and minimized its unpopular views on abortion and gay rights. This compromise was a natural response on the part of a social movement that was an electoral minority but hoped to make the transition from political outsider to political insider. This response also helped sweep the GOP into power in 1994. In 1996, however, political pragmatism failed the Christian Right.

This strategy reinforced the fear among many evangelicals that the movement had become captive to a party that will make gestures toward the Christian Right to get their votes, but if elected to power, would remain moderate on moral issues. Bob Dole was not closely associated with the movement, and few Republican House candidates in California focused on the social issues evangelicals cared about most. Evangelicals who voted in 1996 supported GOP candidates by a large majority, but it stretched the credulity of evangelicals for Ralph Reed to suggest that this was "one of the most important elections of our lifetime." For evangelical voters in California this was apparently not a very important election at all, and it proved difficult for evangelical leaders to rally the troops for the campaign. In the end, evangelicals did not turn out in large numbers for the 1996 elections.

The dilemma for the Christian Right in California and elsewhere is that the movement could have its greatest political and policy impact if it moved beyond its core support among white evangelicals; but forming those kinds of heterogenous coalitions is not easy. The close identification of the Christian Right with the Republican Party appears to have alienated many evangelicals in California who did not vote in the election. Just as important, it undermined the possibility that the movement could expand its support among a growing part of the electorate that is in many ways a natural religious ally: minority evangelicals. African American and Latino evangelicals are a growing part of California's electorate and generally share the traditional-values conservatism of the Christian Right. These voters, however, are uncomfortable with the economic and social-issue conservatism of the Republican Party. The support given to California's anti–affirmative action measure, Proposition 209, by the state GOP and leaders of the Christian Right further antagonized racial minorities.[11]

Indeed, this political division among evangelicals along racial and ethnic lines raises a larger question about the actual impact and true nature of the Christian Right in California. Though evidence suggests that white evangelicals join the movement primarily out of opposition to abortion and gay rights, California's socially liberal political culture makes success on these issues hopeless. Trying to increase their political and policy influence, Christian Right leaders have instead seized upon such populist issues as affirmative action and immigration, which resonate more with the typical California voter. Here the movement appears to have made a real difference. Our analysis strongly suggests that but for white evangelicals, Proposition 209 probably would not have passed.[12] Christian Right voters also provided crucial support for Proposition 187 (which called for cutting off undocumented immigrants' access to most public services) in 1994 (Soper 1995), and Proposition 187's coauthor, Harold Ezell, is a "preacher's kid" with close ties to the evangelical community (McGraw 1994).

This divergence between conservative Christians' motivation for mobilization and their actual policy impact forces us to wonder how Christian the Christian Right in California really is. While a fairly orthodox Christian believer may well find scriptural evidence condemning the killing of human beings (born or unborn), Christian arguments for campaigns to end affirmative action for minorities and to cut off medical and educational services for undocumented immigrants seem much harder to find. The African American evangelical from South-Central Los Angeles is unlikely to see the gospel as opposing pro-equality mechanisms such as affirmative action, and the first-generation, Guatemalan American evangelical from North Hollywood is unlikely to understand how Christ's command to "welcome the stranger" permits Christians to deny health care to undocumented immigrants. Rather, these ethnic evangelicals will more likely conclude that their white brothers and sisters have confused defense of privilege with fidelity to the gospel. Such confusion may seal the doom of California's Christian Right.

Notes

The authors would like to thank Melissa Houghton, Erin Paulsen, Erik Villanueva, and Jane Woodwell for their helpful comments on earlier drafts of this chapter.

1. This figure obviously differs significantly from the percentage of the 1996 electorate categorized as evangelical by the *Los Angeles Times* Exit Poll. This difference may have arisen from dissimilar question wording and from lower evangelical turnout in the 1996 election.

2. The data analyzed in this chapter were collected by the *Los Angeles Times* and distributed by the Roper Center of Storrs, Conn. Responsibility for the analysis and interpretations in this chapter nevertheless rests solely with the authors.

3. This lower apparent turnout probably resulted from a number of causes: Dole's premature concession statement on election night; evangelicals' lack of enthusiasm for Dole; the geater overall turnout in 1996, which reduced evangelicals' impact; slight variations in the order of the "born again" questions in the 1994 and 1996 polls; and possible differences in polling techniques between Mitofsky International (source of the 1994 data) and the *Los Angeles Times* (source of the 1996 data).

4. Evangelicals were defined as respondents who checked the category "born again or evangelical Christian" when answering the grab-bag question "which of these apply to you?" (which was followed by a list of characteristics).

5. To simplify analysis, the eight self-identified evangelicals who claimed to be non-Protestant were eliminated from the sample.

6. Middle class is defined as receiving an annual household income of $20,000 to $59,000.

7. This figure assumes that the number of Eastern Orthodox evangelicals was insignificant. Throughout the analysis, respondents who self-identified as evangelicals and claimed to be "Protestant" or "Other Christian" (most likely a synonym for some Protestant denomination) were coded as evangelical Protestants.

8. For a similar result, see Wilcox (1996).

9. Of course, the relatively pro–affirmative action wording of this question ("to help women and minorities get better jobs and education") might have induced some true opponents of affirmative action to pretend to be more supportive than they really were. It seems more likely, however, that pro–affirmative action "yes" voters misinterpreted the ballot's wording ("The state shall not discriminate against, or grant preferential treatment to, any individual or group on the basis of race, sex, color, ethnicity or national origin in the operation of public employment, public education or public contracting") as simply forbidding discrimination against women and minorities instead of abolishing affirmative action.

10. According to the *Los Angeles Times* (Warren, Cleeland, and Reza 1996), at least nineteen immigrants voted in the Dornan-Sanchez race despite their non-U.S. citizenship (they had passed the Immigration and Naturalization Service's test for naturalization but had not yet officially been sworn in). Dornan's assertions to the contrary (Ayres 1996), it nonetheless seems extremely improbable that enough noncitizens voted to have affected the outcome of this contest.

11. Voter guides by both the Christian Coalition (1996b) and the Traditional Values Coalition (1996) appeared to support a yes vote on Proposition 209 as the solution to a problem that "needs fixing." Though he admitted that some African American churches that support TVC might disagree, he claimed that others would view Proposition 209 as "the fair thing."

12. Nonevangelical respondents to the *Los Angeles Times* Exit Poll divided evenly over the initiative at 50 percent yes versus 50 percent no. If one also includes ethnic evangelicals, the proportion remains 50 percent yes. Only by adding white evangelicals to the mix can one achieve the 51 percent yes votes needed for passage. (This poll's overall results obviously differ by a few percentage points from the actual vote tallies.)

References

Aldrich, John H., and Forrest D. Nelson. 1984. *Linear Probability, Logit, and Probit Models.* Newbury Park, Calif.: Sage.

Ayres, B. Drummond, Jr. 1996. "After Days of Counting, Dornan Race Is Too Close to Call." *New York Times* (14 November): A8.

Bos, Will. 1996. Interview by author, 24 October.

California Opinion Index. 1993. "Religion and Politics" (September).

Christian American. 1996. "California Report" (March/April).

Christian Coalition. 1996a. *1996 Christian Coalition Congressional Scorecard.*

————. 1996b.'*96 Christian Coalition Voter Guide (CA-4)*.

Dart, John. 1996. "Vote Buoys, Bothers Local Faith Activists." *Los Angeles Times* (9 November): A11.

Dunlap, David W. 1994. "Minister Stresses Anti-Gay Message." *New York Times* (19 December): A8.

Gerston, Larry N., and Terry Christenson. 1991. *California Politics and Government*. Pacific Grove, Calif.: Brooks/Cole Publishing.

Gilbert, Christopher P. 1993. *The Impact of Churches on Political Behavior*. Westport, Conn.: Greenwood Press.

Grimaldi, James V., and Dina Elboghdady. 1995. "Rep. Dornan Gets the Hook for Baiting Clinton." *Orange County Register* (26 January): A1.

Jacobs, John. 1996. "GOP Paying at Ballot Box for Gun Issue." *Fresno Bee* (19 November): B5.

Key, V. O., Jr. 1964. *Politics, Parties, and Pressure Groups*. New York: Thomas Crowell.

Lesher, David. 1996. "United Front Key to GOP Hopes for a New Era." *Los Angeles Times* (4 February): A1.

Lutterbeck, Deborah. 1995. "Like Money in the Bank." *Common Cause Magazine*, Summer, 17–20.

Martinez, Gebe. 1996. "Coalition Will Try to Enlarge Voting Flock." *Los Angeles Times* (24 October): B4.

Mayhew, David. 1986. *Placing Parties in American Politics*. Princeton, N.J.: Princeton University Press.

McGraw, Carol. 1994. "Preaching on Prop. 187." *Orange County Register* (16 October): B1.

Morain, Dan, and Carl Ingram. 1995. "Hurrt's Spending Equals His Bold Conservative Agenda." *Los Angeles Times* (24 November): A1.

New York Times. 1996a. "The 1996 Elections, State by State." (7 November): B11–13.

———— 1996b. "Results of Contests for the U.S. House, District by District" (7 November): B8, B9.

————. 1996c. "A Welcome Farewell." Editorial. (26 November): A10.

Nollinger, Mark. 1993. "The New Crusaders—The Christian Right Storms California's Political Bastions." *California Journal*, January, 6–11.

Orange County Register. 1996. "The Final Tally: Dornan Years." (23 November): A1.

Perez, Sue. 1996. Interview by author, 22 October.

Russo, Michael A. 1995. "California: A Political Landscape for Choice and Conflict." Pp. 168–81 in *Abortion Politics in American States*, ed. Mary C. Segers and Timothy A. Byrnes. Armonk, N.Y.: M. E. Sharpe.

Schindler, Jean. 1997. "Voter Education Continues." *California Christian* (a supplement to *Christian American*), January/February, S1, S4.

Sheldon, Lou. 1996. Interview by author, 22 October.

Sipchen, Bob. 1996. "Race Becomes Test of GOP's '94 Ascension." *Los Angeles Times* (25 September): A3, 10.

Soper, J. Christopher. 1995. "California: Christian Conservative Influence in a Liberal State." Chap. 11 in *God at the Grass Roots: The Christian Right in the 1994 Elections,* ed. Mark J. Rozell and Clyde Wilcox. Lanham, Md.: Rowman & Littlefield.

States News Service. 1994. "Dornan's Remarks Draw House Fire." *Orange County Register* (25 March): A5.

Traditional Values Coalition. 1996. *California Voter's Guide: General Election, November 5, 1996.*

Warren, Peter M. 1996a. "Brixley Admits to Taking Down Dornan Signs." *Los Angeles Times* (22 October): B1, Orange County edition.

———. 1996b. "Dornan Faces Tough Challenge in Key Race." *Los Angeles Times* (20 October): A3, 31.

———. 1996c. "O.C. Democrats Say Time to Beat Dornan Is Now." *Los Angeles Times* (19 October): A1, Orange County edition.

Warren, Peter M., Nancy Cleeland, and H. G. Reza. 1996. "Noncitizens Say They Voted in Orange County." *Los Angeles Times* (27 December): A1, 16–17.

Wilcox, Clyde. 1996. "Evangelicals and Racism." Paper presented at the annual meeting of the American Political Science Association, San Francisco.

10

Oregon: The Flood Tide Recedes

William M. Lunch

> There is a tide in the affairs of men, which, taken at the flood, leads on to
> fortune; omitted, all . . . is bound in shallows and miseries.
> —William Shakespeare, *Julius Caesar*

Leaders of the Christian Right sometimes claim the mantle of inheritors of the grand traditions of Western civilization. At least in the Northwest, they might be pondering Shakespeare's warning in *Julius Caesar;* the flood tide of social conservatism that seemed so promising in 1994 rather dramatically receded in Oregon and Washington in 1996.

From the early (January 1996) special-election victory by Democrat Ron Wyden to replace Bob Packwood in the U.S. Senate to the November election results, the leading Christian Right organization in the region, the Oregon Citizens Alliance (OCA), proved far less able than in either 1992 or 1994 to influence the public agenda. Mainstream Republicans avoided public association with the organization, and the OCA itself divided in a schismatic fashion reminiscent of divisions on the left in the late 1940s. In Washington State, the success of Christian Right activists in the primary may well have cost the Republican Party an opportunity to elect a governor in 1996. And in both states, Bill Clinton won easily in the presidential contest. Although 1996 was not without some victories for the Christian Right in the Northwest, particularly in the state legislatures, on balance it was a year that demonstrated the movement's limits.

This chapter (1) summarizes the recent history of Christian Right activism in the Northwest, particularly Oregon; (2) chronicles the failure of most candidates for public office supported by the Christian Right in 1996; (3) analyzes the movement's failure to qualify for the ballot most initiatives sought in 1996; and (4) traces the schisms both within Christian Right organizations and within the Republican Party in the Northwest.

1986–1994: Activism among Northwest Christian Conservatives

In 1986, national antiabortion groups sought to defeat Oregon Republican senator Bob Packwood in the GOP primary because he was identified at the time as the most prominent Republican supporter of women's rights in general and abortion rights in particular. Joe Lutz, then a Baptist minister from Portland, was recruited by national antiabortion groups to run against Packwood in the Republican primary. Expected to receive perhaps 15 percent of the vote, Lutz did far better than expected, attracting 42 percent in a low-turnout primary.

Flush from this "moral victory," Lutz and his supporters created an organization, the Oregon Citizens Alliance (originally named the Oregon Conservative Alliance). The expectation was that Lutz, a handsome and articulate man, would soon run successfully for governor, the U.S. Senate, or perhaps mayor of Portland. Relatively quickly, however, Lutz left his wife to go to California with another woman; given the OCA constituency, he immediately fell from view in politics. But the organization outlived its most prominent founder. Lon Mabon, who had served as a top campaign official in the effort to topple Packwood, was a very effective political organizer who used connections to Christian fundamentalist churches throughout the state to build an organization that has survived, even if it has not quite prospered, for a decade now, influencing politics not only in Oregon but in Washington and Idaho as well.

In 1988, the OCA qualified an initiative to overturn civil rights protections for homosexuals in the state, following an executive order by the Democratic governor, Neil Goldschmidt, extending such protections. The Oregon political establishment did not take this challenge very seriously, but to their surprise, the initiative passed, with 53 percent of the vote. The resulting law was later overturned by the state supreme court, but this victory signaled that the OCA could appeal to voters beyond its core constituency of 10 to 15 percent of the electorate.

In 1990, the OCA returned to abortion, sponsoring a measure that would have outlawed abortion in Oregon except in rare cases. Had the U.S. Supreme Court overturned *Roe v. Wade* (as was widely expected in 1989 following *Webster v. Reproductive Services,* in which the Court majority allowed the states to restrict some abortion rights), the OCA measure would have rewritten state law to make it more restrictive than it was prior to *Roe v. Wade.* The OCA initiative qualified for the ballot as Measure 8. At the same time, less extreme antiabortion groups had qualified an initiative that became Measure 10, to require minors to notify their parents before having an abortion. But swing voters, while uneasy and conflicted about abortion, were not prepared to ban it outright. The opponents tied the two measures together and defeated both; Measure 8 lost by a margin of greater than 2 to 1.

Meanwhile, the OCA had been offended by the nomination of a pro-choice Republican, Dave Frohnmayer, for governor. Frohnmayer is a moderate Republican similar to Mark Hatfield, Bob Packwood, and many other Republicans prominent in the state's history. But OCA leaders were offended when Frohnmayer refused to change any of his positions on abortion, gay rights, or other social issues and also refused to help finance the organization with a contribution from his large campaign treasury. In response, they recruited a spoiler candidate, a retired federal employee named Al Mobley, to run for governor. Though initially given little chance to influence the outcome, Mobley took 13 percent of the vote, almost all of which would otherwise have almost certainly gone to Frohnmayer. The result was a victory for the Democratic nominee, Barbara Roberts, who won with a plurality of 46 percent of the vote.

In the meantime, in Washington State, an initiative that set into state law the criteria for legal abortion established under *Roe v. Wade* passed narrowly in 1991. Efforts by Christian Right activists (not connected to the OCA) to defeat the initiative failed (Hamilton 1991).

By 1992, the OCA had failed in its efforts to ban abortion but had succeeded as a spoiler in a gubernatorial contest. So Mabon shifted the focus back to the OCA's initial success; he cut a quiet deal not to run a spoiler candidate against Packwood in his 1992 reelection contest, as had been threatened (Mapes 1992). Perhaps more important, remembering their success in 1988, OCA leaders qualified a sweeping initiative for the 1992 ballot to limit civil rights and legal protections for homosexuals. The initiative became Measure 9 on the 1992 Oregon ballot. It included hyperbolic language, describing homosexuality as "abnormal, wrong, unnatural and perverse" and compared it to pedophilia, sadism, and masochism. Combined with a similar but less flamboyantly worded initiative that appeared on the Colorado ballot, the measure focused national attention on religious conservative antagonism toward homosexuals. Following a bitter campaign that included a firebombing by racist skinheads, Measure 9 was rejected by Oregon voters, but by the relatively narrow margin of 56 to 44 percent (Sullivan 1992).

In 1993, the OCA pursued a strategy designed to keep its efforts in the headlines—and to keep contributions flowing—by sponsoring a series of local antigay initiatives, mainly in rural communities that had been supportive of earlier OCA measures. Sixteen such local measures were qualified for ballots in 1993–1994 and fifteen of them passed. But the 1993 state legislature passed a state preemption law that had the effect of voiding the local OCA measures (Mapes 1993).

In 1994, the OCA qualified a revised state version of Measure 9, which became Measure 13 on the 1994 Oregon ballot. This version was stripped of much of the hyperbolic language used in 1992, though the legal consequences of the measures would have been almost identical. At the same time, the OCA expanded into the neighboring states of Washington, Idaho, and Nevada and started efforts to put antigay measures on the ballot in all of those states (Rubenstein 1994). Ultimately, an initiative parallel to Oregon's Measure 9 qualified for the ballot in Idaho but failed to qualify in Washington and Nevada, in part because both states have more stringent standards for qualifying measures than Oregon (Church 1994). In the fall, in an upset, the Idaho measure failed as opponents reminded Mormon voters of the discrimination those of their faith had suffered earlier in the century.

The year 1994 was the best for the GOP in half a century; nationally, Republicans took control of the House of Representatives for the first time in decades. In Oregon, the GOP took control of the state senate for the first time in forty years and picked up the open Fifth Congressional District. Nonetheless, Measure 13 was defeated, albeit by a narrower margin—52 to 48 percent—than Measure 9.

So as the 1996 election cycle began, the OCA and religious conservatives in Oregon and Washington were flush from many victories, but they had yet to achieve most of their goals. In particular they had yet to reestablish the social controls restricting women and homosexuals that they had wanted for almost a decade. As it developed, 1996 was not a good year for the Christian Right in the Northwest.

Candidates in 1996: Losses for the Christian Right

Oregon voters made choices among candidates for the U.S. Senate many times in 1996, in part because Bob Packwood did to himself what his opponents on the Christian Right were unable to do—his own behavior forced him into resignation. Ironically, Packwood, a defender of opportunities for women in public policy, behaved as a boor toward women in private (Taylor 1995). Packwood resigned from the Senate in September 1995.

In most states the governor would appoint someone to fill the seat, but in Oregon the resignation triggered a special election, conducted through the mail. A primary held in December 1995 was won among Republicans by Gordon Smith, the presiding officer, or president, of the state senate. A conservative, a Mormon, and a millionaire as a result of his food-packing business, Smith won the endorsement of the OCA in the GOP primary, easily defeating the moderate state superintendent of education, Norma Paulus. To win the primary, Smith positioned himself to the right of Paulus, which was strategic during the primary, given the strong conservatism of the rather small GOP primary electorate (Mapes 1995).

The Democratic primary, between Representatives Ron Wyden (from Portland) and Peter DeFazio (from Eugene, in the Willamette Valley), was closer and nastier. Wyden emerged from his primary somewhat bruised by DeFazio, and his campaign treasury was rather depleted, so it was widely thought among political observers that Smith had the advantage.

During the unusual winter campaign that followed, the wealthy Smith compensated for his low name recognition with a barrage of television ads, particularly in the Portland area, which includes the city of Portland and its suburbs in Washington and Clackamas Counties, where some 40 percent of the total statewide vote is cast. Wyden, well known in the area as a senior member of the House (since 1980), focused his efforts on the Portland suburbs and the Willamette Valley south of Portland, where about a quarter of the state vote is cast.

Both campaigns appeared uncommonly negative to Oregonians, perhaps because the campaigns were presented in isolation, with no other political contests to distract attention. Wyden's campaign, aided by a number of independent expenditure efforts, notably by women's groups, portrayed Smith as a wolf in sheep's clothing, hostile to women, minorities, retired people, and gays and lesbians. The OCA endorsement of Smith was routinely offered in both broadcast ads and print as evidence of his malevolence. Public opinion polls have shown that the OCA and allied Christian Right organizations in Washington are widely perceived—by more than 80 percent of voters—as extreme and antagonistic (Hill 1995).

Ballots arrived in the mail in mid-January, but they could be returned as late as 30 January. During that period of more than two weeks, polls showed Smith with a small but consistent and statistically significant lead. Smith was so confident that he skipped campaigning on the last weekend when ballots were being returned, while Wyden made a point of barnstorming across the state in a seventy-two-hour campaign marathon. When the counting began on 30 January, it was a mild surprise that Wyden started ahead; however, Portland, which is heavily Democratic, often reports early. Smith supporters kept waiting for a surge of rural votes to put their candidate ahead, but Wyden stayed ahead all night, ultimately winning in the crucial suburban Washington and Clackamas Counties, and winning statewide by a narrow margin (Wells 1996).

Exit polling showed that two perceptions hurt Smith: he was perceived as antienvironmental in a state noted for environmental concern and as hostile to the independence of women because of the OCA endorsement and his opposition to legal abortion. These weaknesses were particularly apparent among suburban Republican and independent women, many of whom abandoned Smith to vote for the earnest if rather awkward Wyden (Schneider 1996). Thus the OCA endorsement hurt Smith; after the loss to Wyden,

Smith's campaign manager, Dan Lavey, said, "The OCA's support of Gordon tended to eclipse . . . Gordon's views and record on issues of conscience." (Sarasohn 1996).

Following the special election to replace Packwood, Oregon's senior U.S. senator, Mark Hatfield, announced he would retire, in part because of a threat from Bill Witt, who had run for the House in 1994 with OCA support, to oppose Hatfield in the GOP primary. Once Hatfield withdrew, Republican leaders encouraged Smith to run again. Reluctant at first, he eventually agreed. This time, however, he announced that he would not accept an OCA endorsement, even if it were offered. Lon Mabon, the OCA leader, was furious with Smith; on the last day that candidates could file for the primary, he announced that he would challenge Smith in the Republican primary. Mabon may have thought the primary would offer fund-raising potential for the OCA, which was in precarious financial circumstances, but for Smith, Mabon's challenge was an unexpected gift. Not only could Smith deny any association with the OCA, he would have a primary campaign to demonstrate his relative moderation. And for the moderate Republican establishment, Mabon's challenge allowed support for Smith to be presented as moderate (Green 1996).

In the May primary, Smith won with more than three-quarters of the vote. Mabon attracted less than 10 percent, scarcely beating a nuisance candidate who ran in a clown suit. Smith's repudiation of the OCA helped in the fall to innoculate him against charges of extremism revised by Democrats (Esteve 1996).

Running as a born-again moderate, Smith won in November against a politically inexperienced Democrat, millionaire businessman Tom Bruggere. Thus within a year Oregon replaced two moderate Republican senators with a liberal Democrat and a conservative Republican, albeit one who had to hide his rightist light under a bushel to be elected (Berke 1997). But Smith's candidacy was clearly strengthened by his public differences with the OCA.

Meanwhile, in the House, Oregon's delegation also changed significantly. In 1994, two Republican freshmen had been elected. In the huge Second District in eastern and southern Oregon, state senator Wes Cooley replaced popular Republican Bob Smith, who retired after six terms. State senator Jim Bunn won in the Fifth District in the northern Willamette Valley, which extends south from Clackamas County through Salem, the state capital, to Corvallis. Corvallis, home of Oregon State University, was once a stronghold of moderate-to-liberal Republicanism. It has become increasingly Democratic, in no small measure because of reaction against the perceived intolerance of the OCA and the close links between the GOP and the OCA.

In the Second District, Cooley won a crowded Republican primary in 1994 in part because of the OCA endorsement. But Cooley proved to be his own worst enemy. He claimed in the 1994 state voters pamphlet that he was a Korean war veteran, but in 1996 it was discovered that his military training in North Carolina had extended past the date of the Korean armistice. There were also charges that Cooley's wife, Rosemary, had continued to take a military pension as a widow even after she and Cooley presented themselves as married (Egan 1996). The charges surfaced after the filing date for the Republican primary, so Cooley had no opposition, but he was profoundly damaged. Republican leaders put heavy pressure on Cooley to step down as the nominee; he did so soon after the Republican convention (Lunch 1996).

The Oregon GOP then nominated the popular Bob Smith. Smith agreed to run only after House leaders promised that he would become chairman of the House Agriculture Committee (counting his previous terms toward his seniority). Smith is clearly a conservative, but unlike Cooley, he owes nothing to the OCA or Christian conservatives.

In the Fifth District, Jim Bunn won the Republican primary in 1994 in part because he was endorsed by the OCA. The Democrats had a crowded primary, in which a new state senator was nominated for the House; she was a woman who had been appointed to office to fill a vacancy, not elected. Bunn won narrowly in 1994, the most Republican year in half a century; he would have lost had only the votes cast on election day been counted. The Fifth District is highly marginal; it can be won by either party. Some months into his first term, after winning with active support by Christian conservatives, Bunn divorced his wife and, a few months later, married his chief of staff. Campaign consultants would call these actions "off message" for a cultural conservative. Bunn continued to receive support from the OCA, but once the Democrats nominated a moderate candidate, Clackamas County commissioner Darlene Hooley, who had previously served in the state legislature, he was a marked man. It was not a surprise when Bunn lost to Hooley in November.

In the First District, dominated by Washington County in the Portland suburbs, another candidate associated with the OCA, Bill Witt, lost for a second time against liberal Democratic incumbent Elizabeth Furse. In 1994, Witt had come within about three hundred votes of defeating Furse but fell short. Witt is very conservative and has adopted a public persona that underscores his opposition to legal abortion, homosexuality, and social change in general. In 1995, he had threatened to run against Mark Hatfield in the Republican primary if Hatfield sought a sixth term; with an increasingly conservative GOP primary electorate, it was not a threat Hatfield could take lightly. In 1996, Witt lost to Furse by a substantially larger margin than in 1994 in a campaign marked by very harsh attacks from both sides.

Across the Columbia River from Portland is Washington's Third Congressional District, which extends from Vancouver, a predominantly blue-collar city from which many people now commute to Portland, north through some rural areas once dominated by the timber industry, to Olympia, Washington's capital, on the southern reaches of Puget Sound. In 1994, voters elected Republican Linda Smith, a militant, populist conservative with strong ties to the Christian Right. She won in an upset in 1994, defeating Democratic environmentalist Jolene Unsoeld. Smith secured the Republican nomination through a write-in campaign after the candidate initially favored by Republican Party leaders withdrew from the race (Barone and Ujifusa 1995). Smith established an unusually high profile for a freshman, focusing at first on efforts to repeal or limit environmental laws and then on campaign finance reform. Her high energy mobilized conservative Christian activists, but she alienated some moderate voters with her militant style and socially conservative positions. During the winter and spring months in 1996, however, Smith seemed very popular and was considered a leading candidate to run for governor of Washington. She decided against that race, passing the Christian conservative baton to Ellen Craswell. Smith chose to run for reelection to the House, and her visibility and obvious support among religious activists deterred most prominent Democrats, even though historically Smith's district has leaned Democratic. A political neophyte and professor, Brian Baird, was eventually nominated by the Democrats in Washington's September primary in what most regarded as a suicidal effort. But as it developed, Smith had produced unease among some mainstream voters. Smith had defeated Unsoeld in 1994 by 7 percent of the vote, but on election day in 1996, she appeared to have lost to Baird, if narrowly. However, after the polling place ballots were counted, heavily Republican absentee ballots were tallied. Counting the absentees was slow, but Baird's lead slipped away, bit by bit, until Smith won by a very narrow—less than a thousand votes—margin.

Elsewhere in Washington, in the Second District, a similar pattern emerged; an election-day loss by Republican freshman Jack Metcalf was turned around by absentee ballots. In the end, in 1996, Washington Republicans lost only one of the six seats they had gained in 1994, but the margins for all the freshmen were uncomfortably close. Among the survivors, the two candidates most visibly associated with the Christian Right were also the ones who came closest to losing.

The congressional races in Washington were conducted in the context of a gubernatorial race that probably could have been won by the GOP had the party fielded a mainstream candidate. As 1996 approached, Democratic governor Mike Lowry was in trouble. Like Bob Packwood in Oregon, Lowry had been a champion of women's issues while in Congress; but as in Packwood's case, his own behavior caught up with him. Lowry settled a sexual harrassment complaint by a former aide by personally paying a settlement of almost

$100,000. Lowry, mortally wounded, stepped aside when it became clear that the Democrats would otherwise jettison him (Hamilton and Church 1995). Meanwhile, a number of Republicans had announced that they would run for governor, hoping they could run against Lowry.

Washington has an unusual all-party "bedsheet ballot" primary system in which candidates from all parties run together, but the top Republican and Democrat face off in November. If enough candidates run, it is possible for a candidate with very limited support to capture a major party nomination. That happened among the Republicans: Ellen Craswell, a former state legislator who had strong support from Christian Right activists, gathered only 15 percent of the primary vote—but running against a highly divided field, she had the largest fraction of any Republican. Among the Democrats, the leading candidates were Gary Locke, an Asian American who was the elected executive of King County, where Seattle is located, and the African American mayor of Seattle, Norm Rice. Both Locke and Rice received substantially more votes than Craswell, but as the top Democrat, Locke won the party nomination. Craswell ran on explicitly religious themes, at times calling herself a "Christian radical" (Strinkowski 1997). She frightened many urban voters, but in rural areas the prospect of an Asian American governor was evidently distasteful. Locke ran a weak campaign but still won 60 percent of the vote cast on election day. When the absentee ballots had been counted, his share of the vote dropped to 58 percent. At the same time, Washington voters gave the GOP control of both houses of the state legislature. In retrospect, it seems clear that had Republicans nominated a mainstream candidate, they might well have defeated Locke. Craswell clearly hurt GOP chances, and legislators in Olympia are now discussing repeal of Washington's all-party primary.

Smith, in Oregon, and Craswell, in Washington, show that candidates who are explicitly tied to the Christian Right are likely to lose in the Northwest, except in Idaho. At the same time, Smith's November victory in Oregon shows that if conservative candidates distance themselves from the Christian Right, they have the potential to win.

Some candidates supported by the Christian Right prevailed in 1996. Despite close calls, Smith and Metcalf won in Washington; and in Oregon, two women running with OCA support for seriously contested state senate seats won.

Marilyn Shannon, in the rural Willamette Valley Fifteenth District, was appointed to office when Jim Bunn departed for Congress (Green 1995). She won her own election in 1996 despite bitter primary opposition from a secular but very conservative Republican member of the Oregon House. Representative Cedric Hayden, who had represented a district contained within Bunn's senate district boundaries since 1984, felt that he should have been appointed to the opening in 1995, but the Republican county committees, heavily influenced by the OCA, selected Shannon. In 1996, Hayden ran against Shannon in the primary but lost. Hayden, embittered but prohibited by state law from running in the general election, persuaded a political ally to run in the heavily Republican district as a minor party candidate to punish Shannon. This ploy failed when Shannon was elected with a plurality of the vote.

In Washington County, Eileen Qutub, who was first nominated for the state house in 1994 with OCA support, defeating a moderate Republican woman in the primary, won in the general election that year. In 1996, Qutub ran for an open state senate seat for which the Democrats nominated a strong candidate. The district generally favors Republicans but has been inclined to moderates, so Qutub ran much like Gordon Smith, adopting a moderate persona. Even so, there was no question about her political lineage, and her victory must be counted a success for religious conservatives.

However, in the region many of the most important choices are not in candidate contests but in votes on initiatives and referenda.

Failure to Control the Agenda: OCA Initiatives in 1996

Most of the activity of the OCA over the past decade has been focused not on candidates but on initiatives targeted against legal abortion and the legal rights of homosexuals. The organization has at times attracted substantial contributions (both from Oregon and from other states) for its efforts to qualify such measures and, in the fall, in support of its campaigns. At its high point in 1992, the OCA collected more than $1 million in contributions for its campaign in favor of Measure 9 (Neville 1993).

Thus OCA-sponsored initiatives have become routine on the Oregon ballot in recent years. It is therefore notable—and further evidence of the OCA's troubles—that in 1996 no such measure appeared on the Oregon ballot. It could be argued that the OCA's initiatives have not yet actually changed people's lives. The 1988 vote to reverse the governor's inclusion of sexual orientation under antidiscrimination guidelines was overturned by the courts; the 1990 antiabortion initiative failed by a wide margin; and the 1992 and 1994 anti–gay rights initiatives both failed, if narrowly the second time. But this type of analysis misses the effect these initiatives had in framing public debate.[1] Particularly in 1992, public attention was riveted on gay rights issues, and not just in Oregon, as indicated by the national and even international attention focused on Measure 9 (Sullivan 1992).

The OCA promised to return to the ballot in 1996 with a third antihomosexual initiative. In 1995, Mabon filed a proposed initiative and began circulating petitions. But signature gathering went slowly at first, at least in part because of divisions within the OCA (O'Keefe 1996). Another difficulty was that OCA activists, who had always collected signatures as unpaid volunteers, were often asked to collect signatures for other conservative ballot proposals, for which they were offered bounties of 50 cents or more per signature. For many former OCA activists, the offers were too good to resist.

Then in May 1996, as the deadline for submission of signatures for measures to appear on the November ballot was drawing close, the U.S. Supreme Court issued its ruling in *Romer v. Evans*. Recall that in 1992, when Oregon voters had defeated Measure 9, voters in Colorado had approved Amendment 2, which restricted legal appeals of discrimination for homosexuals in that state. Implementation of the initiative had been enjoined by Colorado courts, eventually resulting in a ruling by the Colorado Supreme Court that held that Amendment 2 was unconstitutional under the federal constitution. The U.S. Supreme Court had accepted the Colorado case, *Romer v. Evans,* for review during its 1995–1996 term. In a somewhat surprising ruling in May, the Court upheld the Colorado Supreme Court ruling, 6-3, that Amendment 2 was indeed unconstitutional (Biskupic 1996). By implication, similar efforts to restrict the legal rights of homosexuals in Oregon would also be found to be unconstitutional. Americans respect the Constitution. Almost immediately, signatures for the proposed OCA measure, which had been slow in coming in any event, all but dried up (O'Keefe and Bates 1996).

The OCA was also circulating petitions for a very restrictive antiabortion initiative, but it had little support from other antiabortion groups. Mabon gathered so few signatures for that measure that he did not submit those he had to the secretary of state. The OCA had also been supportive of efforts by some of its allies on the right to repeal an ambitious state education reform program that attempts to prepare students for either college or work but that increases the state government's control over the K–12 curriculum. That initiative also failed to attract sufficient signatures to qualify for the ballot.

So for the first time in a decade, the OCA in 1996 had neither a candidate running for statewide office nor an initiative on the ballot in Oregon. This failure was, in part, a reflection of internal divisions that developed in the OCA following the successes of 1994.

The Danger of Success: Schisms in the Northwest Christian Right

For Republicans, 1994 was the best year in many decades; and it was the year when many of the political goals of the Christian Right seemed on the verge of being accomplished. But just as the victory of the left in World War II and in the elections that soon followed in England, Italy, and France rapidly proved evanescent, so the moment of triumph for the right may have been brief. Republican Party officials in Oregon and Washington discovered that support from the Christian Right came at a price, and they became embroiled in renewed disputes between the traditional high-status, high-income Republicans and the often less educated, lower-income Christian Right activists.[2]

In Oregon, such differences were long-standing; the OCA has repeatedly battled with moderate Republicans over candidates for the state party chairmanship. In 1987, following the better-than-expected showing by Joe Lutz, a religious conservative named T. J. Bailey was elected to be the state Republican Party chair. But under Bailey's direction, the party was unable to raise funds and did poorly recruiting candidates. In 1989, moderates reclaimed control of the state central committee.

In 1992, after the defeat of Measure 9, OCA members had blamed some traditional Republicans, such as state party chairman Craig Berkman, who opposed the initiative, for its defeat. At the 1993 state party convention, Berkman did not run for reelection. Mainstream Republicans narrowly elected Randy Miller, a quite conservative state legislator, but one without explicit ties to the Christian Right. Miller was reelected state chair in 1995, but despite his success leading the party to legislative victories in 1994, he was opposed by an OCA-supported candidate. And some months later, disputes arose over the composition of both the Oregon and the Washington delegations to the 1996 Republican National Convention (Mapes 1996). In January 1997 the leadership of the Oregon Republican Party was again contested by a candidate identified with the Christian Right running against others associated with very conservative positions but not explicitly religious. In this case, Perry Atkinson, a religious broadcaster and former candidate in the Second Congressional District, faced Deanna Smith, the wife of former U.S. House member Denny Smith, and Don McIntire, an antitax activist and author of a statewide property tax limit. After a first ballot eliminated McIntire, Smith prevailed but by only 1 vote out of 130 (Mapes 1997).

Beyond these factional party battles, which were familiar, the OCA itself divided following the success in 1994. A number of activists who had been deeply involved in the organization openly criticized Lon Mabon in 1995 and 1996. Among them were Al Mobley, the spoiler candidate who ran for governor with the support of the organization in 1990; Mike Wiley, who had served as communications director of the OCA; John Leon, who was the OCA's state coalition director in 1995 but who broke with Mabon in 1996; and Marilyn Shannon, the state senator selected with OCA support to fill out Jim Bunn's term when he was elected to the U.S. House in 1994 (O'Keefe 1996).

The theme running through their criticism of Mabon was that he was increasingly megalomaniacal, claiming that he alone knew God's positions on political issues. Shannon quoted Mabon as saying to her, "I get the message and if they [legislators] want to know how to vote, they should ask me" (Sarasohn 1996).

As severe ongoing financial problems continued at the OCA, many of Mabon's former allies left the organization, although they have not yet formed a group to compete with the OCA for the support of conservative Christians in the state. Still, it seems clear that factionalism among groups on the margins of politics did not end when the American Communist Party attacked the American Socialist Party for violations of ideological purity.

Conclusion: The Northwest Christian Right Encounters Its Limits

As many scholars of the revival of religious activism in American politics have noted, there is a sense of defensiveness among many Christian Right activists (Hunter 1991; Wilcox 1996). They routinely tell interviewers and reporters that they feel under siege in contemporary, largely secular American society.

I have certainly found such feelings in my interviews and surveys of OCA members. I found similar, if less extreme, views among the 1996 Republican convention delegates associated with the Christian Right. Both OCA activists and delegates in my research have cited a wide range of social and political changes that began in the 1960s and 1970s as being catalysts for political activity. They are opposed to much in modern, technological society, but they are completely unreconciled to the changes in social roles, particularly for women, that began in the mid-1960s and relaxed both formal and informal social controls that had previously limited the roles women could play.

This opposition to the relaxation of social controls extends to minorities among Christian conservatives and was reflected in a survey I did at the first statewide convention of the OCA in September 1987. Among the delegates I surveyed, 100 percent opposed legal abortion, 90 percent opposed the Equal Rights Amendment, then under serious consideration, 80 percent opposed the Civil Rights Act, and 57 percent opposed the Voting Rights Act (Lunch 1995). In my survey of Republican delegates to the 1996 Republican convention in San Diego, the results were less extreme, but there were similar reflections of opposition to social changes—notably to civil rights laws and policies—that many delegates perceived as undermining the God-given social order.

So the activities of the OCA in Oregon and its organizational siblings in Washington and Idaho opposing legal abortion and equal status for homosexuals reflect deeply held beliefs among conservative religious activists. Activists such as Mabon appeal to, and have mobilized much of, a constituency that is motivated to participate in the political system at rates higher than those found among ordinary citizens.[3]

But the strength of such polarized views among the supporters of the OCA in Oregon and similar groups in the nation frequently alienates moderates. It is sometimes charged that politicians are insensitive to the views of ordinary people, but Gordon Smith's remarkable reinvention of himself as a moderate— after concluding that association with the Christian Right in general and the OCA in particular may have cost him the Oregon special election for the U.S. Senate in January 1996—shows a high level of sensitivity to the nuances of public sentiment. By contrast, the resigned acceptance among Washington GOP campaign consultants (and most GOP candidates) of Ellen Craswell's defeat in 1996 suggested that close public association with the Christian Right was a liability of overwhelming proportions.

As these examples should suggest, the Christian Right in the Northwest, at least in Oregon and Washington, mobilizes a committed and energetic constituency. But while commitment and energy can go a long way in American politics, the Christian Right is now approaching—if it has not already reached—its limits. It will hardly disappear from politics in the Northwest, but neither should the Christian Right expect successes in the region comparable to those it has achieved in the South or even in the Midwest.

Notes

1. My thanks to David Magleby of Brigham Young University for reminding me of this point.

2. Pollster Andrew Kohut warned in 1994 that "the Moralists" have expanded the Republican Party base but have also increased party fragmentation and factional conflict within the GOP. See Kohut 1994, 66.

3. See Kohut 1994 on rates of participation among "the Moralists," as he calls the constituency that supports the OCA in Oregon. For more recent evidence showing these patterns in 1996, see Kohut 1997, 2–3, 16–17.

References

Barone, Michael, and Grant Ujifusa. 1996. *The Almanac of American Politics, 1996.* Washington, D.C.: National Journal.

Berke, Richard. 1997. "Trent Lott and His Fierce Freshmen." *New York Times Magazine,* 2 February, 40-48.

Biskupic, Joan. 1996. "Gay Rights Ruling Threatens OCA Drive: U.S. Supreme Court Voids a Colorado Constitutional Amendment." *Oregonian* (21 May): 1.

Church, Foster. 1994. "Frontier Values Not Always the Same as Traditional Ones." *Oregonian* (26 June): B1.

Egan, Timothy. 1996. "Of Marriage, Money, and a Lawmaker's Woes." *New York Times* (2 May): A8.

Esteve, Harry. 1996. "Smith Scores with Gentler Campaigning." *Eugene Register-Guard* (10 November): 1.

Green, Ashbel S. 1995. "Commissioners Select Shannon for State Senate Seat." *Oregonian* (11 January): B1.

———. 1996. "GOP Backs Off, Shuns Support from OCA." *Oregonian* (9 March): C1.

Hamilton, Don. 1991. "Abortion Foe Stirs Comment," *Oregonian* (7 November): B1.

Hamilton, Don, and Foster Church. 1995. "A Governor in Trouble." *Oregonian* (16 February): A14.

Hill, Gail Kinsley. 1995. "OCA Gets behind Gordon Smith." *Oregonian* (22 September): B1.

Hunter, James Davidson. 1991. *Culture Wars.* New York: Basic Books.

Kohut, Andrew. 1994. *The New Political Landscape.* Washington, D.C.:Times-Mirror Center.

———. 1997. *Scene 96, Take 2.* Washington, D.C.: Pew Charitable Trust.

Lunch, William M. 1995. "Oregon: Identity and Politics in the Northwest." Chap. 12 in *God at the Grass Roots: The Christian Right in the 1994 Elections,* ed. Mark J. Rozell and Clyde Wilcox. Lanham, Md.: Rowman & Littlefield.

———. 1996. "Happy Days?" *Willamette Week* (21 August): 7.

Mapes, Jeff. 1992. "Mobley, OCA Consider Independent Senate Race." *Oregonian* (16 January): B1.

———. 1993. "Compromise Bill on Gays May Bring Confusion." *Oregonian* (8 July): B1.

———. 1995. "Right Gives Its Might to Gordon Smith." *Oregonian* (20 September): B1.

———. 1996. "GOP Right Fights over Oregon's Delegates." *Oregonian* (26 June): 1.

———. 1997. "Choosing a Chair Sits Better with Republican Party This Time." *Oregonian* (28 January): B1.

Neville, Paul. 1993. "Money, Power, and the OCA." *Eugene Register-Guard* (24 October): 1.

O'Keefe, Mark. 1996. "OCA Founder Confident amid Myriad Problems." *Oregonian* (2 March): 1.

O'Keefe, Mark, and Tom Bates. 1996. "OCA Decides to Abandon '96 Campaign on Gay Rights." *Oregonian* (7 June): 1.

Rubenstein, Sura. 1994. "Washington Faces Gay Rights Issue." *Oregonian* (11 January): B1.

Sarasohn, David. 1996. "To Some, Real Mabon a New Revelation." *Oregonian* (15 March): B4.

Schneider, William . 1996. "Women Made the Difference in Oregon." *National Journal*, 10 February, 342.

Strinkowski, Nicholas. 1997. "God among the Evergreens: Religious and Secular Politics in the 1996 Washington Gubernatorial Race." Paper presented at the annual meeting of the Western Political Science Association, Tucson, Ariz., 14 March.

Sullivan, Robert. 1992. "Revolution Number 9." *New Yorker,* 9 November, 67–69.

Taylor, Paul. 1995. "His Home—the Capitol—Was His Castle." *Washington Post* (8 September): A1.

Wells, Robert Marshall. 1996. "Wyden Narrowly Scores Win in Bid for Packwood Seat." *Congressional Quarterly Weekly Reports,* 3 February, 310–12.

Wilcox, Clyde. 1996. *Onward Christian Soldiers.* Boulder, Colo.: Westview.

11

Washington: Mobilizing for Victory

Andrew M. Appleton and Daniel Francis

Washington State provides an interesting laboratory in which to assess both the capacity and the limits of the Christian Right to influence and/or control political outcomes. Political parties (and other political organizations) are heavily regulated by state law and have historically been somewhat weaker than in other states. Although parties in Washington are far from irrelevant, the populist political culture that underlies the electoral dynamics of the state, combined with the porousness of state party organizations, makes the political process more open to grassroots insurgency than might be the case elsewhere.

The 1996 election campaign for governor in the state of Washington highlights the potential for the Christian Right to be a major player in the political process at the state level; however, paradoxically, while demonstrating that the Christian Right has carved out a niche as a player that cannot be neglected, the 1996 gubernatorial campaign also exposes the fundamental weaknesses of the Christian Right in the quest for control of statewide offices. The failure of the campaign of Ellen Craswell for the governorship of Washington revealed that the extraordinary mobilization of the conservative Christian grass roots could not alone displace the political agenda and catapult one of its most outspoken members to office. Rather than winning a historic victory in the 1996 election, the Christian Right was placed on the defensive and even ridiculed in many quarters; the erosion of the moderate Republican electorate's support for the party candidate in the gubernatorial election is the most telling indicator of the failure of the Christian Right to mobilize outside its core committed constituency.

Before turning to the emergence of the Christian Right in Washington and the detailed analysis of the 1996 election campaign, this chapter will begin by examining the important contextual factors that have influenced the rise of the Christian Right.

169

The Political Context: Party Politics in the State of Washington

One of the most important features of party politics in the state of Washington is the existence of the blanket, or so-called wide-open, primary (Appleton and DePoorter 1996). This electoral mechanism was adopted by voter initiative in 1935 and has remained ever since, a by-product and a symbol of the enduring populist, antiparty tradition in the state political arena. Even before this reform, the state was heavily involved in the regulation of state party organizations, and today Washington remains one of the states with the highest level of legal restraint on the organizational capacities of its political parties. Importantly for those organizing at the grass roots, state law effectively prescribes a very decentralized party structure, with much of the power over delegate selection and the programmatic functions of the parties being vested in the county party committees (Mullen and Pierce 1985; Nice 1992). The preponderance of less-populated rural counties in the state, counties that also tend to be more socially conservative, means that the state-level party organizations are susceptible to vigorous grassroots activism in targeted areas of the state.[1]

The wide-open primary, and the banning of preprimary endorsements that was enshrined in the same piece of legislation, effectively removed the state party organizations from the process of candidate selection; nowhere is this more true than at the statewide level. Given the paradox that the county party organizations have more leverage over internal party politics than in many states as a result of the statute, while the same organizations have historically had trouble filling all their elected positions (particularly in the more rural counties), the institutional context is one that was ripe for the influx of a well-organized, active grassroots insurgency. The Democrats had to deal with such an insurgency in the late 1970s that split the party asunder for several years; in that case, it was led by those from the liberal bastion of King County (Seattle) who wanted to assert more control over the state party. In the late 1980s and early 1990s the Republican Party also faced a grassroots insurgency, although this time it came from the increasingly well organized Christian Right.

Historically, the state of Washington has been dominated by a populist tradition that defies easy characterization. In terms of the balance of party politics at the state level, the period since 1960 has been marked by a competitive balance between the two main parties (Appleton and DePoorter 1996). However, the political geography of the state is such that both parties have had to contend with significant internal differences. In general, the western third of the state is rather more socially liberal than the more agricultural and less populated eastern two-thirds. This does not, however, negate the presence of social conservatives in the political life of the major population center, King County.

In the historic 1994 election, Washington experienced the greatest swing at the congressional level from Democrats to Republicans. The historic defeat of the sitting Speaker of the House, Thomas S. Foley, perhaps overshadowed the defeat of many of his fellow Democrats in the Washington House delegation. The Republican Party of Washington understandably claimed the 1994 election as a great success for its candidates and its organizational prowess; indeed, several of the new Republican members of Congress were social conservatives who were representative of the new activism within the party. However, the success of the Republicans at the general election polls perhaps masked some of the deeper divisions that had marked the organization in recent years and that had alienated many former party leaders.

The Republican Party in Washington has not been immune to the kind of factional divisions that pervade state party organizations. In the mid-1960s, the party faced a bitter insurgency waged by members of the John Birch Society, based mainly in the eastern part of the state. Although the insurgency ultimately failed to wrest control of the central party organization from moderates, the schism offered a taste of things to come in the 1990s. At the beginning of the decade, the conservative faction of the party, closely identified with the emergent Christian Coalition, began to capture important posts in the party apparatus. However, social conservatives and the Christian Right did not always achieve a coalition on all issues; indeed, there was often friction between these two factions. In sum, the recent history of the party is marked by internal feuding and ideological dispute.

The Republican Party has had little peace since the 1992 state party convention. That year the annual convention was held in Yakima, and it became the stage of a couplike showing by the Christian Right, particularly the Christian Coalition of Washington. Using its grassroots strength, the Christian Right was able to control the agenda of the convention, which included several "cultural war" speeches reminiscent of Pat Buchanan's speech at the national convention in Houston the same year. The Christian Right was able to pass a state party platform that emphasized social issues (it even included denunciations of yoga and witchcraft!). The Christian Right's clout within the state Republican Party was even more evident in the selection of state delegates to the Republican National Convention. Effectively, the Christian Coalition was able to supplant the state party organization in the composition of the delegation to the national convention. David Welch, director of the Christian Coalition of Washington, was able to gain control of the chairman's seat to the convention, at the expense of GOP chairman Ken Eikenberry (a conservative), who was rejected even as a delegate. Welch and the Christian Coalition organized the delegation and drew on the strength of their grassroots organization at the GOP caucuses and the state convention.

The result was to exacerbate and expose the division within the Republican

Party. Where in the previous decade the party had been able to maintain some semblance of internal unity based on a coalition of Goldwater conservatives, Rockefeller moderates and progressives, fiscal conservatives, Reaganauts, and Cold War hawks, the massive infusion of social conservatives prompted many Republicans to choose sides and form alliances to counter the surge of the Christian Right.

In fact, the 1992 election was not a good one for Republicans at the state level, where the party lost several seats. But the reaction posted by many Republicans to losses by key religious conservatives such as Ellen Craswell (who lost the seat in the legislature that she had held since 1976) best exemplified the division within the party. Moderates and fiscal conservatives were heartened by her defeat and let it be known publicly that they hoped it would temper the influence of Christian Right. For those in the vanguard of the Christian Right activism, it signaled the moment to push for more control over the party apparatus and to oust moderate Republicans from leadership positions.

Despite the continued feuding, neither faction was able to assert uncontested dominance within the party. In an attempt to avert the same fate the Republicans had suffered in 1992, motions were made to call a truce before the 1994 election. Thurston County auditor Sam Reed, the unofficial leader of mainstream Republicans, and Thurston County state committeeman and chairman of the state chapter of the Christian Coalition David Welch called upon the state party chairman, Ken Eikenberry, to form a meeting of party leaders. They agreed to call ten members of each camp together, and the two factions met in Tukwila before the state convention. The result was an agreement based on three principles: the convention would be open, giving all a lot of time to speak; the majority would rule; and neither side would try parliamentary trickery like that practiced by the Christian Right and the Christian Coalition in the 1992 state party convention. Finally, they also agreed not to speak ill publicly of the resulting party platform.

The Tukwila summit did not totally eliminate the lack of trust between the two main factions. Furthermore, certain other factions (such as tax-and-spend conservatives, who disagreed with the Christian Right on social issues) were left out. The peace was fragile, but the 1994 convention was much less fractious than the preceding one. In addition, Christian Right candidates tempered their rhetoric in the 1994 campaign to a degree acceptable to most in the party. Perhaps equally important, the wave of protest that motivated many to vote for the Republican ticket in the midterm election was fueled less by massive sympathy for the Republican platform than by a reaction to the incumbent Democratic Party (symbolized in part by the defeat of Speaker Thomas S. Foley).[2] The result was much more success for the Republican Party in the 1994 general election than in 1992.

The New Christian Right Movement in Washington

From the vantage point of 1994, the Christian Right seemed to be enjoying substantial success in Washington State. The future of the movement, both within and beyond the Republican Party, seemed bright. After all, Christian conservative and longtime Republican state legislator Ellen Craswell had just helped dozens of Christian candidates around the state win office in 1994. Craswell's political action committee, Impac, had endorsed fifty-two victorious members of the new state legislature because they were both Christian enough and conservative enough to win Craswell's endorsement. Thus it can be argued that those backed by the Christian Right formed the largest faction in the legislature; certainly they outnumbered more moderate conservative Republicans.

This reversal of fortune for the Christian Right, after the fiasco of 1992, was, according to Craswell herself, all part of God's plan for government. From an institutional perspective, much of the success of the Christian Right in the 1994 elections can be attributed to qualitative changes within the Christian Right organizations. The Christian Coalition, for example, worked hard prior to the elections to broaden the appeal of its candidates and to present a more moderate and mainstream public face. In 1993, the Coalition held several training sessions where they encouraged young conservative Republicans to broaden their appeal by including issues in their rhetoric not easily identifiable with the Coalition or the Christian Right. They were urged to talk about tax cuts and curbing the role of government, property rights, opposition to gun control, and more local control of education. As veteran Democratic strategist Elden Rogers of Olympia, Washington, said, "It's impossible to sort out what Christians are doing from the rest of the right wing" (Simon 1994).

Soon after the 1994 elections, however, a number of circumstances highlighted the continued limits to the power of the Christian Right in Washington. One limitation was the lack of support for local Christian interest groups such as the Washington Citizens Alliance (WCA). The Citizens Alliances are a network of state organizations that began in Oregon and have since emerged in Washington, Idaho, Nevada, and Ohio. The main objective of these groups is to use citizen initiatives to enact laws that repeal or limit rights of homosexuals. In Washington State, however, the Citizens Alliance counted only five hundred members and a minimal budget. In 1994 they were unable to get an anti–gay rights initiative on the ballot, unlike their neighbors in Idaho.[3] In 1996, the WCA attempted a less ambitious proposal that focused on gay rights with respect to adoption and child care, but again they were unable to collect enough signatures.

Another limitation of the Christian Right was exposed following the 1994 elections when a number of countermovement organizations emerged. The most notable organization is the Interfaith Alliance, which formed in 1994 and claimed at least some credit for the failure of Oliver North's bid for a U.S. Senate seat in Virginia. The Washington chapter of the Interfaith Alliance was established in May 1995 with the goals of conducting educational forums on religious tolerance and setting up telephone trees that can turn out quick-response teams to attend school board meetings or other public events if intolerance and hatred arise. More specifically, their goal is to clash with, and debate the goals and initiatives of, Christian Right organizations.

Prior to the 1996 elections, the Alliance was able to hinder substantially the activities of the Christian Coalition of Washington by calling on pastors throughout the state to refuse to distribute voters guides passed out by the Coalition and to refrain from all political activity. They argued further that under federal tax laws, churches cannot participate in partisan politics without losing their tax-exempt status. Finally, the Alliance passed out its own guides to pastors giving detailed descriptions of what is and is not permissible from the pulpit.

The strength of the Christian Right in Washington is therefore difficult to define. Prior to 1994, it had limited successes such as Pat Robertson's 1988 caucus victory, the election to the state legislature of a few key Christian conservatives such as Ellen Craswell, and the primary victory of Representative Bob Williams in the gubernatorial race of 1988. The election of 1994, however, seemed to indicate the growth and maturity of the Christian Right and firmly establish the movement as a major faction in state party politics. Yet the experience of the 1996 election campaign perhaps signaled that, although the Christian Right is a major player within the Republican Party, it still cannot parlay that position at will into electoral success. With an electorate that was more prepared to look closely at the Republican candidates (many of whom were now running as incumbents), the Christian Right found that it was unable to consolidate even traditional Republican electorates when the religious affiliation and beliefs of its members came into the public spotlight.

The 1996 Election Campaign

Ellen Craswell's campaign to replace the retiring Democratic governor, Mike Lowry, placed the politics of the Christian Right squarely in the public spotlight. Lowry's retirement signaled a real possibility for the Republican Party to capture the governorship; the Lowry administration had struggled with a poor public image, and Lowry himself was the subject of sexual harassment charges from former employees. The incumbent governor's indecision as to whether to run again added to the air of disarray that permeated the Democratic camp in late 1995 and early 1996 and that seemed to make the Republicans favorites to win the office.

The election year of 1996 witnessed the continuation of the fragile peace within the Republican Party organization, much in the mold of 1994. In an attempt to keep the peace during the 1996 primaries and to continue rebuilding the image of the Republican Party after the 1992 fiasco, all Republican candidates for governor signed a pledge (known as the "Eleventh Commandment") to refrain from attacks on fellow GOP candidates during the campaigning season. This pledge proved difficult to keep for many of the candidates, however, as Craswell led a charge of loyal Christian soldiers into the election campaign. Perhaps no other candidacy more exemplified the fragility of that truce and the attendant strains on the Republican Party than that of Ellen Craswell. She was the first to announce her bid for the post of governor and was the only Christian Right candidate to do so. But she had strong support and strong opinions about social issues and the role of religion in politics; in no way was she one of the "new moderates" that the Christian Coalition had tried to foster.

Ellen Craswell: Foot Soldier of the Christian Right

A retired medical technologist, a strongly committed Baptist, and a University of Washington graduate, Craswell has four children and fourteen grandchildren. Her grandchildren are all either home-schooled or attend private schools. Her entry into politics was largely the result of her husband's career as a politician. In the 1960s, Bruce Craswell was a moderate Republican who volunteered on Dan Evans's gubernatorial campaigns and later served on the local school board. He ran unsuccessfully for the state house in 1974 and was called upon by state Republicans to run again in 1976. But he was in the middle of a change of careers from dentistry to managing a prepaid dental plan and decided not to run. The Republican Party was left without a candidate for the Kitsap seat. In an emergency meeting of Kitsap Republicans, Ellen Craswell was asked to run. She subsequently won the race and served in the state house from 1977 to 1980 and in the state senate from 1981 until her failed reelection bid in 1992.

Craswell's legislative career did not begin as a religious crusade, as neither she nor her husband was particularly religious at the time. Rather, she was a fiscal conservative, voting against tax increases so often that she earned the nickname "Representative No." With her record on tax votes, she quickly fell into favor with Bellevue representative Ron Dunlap. As one of the products of their increasingly close collaboration, together they sponsored a tax-limitation plan, Initiative 62. It was Dunlap and his wife, Allison, who were instrumental in turning the Craswells to God.

As Craswell and Dunlap campaigned around the state before the 1980 election, Allison Dunlap and Bruce Craswell would join them for the long car rides. Craswell's husband would often get into discussions with Allison Dunlap about the Bible. Unable to shake her belief in God and God's Word, Bruce decided to devote his life to God. Soon after, on 15 April 1980, Ellen also devoted her life to God and became a born-again Christian. "I remember feeling suddenly it was like the weight of the world was off my shoulders," Craswell was to say. "I think that's part of what gives you strength. You don't have to do it alone. You have this inner strength. Somebody else is there to hold you up" (Matassa 1995). From that moment, Craswell used the Bible as her guidebook for political life.

Her religious conversion also led to her political conversion, as all issues became issues of faith. Although she was unsuccessful on almost all her legislative initiatives in the state senate, she became well known in Olympia and was often sought out for her religious perspective on bills. Among those with whom she shared that religious perspective, she was a leader. For those with whom she did not, she became an enemy. Her religious conviction, however, led her to adopt uncompromising positions on bills, even those with which she agreed. For example, she opposed a bill that legalized home schooling because she disagreed with some minor details. Hence, she was unable to garner support for many of her own ideas. Perhaps Craswell's most notorious proposal was the 1990 plan to castrate sex offenders. The bill failed, but this indelibly labeled her as a social and religious conservative. This uncompromising and conservative image in large part led to the failure of her reelection bid in 1992.

For the latter part of her senate career and to the time of this writing, Craswell has been director of a socially conservative PAC called Impac. The PAC's literature states its purpose as putting "Bible-believing Christians in leadership of our state." The literature also describes homosexuals as "sodomites" who must be stopped in their effort to gain "special rights." Craswell herself said that homosexuality was "a life-style choice" that would cause people to live thirty-five years less than the typical life expectancy. She added that homosexuality is not "something that is unchangeable" and that she had a friend who was a lesbian but "she came out of it" (Postman 1996b).

Her religious conversion and her work with Impac have shaped her attitudes and positions on many key issues in the state. Craswell was prone to discussing openly religion and politics. She argued that the state's laws are being corrupted by legislators who "don't know God's plan," and she believes that voters should ask legislative candidates whether they have a "personal relationship with Jesus Christ" (Matassa 1995). According to Craswell herself, all that she does in her life is one way or another a reflection of God. For her, the way to solve the social problems that beset contemporary American society is to elect more people like her: Bible-believing Christians. "Christians should be outraged at the secularization of government," she has been reported as saying. "A lot of people say religion and politics don't mix. Well, they better start mixing" (Postman 1996c).

Ellen Craswell's Political Program for Reform

Craswell's campaign arguments in the 1996 gubernatorial elections emphasized the notion that it is America's turning away from God and morality that has given rise to a scourge of recent problems; those ills include crime, drugs, divorce, suicide, teen pregnancies, abortion, worse schools, more welfare, and less goodwill. And her beliefs are founded on the idea that it was not only God's plan but also the nation's founding fathers' plan to inject more religion into politics. "We went from one extreme where something like 50 of the 52 founding fathers were Christians to a total turnaround, to believing Christians shouldn't be involved at all politically. Naturally that's changed the outcome of what government's doing." Craswell has also contended that the Bible and the Constitution are intertwined—the latter being inspired by the former, so that "upholding the law of the Bible is the same as upholding the Constitution" (Matassa 1995). There are three basic institutions in life, according to Craswell—the family, the church, and the government—and God has a plan for all three.

On the top of the list of God's plan as interpreted by Craswell was governmental promotion of the family. In 1990, she introduced a bill in the state senate to end no-fault divorce; divorce would be granted only if a court finds adultery, abuse, abandonment, neglect, habitual drug or alcohol abuse, or impotence. She also wanted to dismantle the state agency of Child Protective Services (CPS). The rationale for this move came from the perception that CPS is too quick to pull children out of their homes. The alternative, from her perspective, was that such cases be dealt with in a criminal manner. Furthermore, she has voted against child abuse laws that aimed to make it illegal to shake a child under three or to throw, kick, burn, or cut a child or to strike the child with a fist; according to her, the laws were too "vague." Finally, her program sought to enable day-care centers to employ corporal punishment. The plight of the family, argued Craswell and her supporters, has been exacerbated by multiple negative influences on moral values, including more permissive attitudes toward homosexuality and unwed mothers, popular entertainment, the news media, divorce, the increase in working mothers, schools, government, and the courts. Craswell is typical of supporters of traditional social value issues among Christian Right advocates. She is a longtime abortion foe who hopes to make abortion illegal in *all* circumstances. She claims that too many people with harmful lifestyles pose a greater danger than a lack of tolerance for the lifestyles of others, and she has consistently opposed any and all gay-rights initiatives.

Craswell has also emphasized educational reform as an important issue facing the state. Her platform would have had the state remove many state rules over schools in order to give local school boards more control. She opposed state licensing of private schools (as well as home child-care centers), and she opposed state laws requiring local schools to provide bilingual education and social services. Craswell was also opposed to AIDS-awareness and antidrug education classes, arguing that these often send a permissive message to students. Her campaign targeted as negative the state education reform law, which requires schools to impose tougher academic requirements, gives students more comprehensive tests, and ties some federal funding to measurements of how well a school educates its students. In the long run, Craswell stated, "the government needs to get totally out of education," including the privatization of state-run universities (Simon 1996c).

When Craswell began her campaign for governor in 1994, she was very specific about her reasons for running. She said that she wanted to inject a little religion into politics and that it was clear to her that the state—the entire country, really—began a slide into immorality, crime, drugs, and abortion as laws were passed and court decisions were made that excluded religion from public life. "I believe we're seeing the country destroyed from within." To change that, she was wont to state, it will "take somebody willing to be a radical" (Simon 1996a).

The 1996 Gubernatorial Election Campaign

Perhaps most radical was Craswell's method of campaigning. Particularly in the primary, her campaign was legitimately grassroots. Drawing upon the organizational capacities of the Christian Right groups in Washington, whose strength had been evident in Buchanan's strong showing in the late presidential caucus, Craswell was able to mobilize a large number of people within the state who volunteered time and money to her campaign. By July 1996, Craswell had attracted 6,393 contributors, most giving as little as $5 to $10. Early in her campaign, volunteers organized five "coffee hours" in different homes each month, where attendees would watch Craswell in an eleven-minute video. All her political appearances were preceded by a group of "Prayer Warriors" who saw to it that all went well with Heaven's blessing. By August, her campaign had attracted 10,000 volunteers around the state and the campaign had organized a "Foundation Club" with 3,500 tithing volunteers who gave her campaign $10 to $50 a month. All of this was achieved without campaigning on Sundays, which she eschewed out of religious conviction.

Her campaign, focusing on individual rather than business or PAC donations, had raised $546,000. The Craswell team also accepted other types of donations. At the top of the recommended ways to help the campaign, in pamphlets sent to voters, was a check-box for people willing to pray for her victory. Craswell's Republican opponents, most prominently Dale Foreman, used million-dollar campaigns and television ads to promote their candidacy. Foreman, one of the most prominent Republican lawmakers in the state legislature, was clearly the favorite to win the Republican nomination and was the choice of most of the party leaders (although the party remained officially neutral, unable to endorse any candidate in the primary election, as prescribed by law). But Craswell did not run a single television commercial, relying instead on a mobilized grassroots network of volunteers who canvassed, put up thirty-five thousand yard signs, and distributed information.

Because of the Eleventh Commandment, Craswell's more moderate Republican opponents had difficulty questioning her about the role of religion in politics. Only Tacoma lawyer Jim Waldo worried aloud whether Craswell's beliefs would threaten the separation of church and state. The result of this diffidence was a dramatic Craswell victory in the primary held on 17 September 1996 (see table 11.1).

Although she had less money and less support among business interests and mainstream Republicans, Craswell was able to use committed grassroots Christian support to obtain her party's nomination. But the final results of the open primary were not very impressive; Craswell actually finished third. The Democratic nominee, Gary Locke, received 24 percent of the vote, Norm Rice received 18 percent, Craswell 15 percent, and Republican runner-up Dale Foreman took 13 percent. However, Craswell's strength was concentrated in a limited number of counties; Foreman actually won in nineteen of the thirty-nine counties, and two more were statistical dead heats.

Other indications also point to the weakness of her primary victory. Surveys of voters showed 38 percent of voters had a negative impression of Craswell while only 29 percent gave her favorable marks (Broom and Varner 1996). Craswell's supporters indicated that the main reason for supporting her was her moral character. It was clear that the Christian Right was very instrumental in her bid for the party's nomination. But what was unclear was whether this could translate into a general election victory. Following her victory, Craswell obtained only weak support among the leaders of her own party, which presaged the difficulties she would face in the November general election. Secretary of State Ralph Munro and Thurston County Auditor Sam Reed both publicly declared that they would have difficulty supporting her. Munro was quoted

Table 11.1
Primary Election Results, Governor of Washington State

Candidate	Votes	Percentage
Gary Locke (D)	287,762	23.7
Norman Rice (D)	212,888	17.5
Ellen Craswell (R)	185,680	15.3
Dale Foreman (R)	162,615	13.4
Jay Inslee (D)	118,571	9.7
Norm Maleng (R)	109,088	9.0
Jim Waldo (R)	63,854	5.2
Pam Roach (R)	29,533	2.4
Nona Brazier (R)	21,237	1.7
Bryan Zetlen (D)	6,152	0.5
Warren E. Hanson (R)	4,886	0.4
Bob Tharp (R)	4,825	0.4
Jeff Powers (Socialist Workers)	3,742	0.3
Mohammad H. Said (D)	3,007	0.2
Max Englerius (D)	2,837	0.2
TOTAL	1,216,677	100.0

Source: Secretary of State, Washington

as saying, "She describes herself as a radical and the question is, I'm not sure if the state is ready for that or wants that." Reed added that the philosophical rifts were simply too large for him to support Craswell (Simon and Postman 1996).

Immediately following Craswell's victory in the primary, Republicans and the Craswell campaign team recognized that she must temper her rhetoric in order to have any chance of success in the general election. As GOP consultant Brett Bader, who ran the campaign for the Republican runner-up, House Majority Leader Dale Foreman, said, "Gary [Locke]'s advantage is that he won't have to change a thing in his campaign" (Simon 1996b). But it was unavoidable that Craswell would. Even David Welch of the Christian Coalition argued that Craswell would have to put more divisive social issues in the background and stress her "mainstream" positions on cutting taxes, paring state government, and fighting crime. Craswell took the suggestions to heart and soon began a campaign that emphasized tax and budget cuts. The GOP nominee for governor immediately began to emphasize her plans for cutting in half three major state taxes that constitute 30 percent of state revenues: the motor vehicle excise tax, the state property tax, and the business-and-occupation (B&O) tax. She also argued that if the economy remained stable after the first two years, she would strive to eliminate those taxes entirely. Craswell called upon Michigan governor John Engler, a rising GOP star credited with major tax and spending cuts, to help her devise her tax-slashing plan.

The other part of the Craswell strategy was to attack her opponent, Gary Locke, the incumbent King County executive. Locke proclaimed after the primary that he would launch no attacks on Craswell; yet the Democratic Party did not feel bound to abide by this truce. In $100,000 worth of ads that noted Craswell's pro-life position and her suggestion that the University of Washington might be better run by private industry, the ads concluded that "when the smoke clears, Ellen Craswell is an irresponsible choice for governor." Republicans reacted by attacking Locke with ads proclaiming that his votes for tax increases as a legislator indicated that he is "another extreme liberal we can't afford." Furthermore, the Republican Party attacked Locke for his previous support for a state income tax. Craswell also battered Locke, particularly in the first televised debate, about his record on taxes, calling him another "Lowry liberal" (Serrano 1996).

Despite these efforts, Craswell continued to obtain her major support from her grassroots army of Christian Right supporters. There is no question that the support she received was quite impressive. By election day, she had garnered fifteen thousand volunteers statewide and had collected $1.59 million (Locke had raised $1.79 million, mostly from large contributions) from over a thousand loyal supporters and tithing individuals. However, support from the corporate sector, a typical Republican strength, was more difficult for Craswell to obtain. According to Carolyn Logue, state director of the National Federation of Independent Business (NFIB), this was largely because some did not believe Craswell could win and because many businesses worried that her budget-cutting plans would damage the state's higher education system. Even when business support was obtained, it was never enthusiastic. The Building Industry Association of Washington, for example, voted to endorse Craswell despite a denunciation of Craswell's candidacy by the group's president. Again, Craswell had to rely on the support of Christian Right activists rather than traditional Republican strongholds.

Other problems permeated Craswell's campaign. When speaking of morality or God's plan for government (talk that, to the dismay of many Republicans and campaign leaders, continued), Craswell was knowledgeable and fluent. But when discussing mainstream Republican issues such as budget and tax cuts, she often became flustered, particularly when asked about specifics. For example, when asked on a radio talk show how she planned to cut the budget by 30 percent, she asserted that the government should sell or even *give away* enterprises best run by private industry.

The biggest public relations problem to emerge in the campaign, however, was her involvement with Texas Christian historian David Barton. Barton has been a fervent proponent of the position that the separation of church and state is a myth; in this view, the moral decline of America can be directly attributed to the Supreme Court rulings in 1962 and 1963 that abolished state-sponsored school prayer and Bible reading. His popularity and notoriety, however, came mainly from his ability to give eloquent speeches. He remains one of the Christian Right's most popular speakers and is a regular headliner at national conventions. David Welch said, "I've seen people coming away from his programs just literally weeping, saying: 'I just never knew this. Why didn't I learn this in school?'" Barton appeared for Craswell on several occasions during the primary campaign, particularly in front of Christian groups, in order to gain support and funding. Unfortunately for Craswell, organizations such as the Anti-Defamation League (ADL) were able to point out that twice in 1991 Barton spoke to groups associated with Christian Identity, a white-supremacist movement. Barton claimed that he did not know that the group was "a bunch of separatists" (Postman 1996a). But the ADL was quick to point out that after this statement, Barton visited the group again four months later. When Craswell learned of this, she was able to quiet her critics by explaining her ignorance about Barton's past. But Craswell brought Barton back five months later, during the general election campaign (this time behind doors closed to the press), to speak at fund-raising events. Not only did this garner bad press for Craswell, but also it further marked her as a religious candidate rather than as a mainstream Republican candidate for governor.

Not surprisingly, Craswell did poorly at the ballot box. She lost by more than 16 percent of the vote to Gary Locke (see table 11.2). Both candidates for governor did better than the presidential nominees from their respective parties. However, Locke added nearly seventy-four thousand votes more than his Republican rival in his winning bid. Just as tellingly, in the race for lieutenant governor, Republican Ann Anderson ran a close race with Brad Owen, losing by only 2 percent. And in the races for U.S. House of Representatives, Republicans were victorious in five of the six districts. These figures are indicative of the lack of broad appeal that the Christian Right has within Washington State. Despite having a more substantial campaign following and volunteer organization than Gary Locke, Craswell was unable to appeal to moderate independents in the race.

Other Christian Right candidates in Washington have had similar difficulties in obtaining broad support. State representative Bob Williams, for example, lost in similar fashion to incumbent Democratic governor Booth Gardner in 1988. It is difficult for a Christian Right candidate to win a statewide election given the tendency of moderate Republicans not to support such candidates. Postelection surveys indicated that one in every five Republican voters abandoned Craswell in favor of Locke in 1996 and that many were turned off

Table 11.2
General Election Results, 1996, Washington State

Ticket	Votes	Percentage
Gary Locke (D)	1,296,492	58.00
Bill Clinton and Al Gore (D)	1,123,323	49.80
Difference (Locke-Clinton)	173,169	8.2
Ellen Craswell (R)	940,539	42.00
Bob Dole and Jack Kemp (R)	840,712	37.30
Difference (Craswell-Dole)	99,827	4.7
Difference (Locke-Craswell)	355,953	
Difference (Clinton-Dole)	282,611	
Lieutenant Governor's Race		
Brad Owen (D)	1,022,878	48.0
Ann Anderson (R)	989,661	46.5
Shawn Newman (Reform)	78,510	3.7
Art Rathjen (Libertarian)	39,277	1.8

Source: Secretary of State, Washington

by the role of religious values in her campaign (Egan 1996). Even several prominent Republicans voted for Locke, among them Sandra Brady, the campaign manager for the Republican candidate for governor in 1992. In sum, the 1996 gubernatorial election campaign shows that even when the party organization can retain a fragile truce in the face of active insurgency from the highly mobilized Christian Right organizations at the grass roots, it is not able to pull the moderate rank-and-file voters into effective and winning support for a candidate identified with the Christian Right.

Conclusion

The 1996 election in the state of Washington reveals the possibilities and limits of Christian Right activism in the electoral arena. Institutional mechanisms, such as the open primary and the voter initiative process, make it possible for the highly mobilized Christian Right to penetrate both the Republican Party and the legislative process. Although the Washington Citizens Alliance has not been nearly as successful or powerful as its counterparts in neighboring Oregon and Idaho, the Christian Coalition of Washington has been an important and disciplined force in the party politics of the state in recent years. Thus, as far as the possibilities are concerned, the Christian Right has demonstrated its power to infiltrate the Republican Party, to back candidates in particular areas of the state, and to get them elected. Furthermore, the Christian Right has not crumbled after one election. Part of this success can be attributed only to the motivation and energy of its grassroots supporters.

Yet once the Christian Right attempts to move beyond targeting specific candidates and races, the limits of its power are clearly exposed. Although Craswell did not completely alienate all Republicans in the 1996 election, she failed to mobilize critical support from the moderate faction of the party. The notion of the Republican Party as a "big tent" cannot be said to have much credence in the 1996 gubernatorial election in Washington. The very attributes that led to Craswell's somewhat unexpected success in the primary election paradoxically hastened her defeat in the general election. Despite the attempts of some in the Christian Right to present a more moderate and less religiously defined public image, Craswell was never able to overcome the depth of identification as an explicitly religious conservative with themes that scare off moderate Republicans. Porous parties may make for a greater possibility of grassroots insurgency, but the electorate remains sufficiently centrist to block the pathway to power for candidates who are seen as too extreme.

Where the Christian Right will go from the 1996 election in the state of Washington is unclear. The movement is still powerful inside the Republican Party, and many of the aims of the WCA (e.g., voter initiatives to restrict and outlaw homosexual rights) are still live ones for those on the Christian Right. For those who will point out the heavy defeat of Craswell, there are others who will note that she still garnered nearly one million votes, outstripping Bob Dole by about 10 percent. It is clear that the Christian Right is far from spent as a political force and will be deeply involved in the politics of the state for many years to come. Whether that involvement can be translated into capturing the governor's mansion and overcoming the current barriers to achieving statewide office remains to be seen.

Notes

1. Washington State has thirty-nine counties, each of which has equal representation on the state central committee, under state law. Thus it is theoretically possible that "the twenty smallest counties with a population of around 265,000 people could outvote in the Central Committee the nineteen counties representing more than 3,700,000 people" (Mullen and Pierce 1985, 59).

2. In Washington State, the Republican Party emulated the national platform promoted by Representative Newt Gingrich and adopted a "Contract with Washington."

3. The ICA sponsored Proposition 1, which sought to remove any "special protection" for homosexuals as a group and to limit public information about homosexuality; the proposition failed by a very slim margin.

References

Appleton, Andrew, and Anneka DePoorter. 1996. "Washington." In *State Party Portraits: Organization, Adaptation, and Resources,* ed. Andrew Appleton and Daniel S. Ward. Washington D.C.: Congressional Quarterly Press.

Broom, Jack, and Lynne K. Varner. 1996. "Poll Shows Strong Locke Support," *Seattle Times* (18 September): A1.

Egan, Timothy. 1996. "Election Results," *Seattle Times* (20 September): C6.

Matassa, Mark. 1995 "Craswell's Crusade: This Long-Shot Candidate Dares to Mix Religion and Politics." *Seattle Times* (5 February): Pacific 10.

Mullen, William, and John Pierce. 1985. "Political Parties." In *Government and Politics of Washington State,* ed. William Mullen et al. Pullman: Washington State University Press.

Nice, David. 1992. "Political Parties in Washington." In *Government and Politics in the Evergreen State,* ed. David Nice, John Pierce, and Charles Sheldon. Pullman: Washington State University Press.

Postman, David. 1996a. "Controversial Speaker to Appear for Craswell." *Seattle Times* (10 April): B1.

———. 1996b. "Debate Spotlights Differences—Religion, Taxes, Privatization of Schools." *Seattle Times* (11 October): B1.

———. 1996c. "Ellen Craswell's Plan for State Government." *Seattle Times* (22 October): A1.

Serrano, Barbara A. 1996. "Campaign Dollars Rerouted, Not Cut, Since Law Revised." *Seattle Times* (4 November): B3.

Simon, Jim. 1994. "More Pragmatic Christian Right Gets Poll Results." *Seattle Times* (13 October): A1.

———. 1996a. "Craswell Shaking Up GOP on 'Quiet Revolution' Circuit." *Seattle Times* (30 August): A1.

———. 1996b. "Primary Win Presents Locke with a Whole New Set of Issues," *Seattle Times* (20 September): A1.

———. 1996c. "State's Powerful Role in Classroom Divides Gubernatorial Candidates," *Seattle Times* (7 October): A1.

12

Minnesota: Onward Quistian Soldiers? Christian Conservatives Confront Their Limitations

Christopher P. Gilbert and David A. M. Peterson

Traditionally considered one of the nation's most progressive states, Minnesota has nevertheless been a hotbed of Christian Right activism in the last two decades. The state's political culture and structure provide windows of opportunity for electoral movements founded on social or moral grounds, and several groups and candidates with ties to Christian conservative causes have taken advantage. The track record of Minnesota's Christian Right activists at the polls, however, is decidedly mixed, and 1996 proved to be no exception.

Indeed, the most notable "victory" of Minnesota Christian conservative activists in 1996 came through a name change the previous fall. Twenty-one years earlier, reacting to the Watergate scandal, the state Republican Party rechristened itself the Independent Republican (IR) Party. The IR label in recent years had come to symbolize an underlying, uneasy coalition of social moderates and a strongly conservative wing dominated by the Christian Right. In the fall of 1995, the IR state party convention decided to drop "Independent" and become again the Republican Party of Minnesota. The apparent unity displayed then and later at the 1996 state convention, however, only highlighted the deep divisions and contrasting worldviews of the party's twin cores and hampered the state Republican Party's drive to replicate in the Minnesota state legislature and congressional delegation the national party's ascendance.

This chapter describes the tactics and strategies of the Christian Right in the 1996 Minnesota election cycle, with particular attention to the U.S. Senate race, the state party convention, and the composition of the state delegation sent to the Republican National Convention in San Diego. We will contrast a relatively successful 1994 election year with the mixed record of 1996, evaluating media coverage of Christian conservative candidates and the contrasting fortunes of the Republican U.S. Senate candidates in 1994 and 1996. Christian conservatives played an important, if somewhat quiet, role in the

1996 elections. The patterns of success and defeat for Christian conservatives provide evidence that their extensive influence shows no sign of dissipating in the future.

The Background

Against the backdrop of towering Democratic-Farmer-Labor (DFL) figures such as Hubert Humphrey, Eugene McCarthy, and Walter Mondale, Christian conservatives have been active and influential in Minnesota politics since the early 1980s, gaining strength within the Republican Party and forming a reliable core constituency for several prominent conservative officeholders (Haas 1992). The old label Independent Republican came to represent two very distinct and conflicting worldviews: a primarily secular constituency advocating moderate to progressive social policies combined with fiscal restraint (the "I" side), and the increasingly Christian conservative–dominated "R" wing that stressed a social agenda centered on opposition to abortion and the restoration of traditional values and family structures. The conflict remains, even as the label has changed.

Some leaders have successfully merged these two strains of ideology. By the late 1980s the state's acknowledged key Republican figure was Second District U.S. representative Vin Weber, who eventually became a member of the House minority leadership and an early ally of Newt Gingrich. An articulate, effective spokesperson, Weber possessed the ability to meld the two wings of the state party into one cohesive base from which he and others drew votes. The conceptual leadership of Weber, married to a vigorous set of pro-life activists and organizations, provided the foundation for the strong emergence of the Christian conservatives in the 1990s, a fact that Weber (who is not himself a Christian conservative) has publicly acknowledged numerous times (Schmickle 1996; *Minneapolis Star Tribune* 1996).

The commitment of the IR's Christian conservative wing was tested by election results in 1990 and 1992. In both years Christian conservative candidates and groups were anything but victorious. In 1990 the gubernatorial candidate endorsed by the IR party, Christian conservative Jon Grunseth, had to bow out of the election in bizarre circumstances and was replaced by pro-choice, pro–gay rights Arne Carlson, who managed to defeat weak incumbent Rudy Perpich in the general election (Hoium and Oistad 1991). Coupled with the loss of a U.S. Senate seat to the DFL, Carlson's victory made 1990 a near disaster for Christian conservatives.

The 1992 elections were not much better. While Christian conservatives gained control of the IR Party apparatus, and hence control over candidate endorsements and party resources, electoral results remained mixed. The most alarming defeat came in the Second District, where Vin Weber had decided not to seek reelection. The IR nominee to replace him was Cal Ludeman, a former legislator and unsuccessful 1986 gubernatorial candidate with unimpeachable Christian conservative credentials. Despite having higher name recognition and far more money than his opponent, DFLer David Minge, Ludeman lost the election by 569 votes (Barone and Ujifusa 1993, 690–91).

The defeat of Ludeman and the very poor showing of President Bush in Minnesota (he received only one-third of the vote in the state) overshadowed one minor success, the victory of former television anchor and political new-comer Rod Grams over a DFL incumbent in the Sixth Congressional District. The overall results led many moderate Republicans to warn of the impending doom brought on by the increased influence of the Christian conservatives, who responded in turn by exerting even more influence over the party (Smith 1992). In 1993, activists installed a new party chair after ousting the moderate who had presided over the tumultuous past few years (Smith 1993).

All of this set the stage for the monumental struggles that took place in 1994, both within the IR Party and between the IR and the DFL. The first sign of internal problems arose at the precinct caucuses in early March. Christian conservatives turned out in large numbers to support the gubernatorial bid of former state legislator Allen Quist, who essentially wrapped up the party endorsement over Governor Carlson that first night. The sizable advantage of Christian conservatives at these caucuses also kept a number of prominent Republicans from becoming delegates to the county, and eventually the state, convention. Quist's candidacy eventually petered out. Carlson soundly defeated him in the primary, where Quist supporters could not silence dissenting voices. In fact, the publicity created by Quist's caucus success helped to fuel the huge primary turnout that led to his defeat. Carlson went on to swamp DFL candidate John Marty in the general election, winning reelection by a record margin (Whereatt 1994).

Underappreciated during all of this were the successful candidacies of Rod Grams and Gil Gutknecht. First-term representative Grams won a close, bitter race for the open U.S. Senate seat vacated by fellow Independent Republican David Durenberger. Grams benefited from his perfect congressional rating from the Christian Coalition and from the fact that moderate and independent voters did not connect Grams strongly to the Christian conservative move-ment. Another candidate enthusiastically supported by Christian Right groups, former state legislator Gutknecht, won his bid to replace moderate DFLer Tim Penny in the First District. Gutknecht's connections to the Chris-tian Right and his endorsement of the Contract with America were considered essential to his victory.

Structural Factors

No understanding of Minnesota electoral outcomes is complete without consideration of the state's party caucus-convention system. The structure of the endorsement process in Minnesota is advantageous for well-mobilized factions within the parties. The endorsement process begins in late February or early March when all three major parties hold precinct caucuses, open to every party member who chooses to attend, to pick delegates for the county conventions held a few weeks later. These conventions in turn select delegates to the state and congressional district conventions, held in late May or early June. Each caucus and convention endorses candidates for local elections: the county conventions endorse for local and county offices, state representatives, and state senators; district conventions endorse congressional candidates; and the state convention chooses candidates for statewide offices.

These endorsements pertain only to each party's primary election, and candidates who are not endorsed are free to contest the primary in September. The importance of the endorsement is that it provides financial and organizational support from the party, as well as considerable free publicity from coverage of the caucus-convention season. Party support takes the form of party contributor and membership lists, printing of sample ballots, poll data, and access to the party booth at the state fair in late August. For many local candidates, a viable campaign without the benefits of party endorsement is hardly possible.

Tradition holds that unendorsed candidates should not contest the primary, but recent elections have seen a reversal of this trend and a corresponding reduction in the importance of the party endorsement. The 1994 Republican race for governor is the prototypical example of both the importance and the limitations of the endorsement. Allen Quist gained the IR endorsement with little difficulty at the June convention but was trounced by Governor Carlson in the September primary. While the endorsement could not guarantee a victory for Quist, it did give him a platform and visibility he could not otherwise have attained.

Since a very small proportion of the electorate attends the county caucuses (usually about 1 percent), a small and well-organized group of individuals can have a disproportionate impact on the decisions of their party. This is precisely what happened in 1994 with the so-called Quistians. In 1996, however, there appeared to be no single candidate behind whom Christian conservatives could unify.

The Republican Senate Nomination Race

The U.S. Senate race of 1996 was pegged early on as a potential rematch between DFL incumbent Paul Wellstone and the man he replaced, Rudy

Boschwitz. In 1990, Boschwitz's campaign was memorable for a stunning mistake followed by a stunning defeat. With a slim lead in the polls the week before the election, Boschwitz sent a letter to Jewish leaders in Minnesota calling Wellstone a "bad Jew" for marrying outside the faith and allowing his children to be raised as Christians. Boschwitz, who is also Jewish, was lambasted in the media, and conventional wisdom now cites the infamous letter as a critical factor in Wellstone's narrow victory (McGrath and Smith 1995).

Republican Party leaders never seemed eager to embrace a Boschwitz comeback; this probably spurred on Boschwitz's natural inclination not to quit, an inclination formed early in his life. Boschwitz emigrated to the United States at age four, when his parents fled Nazi Germany. After earning a law degree and serving a short stint in the army, Boschwitz founded what would become a multimillion-dollar home improvement company. He entered state politics as Minnesota campaign coordinator for Richard Nixon in 1968 and went on to score impressive Senate election victories in 1978 (defeating incumbent Wendell Anderson with 57 percent of the vote) and 1984 (58 percent) (Smith 1996i).

Boschwitz was considered a conservative by the standards of his era in the Senate. His voting record as compiled by *Congressional Quarterly* shows that he supported a conservative position on economic and foreign policy issues more than 70 percent of the time but only 60 percent of the time on social issues (Smith 1996g). Moreover, as the 1996 campaign wore on, it became apparent that Boschwitz had moved further to the right during his time out of office (Smith 1996g).

Despite a solid conservative record and stance on issues, Boschwitz conflicted on several fronts with Minnesota's Christian conservatives. The initial problem was his own faith, which, while not a fatal problem for Christian Right activists, nevertheless did not mesh well with their worldview. Further, his Senate voting record was notable for the handful of votes that stood out against his overall conservatism: he voted against the school prayer amendment, in favor of funding the National Endowment for the Arts, and in favor of the 1982 and 1990 tax increases. Finally, Christian conservatives had not fully forgiven Boschwitz for so quickly distancing himself from Jon Grunseth's troubles in October 1990 (Smith 1996g). Taken as a whole, Boschwitz's background and record made Christian conservatives wary, to say the least (Schmickle 1996). Not surprisingly, then, like Arne Carlson in 1994, Boschwitz early in 1996 perceived the reality of his standing with party activists and declared that he would not respect the convention endorsement—he would challenge all comers in the primary no matter what (Smith 1996a).

Boschwitz's main opposition for the endorsement was Bert McKasy, a former state legislator and commerce commissioner. McKasy's campaign was centered on the notion that Boschwitz's time had passed and that McKasy was the candidate who could best carry the party banner. To win the endorsement on this slim platform, McKasy needed to court the Christian conservatives who dominated the nomination process. His quest had actually begun two years earlier when he ran for the U.S. Senate endorsement, only to bow out when it became clear that the state convention would endorse Rod Grams. McKasy claimed this showed his dedication to the party, in contrast to Boschwitz's disrespect toward the endorsement process. In a more direct outreach effort, nearly two-thirds of McKasy's campaign staff had worked two years earlier for the unsuccessful Quist campaign (deFiebre 1996b).

Despite these endeavors, McKasy faced two difficulties. First, he was an undistinguished campaigner and never developed a coherent, visible ad campaign in the weeks leading up to the state convention (Baden 1996b). Second, McKasy was perceived by Christian conservatives as somewhat disingenuous about his own social conservative credentials. He had never campaigned on a strong social-issues platform in the past, and he had worked previously for moderate Republicans Carlson and Durenberger.

In short, McKasy was not an effective candidate, and his chances of defeating the well-financed Boschwitz were further reduced by the attacks of a third GOP contender. Monti Moreno—a political newcomer, evangelical Christian, former Golden Gloves boxer, and hairdresser by trade—made his mark in the race by distributing photocopies of AIDS awareness pamphlets that included graphic illustrations of gay sex, which he claimed came from a high school sex-education class. In passing out this literature, he would point out that McKasy had voted to legalize sodomy as a state legislator in 1983 (Smith 1996k). Throughout the campaign Moreno was relentless in his assaults against McKasy and "the homosexual agenda."

In a straw poll conducted on the first caucus night, McKasy received nonbinding support from 40 percent of the delegates (60 percent is required for convention endorsement), while Moreno and Boschwitz gained 20 percent each (Smith 1996k). As the convention neared, the endorsement choice for Republicans came down to McKasy or nobody; Moreno was considered too much of an unknown and extremist, while Boschwitz burned his bridges by flouting the endorsement process in favor of the primary, regardless of the convention outcome. Even local media began to refer to McKasy's "presumed victory" (Smith 1996h), and when the convention began, Boschwitz aides conceded that a McKasy endorsement was inevitable despite the favorite's weaknesses (Smith 1996d).

From the outset, the state convention did not go as planned. Moreno energized the crowd with a rousing speech, during which he raised a musket over his head and proclaimed, "If you can't do it by ballots, you've got to do it with bullets" (Smith 1996f). This speech, combined with the questions about McKasy's commitment to their agenda, led Christian Right activists in the end not to support McKasy strongly enough. Boschwitz still had no chance of gaining the endorsement for himself (never topping 40 percent), but he was able to prevent a McKasy triumph through the combination of his own support and the action of delegates who became fed up and left the convention, effectively abstaining. After fourteen ballots spanning two days, the delegates finally decided to endorse no Senate candidate in the Republican primary (deFiebre 1996a).

The failure to gain the endorsement was the final blow to McKasy's candidacy. Without the support of the party to give him a needed boost for the primary, and more than forty points behind in the preprimary polls, McKasy withdrew from the race (Baden 1996a) and cleared the way for Boschwitz to win the primary with more than 80 percent of the vote (Baden 1996c).

The perception arising from the convention endorsement fiasco was that Republicans rejected McKasy because they were unwilling "to make the same mistake they'd made in 1994" (*Minneapolis Star Tribune* 1996a). This reasoning suggests that McKasy was indeed the candidate of Christian conservatives and these conservatives had become less dogmatic in the past two years. In reality, the situation differed significantly from the perception and from the 1994 circumstances. Boschwitz was clearly not a perfect candidate from the Christian Right's perspective, but he was not nearly as anathema as Governor Carlson. On the other hand, McKasy may have actively courted the Christian Right, but he did not have the same natural attraction and credentials as Allen Quist. In short, 1996 turned out different from 1994, not because of any change in the makeup of Republican convention delegates, but because of the differences between the candidates involved.

Media Coverage of Candidates and Religious Ties

A content analysis of political coverage by the *Minneapolis Star Tribune* also supports the notion that the 1996 Republican Senate race differed significantly from the 1994 race, most notably in the degree to which endorsement candidates were described in religious terms. The *Star Tribune* has the largest readership of any paper in the state, and therefore the largest probable impact on the public. We examined all articles published from 1 January through 29 October 1996. The tables also include findings from a similar content analysis done during the 1994 campaign, to serve as a benchmark.

We hypothesize that among the 1996 candidates, newspaper coverage will describe Moreno most often in religious terms, followed by McKasy and

Boschwitz. And in comparison to the two main Christian conservative candidates of 1994, Allen Quist and Rod Grams, the number of references will be substantially lower in 1996.

Coding

Star Tribune articles were coded to differentiate among sections of the paper, date, and length of stories. Word counts were used to balance the discrepancies in the number and length of articles that cover the three candidates; not surprisingly, Moreno received lighter coverage throughout the campaign.

Once we identified and sorted articles by type, we analyzed the data base to find religious references to Boschwitz, McKasy, and Moreno. The terms selected for testing were: *religion* (or any word with the root *relig*), *Christian* (or any word with the root *Christ*, excluding *Christmas*), *church*, *Lutheran*, *Evangelical*, *fundamentalist*, *theology* (or any word with the root *theol*), *pray/prayer/praying*, *Bible/biblical*, *born again*, *worship*, *zealot*, *God*, and *cult*. With appropriate controls for article length and type, the results of the analysis are presented in tables 12.1and 12.2.

Frequencies of Religious References

Within this period, the selected terms were used a total of 94 times in articles referring to the three Republican candidates. Table 12.1 shows that while 52 percent of the references describe Boschwitz, 28 percent describe McKasy, and only 20 percent describe Moreno, the amount of coverage drives these differences. Once this is controlled for, as predicted, the references to Moreno

Table 12.1
Frequency of Religious References for Selected Republican Candidates, 1994 and 1996 Campaigns, *Minneapolis Star Tribune*

	References	Words	Words per reference
1996			
Boschwitz	49	273,184	5,575.18
McKasy	26	92,905	3,573.27
Moreno	19	33,899	1,784.16
1994			
Quist	251	92,432	368.26
Grams	83	152,333	1,835.34

Source: Author's calculations from 1994 and 1996 *Minneapolis Star Tribune*.

Table 12.2
Content of Religious References for Selected Republican Candidates, 1994 and 1996
Campaigns, *Minneapolis Star Tribune* (percentages in parentheses)

Term	Quist	Boschwitz	McKasy	Moreno
Religion/religious	88	10	7	2
	(35.1)	(20.4)	(27.0)	(10.5)
Christ/Christian	41	13	3	7
	(16.3)	(25.5)	(10.3)	(36.8)
Church	30	11	5	2
	(12.0)	(22.4)	(17.2)	(10.5)
Lutheran	40	0	0	0
	(15.9)	(0.0)	(0.0)	(0.0)
Evangelical	4	0	1	1
	(1.6)	(0.0)	(3.4)	(5.3)
Fundamentalist	8	1	1	0
	(3.2)	(2.0)	(3.4)	(0.0)
Pray/prayer	6	10	8	0
	(2.4)	(20.4)	(27.6)	(0.0)
Bible/biblical	2	0	0	2
	(0.8)	(0.0)	(0.0)	(10.5)
Theology/theologian	1	0	0	0
	(0.4)	(0.0)	(0.0)	(0.0)
Worship	3	0	0	0
	(1.2)	(0.0)	(0.0)	(0.0)
Zealot	7	1	1	3
	(2.8)	(2.0)	(3.4)	(15.8)
God	12	2	0	1
	(4.8)	(4.1)	(0.0)	(5.3)
Cult	4	1	0	0
	(1.6)	(2.0)	(0.0)	(0.0)
Born again	5	0	0	1
	(2.0)	(0.0)	(0.0)	(5.3)

Source: Author's calculations from 1994 and 1996 *Minneapolis Star Tribune.*

appear about three times as often as references to Boschwitz and twice as often as references to McKasy.

More interesting is the comparison between 1994 and 1996. The lower part of table 12.1 shows that in 1996 the *Star Tribune* referenced religious cues about the candidates much less often than in 1994. Certainly Quist was tied more closely to religiously motivated activists than was McKasy or

Boschwitz. However, Christian conservatives played a much more prominent and visible role in Moreno's campaign than in Rod Grams's, yet the two candidates are described at essentially the same rate. McKasy, depicted by the press as the candidate of Christian conservatives in 1996, is described in religious terms less often than either Quist or Grams was in 1994.

Specific Content of References

Table 12.2 indicates the differences in the content of the religious references made about the three candidates in 1996, with data for Allen Quist in 1994 again included. Nearly half the references (48 percent) describing Boschwitz are either *Christian* or *church*—a faith he does not hold and a place he does not attend. These references arise primarily in articles describing his difficulties with Republican Christian conservatives. The references to *pray/prayer* also fit this pattern, involving instances when Boschwitz voted against school prayer restoration while in the Senate.

Another pattern helps to develop a clearer picture of the impact of these terms. Three-fourths of the references to Quist and Moreno are descriptive— that is, they are adjectives that indicate something about the candidates themselves—while less than half the references to Boschwitz or McKasy are descriptive. Thus, the small number of religious cues about these candidates describes them personally less often than do references for Moreno and Quist.

Content Analysis Conclusions

The findings outlined in the tables lead to two different judgments about the 1996 Republican Senate campaign. First, Bert McKasy was not the candidate of the Christian conservatives that popular wisdom made him out to be. Second, religious cues about the candidates were less salient to the media than in 1994. Neither conclusion is surprising in light of how the state convention turned out. The amount of coverage and cues does not reveal the difficulties; Christian conservatives are organized enough that they do not rely on the popular media for voting cues, as evidenced by Rod Grams's success among the Christian Right in the 1994 Senate campaign. Rather, the content of the coverage indicated that McKasy was not truly a Christian conservative. He never publicly specified his religious beliefs or identification; in combination with his legislative voting record and ties to GOP moderates, this fact makes McKasy's problems clear and shows why they were insurmountable.

As to the second idea, neither of the two main candidates for the 1996 endorsement was described in religious terms nearly as frequently as Quist or Grams was in 1994. In fact, the number of religious references made in 1996 is dwarfed by references during the previous campaign, indicating that the media did not see the issue as relevant in 1996. As opposed to 1994, where religion had to be included in the coverage because it appeared to be the only way to explain the success of the Quist candidacy, in 1996 no candidate (save perhaps Moreno) prompted this type of explanation.

Presidential Politics

Christian conservatives may have played a much smaller role in the high-profile races of 1996 than in 1994. However, an examination of the Minnesota delegation to the Republican National Convention in San Diego reveals that not all influence is geared toward success at the ballot box. The delegates to the GOP national convention from Minnesota are selected in the same state convention that endorses statewide candidates. Thus the composition of this delegation indicates exactly where the power in the party rested in 1996. It turns out that Christian conservatives dominated the Minnesota Republican convention delegation as they did few others in the country.

A survey of the national convention delegates indicates this dominance. Table 12.3 shows the thirty-three-member Minnesota delegation clearly sitting further to the right than national convention delegates. On abortion, the Minnesota delegates are solidly pro-life and more likely to be personally involved in the issue by belonging to at least one pro-life organization. Furthermore, the

Table 12.3
Opinions of Minnesota versus National Republican Convention Delegates
on Social Issues (in percent)

	Minnesota Delegates	National Delegates
Abortion		
"Should be up to a woman and her doctor."	0	24
"Should be legal only in cases of rape, incest, or when mother's life is at risk."	64	47
"Should be illegal in all circumstances."	27	12
"Are you a supporter of . . . an antiabortion group." (yes)	64	47
Issue Importance		
Social issues are more important.	39	21
Fiscal issues are more important.	21	56

Source: Minneapolis Star Tribune, 4 August 1996.

Minnesota delegates are more likely to emphasize social issues over fiscal ones and more likely to support an increased role for the Christian Right in the Republican Party.

Perhaps the strongest indicator in table 12.3 is the apparent litmus test on abortion. No Minnesota delegates believed abortion should be up to a woman and her doctor. When confronted with this, members of the delegation pointed to a single alternate delegate who was pro-choice as a sign of inclusiveness within the party (Smith 1996c). Even with this token exception, Minnesota's delegation was without doubt a stronghold of social conservatives.

The demographic composition of the delegation provides further evidence on this point. The delegate survey shows that although 40 percent of all delegates earned more than $100,000 a year and only 15 percent earned less than $50,000, the numbers for Minnesota delegates are 12 percent and 42 percent, respectively (Smith 1996j). Only 6 percent of Minnesota's delegates held elective office, versus 38 percent of all delegates. In this and other respects, the Minnesota delegation reflected the caucus-convention selection process that continues to be controlled by the Christian Right.

A final indication of the distinctiveness of the members of the Minnesota delegation to San Diego comes from their presidential preferences. Minnesota has no presidential primary, and with its small number of delegates chosen late in the presidential primary season, the state is essentially irrelevant to the nomination race. Based on the survey results, this constituted good news for Bob Dole, for table 12.4 indicates that Minnesota delegates were not among Dole's earliest or most ardent supporters. Phil Gramm was the clear first choice of Minnesota delegates. Allen Quist, who helped organize the original effort for Gramm, publicly backed Pat Buchanan after Gramm withdrew from the race (Smith 1996b). While we do not suggest that Christian conservatives are a monolithic group that would follow Quist anywhere, the survey results and the issue positions of the candidates imply that Buchanan and Alan Keyes were the most immediate beneficiaries of Gramm's early departure from the race.

Support for presumptive nominee Dole remained lukewarm even in San Diego. Only 52 percent of Minnesota delegates were "very favorable" toward Dole, versus 72 percent of all delegates. By contrast, the numbers for Newt Gingrich were almost the exact opposite, with 73 percent of Minnesotans giving him a "very favorable" rating compared to 54 percent of national delegates (Smith 1996j).

Overall, the San Diego delegation may be the best indicator of the dominance of Christian conservatives in Minnesota. National convention delegates are chosen from within the ranks of party activists and elected officials. A quick perusal of the thirty-three names reveals the leaders of the state's three most influential Christian Right groups: the Minnesota Concerned Citizens for

Table 12.4
Presidential Preferences of Minnesota versus National Republican Convention
Delegates (in percent)

	Minnesota Delegates	National Delegates
Candidate Originally Supported		
Bob Dole	21	62
Phil Gramm	55	11
Alan Keyes	15	2
Pat Buchanan	3	9
Impression of Dole		
Very favorable	52	72
Somewhat favorable	39	19
Somewhat unfavorable	3	2
Very unfavorable	0	1
Impression of Gingrich		
Very favorable	73	54
Somewhat favorable	15	30
Somewhat unfavorable	3	5
Very unfavorable	0	1

Source: Minneapolis Star Tribune, 4 August 1996.

Life (MCCL), the Minnesota Christian Coalition (MNCC), and the Minnesota Family Council (MFC) (Smith 1996j). Several other delegates represent conservative groups or are often quoted by the media and appear on public affairs programs. The strong social conservative slant of this delegation indicates that Christian conservatives remain well positioned in the state GOP, regardless of the outcome of endorsement or electoral battles.

General Elections Results

Senate and President

In the Senate race, Paul Wellstone won a surprisingly decisive victory over Rudy Boschwitz. While preelection polls indicated a modest Wellstone lead, he was declared the victor immediately after the polls closed (Ragsdale 1996). Christian conservatives had a clear choice in this race between the most liberal member of the Senate and the good but less-than-perfect Boschwitz. Wellstone counted on his grassroots mobilizing efforts, developed during his first campaign and maintained through successive election cycles. Boschwitz hoped that the mobilization of Christian conservatives would help offset this advantage. In the end, Wellstone's success may indicate the weakness of these groups in Minnesota, particularly in higher-turnout elections. While Christian conservatives get the motivated core to the caucuses in March, they have not been able to replicate this success in November to the same degree as in other states. Thus, the difference between 1994 and 1996 may come down to the fact that in 1994 there was no presidential election to help mobilize voters, and the 1994 Democratic Senate candidate did not have the same organizational capabilities as Wellstone in 1996.

The Republicans more or less conceded the presidential race in Minnesota from the outset. While Bill Clinton made frequent trips to the state throughout his presidency, Bob Dole hired "one lone operative" to staff his Saint Paul headquarters and made but one personal appearance during the race. Minnesota may not be as liberal as it once was, but in this election it was clear from the beginning that Clinton was unbeatable, and in fact he gained a decisive victory in November. No amount of Christian conservative activity would likely have prevented such an outcome; nevertheless, the movement's failure to mount any type of opposition is striking.

County-Level Vote Analysis

In the 1994 elections, our aggregate analysis of county voting patterns showed that candidates affiliated with the Christian Right gained more votes in counties with higher levels of religious adherence (Gilbert and Peterson 1995, 182–85). Absent a clear Christian Right candidate in 1996, the patterns emerging from county-level data are murky, to say the least. The best extant measure of Christian conservative strength in a county is its share of the 1994 primary vote for Allen Quist; this factor correlates positively with voting for Dole but not with voting for Boschwitz. Dole also gains from counties that have shown long-term support for GOP candidates. By contrast, Boschwitz was hurt by the inability of the Christian conservatives to match Wellstone's mobilization efforts on election day; he gains little from the religious characteristics of Minnesota counties.

Congressional Races

One explanation for the lack of Christian Right involvement in the presidential race is that scarce resources were directed instead to congressional and state legislative races. Three of Minnesota's eight congressional races stand out in this regard. In the First District (southeast), first-term GOP incumbent

Gil Gutknecht was opposed by college professor and former Republican Mary Rieder. This race pitted the two most active interest groups in the campaign head to head in a key swing congressional district. Beginning early in the campaign, the AFL-CIO aired ads against Gutknecht in its campaign to win back the House for the Democrats. The Christian Coalition countered with large amounts of soft money supporting Gutknecht. Rieder closed a 20-point gap, but Gutknecht prevailed with 52 percent of the vote. The national office of the Christian Coalition was a decisive factor in the race, compensating for the relatively weak organization of the MNCC in the state.

In the Sixth District (northern Twin Cities suburbs) Minnesota's other first term representative, Democrat Bill Luther, faced a rematch with Republican opponent Tad Jude. In 1994, Jude ran on a strident antiabortion, social-issue platform, hoping to ride the tide of the Quist and Grams campaigns. In a year when this strategy might have been expected to work, Luther prevailed by only 550 votes. Believing that the political winds had shifted, in 1996 Jude ran as a fiscal conservative, distancing himself from the Christian Right and its core social issues. The results were the same, but the outcome was more decisive, as Luther outspent Jude by a wide margin and won reelection with 56 percent of the vote. Jude's campaign tactics and the outcome again point to the weakness of the Christian Right in elections with higher voter turnout.

Finally, the race in the Seventh District pitted three-term DFL incumbent Colin Peterson against first-time candidate Darrel McKigney. The Seventh District covers the northwestern region of Minnesota, an area more socially conservative than the rest of the state. Peterson fit the district well, frequently deserting congressional Democrats on spending and social-issue votes. In fact, for several months prior to the election, he contemplated switching over to the GOP. McKigney also possessed impeccable Christian conservative credentials, serving as a very effective and visible legislative director for the Minnesota Family Council; prior to that, he worked as an aide to Representative Jim Ramstad and former representatives Vin Weber and Rod Grams (Smith 1996e). While McKigney was unsuccessful in his bid (he received only 32 percent of the vote), his candidacy itself illustrates how Christian conservatives in Minnesota have sought to gain power at different levels of office.

State Legislature

This was billed as the year that the Republican Party would take over the Minnesota House of Representatives. The party made significant gains in 1994 by electing eleven new Christian Right–backed candidates (Baden 1994), and the intervening two years saw a remarkable series of scandals rock the DFL in the state house, leaving a tight 68-66 DFL margin heading into the

1996 contest. Consistent with the other results in November, the Republicans were shocked to discover that not only did they fail to retake the House, but also many of the Christian conservatives who had stormed into office in 1994 were defeated, leaving a 70-64 DFL majority in place (Whereatt 1996). This is perhaps the most surprising of any of the election results. Christian conservatives usually have the biggest organizational advantage at the local levels, as demonstrated in 1994. This time, the dominant pro-DFL voting pattern of the state, buoyed by strong showings from Clinton and Wellstone at the top of the ticket, emerged again to overcome any organizational advantages held by the Christian Right.

Lessons from Christian Right Activity

In the end, the state legislative results demonstrate the limitations of Christian conservative influence in Minnesota. While Christian conservatives can dominate the Republican Party and be successful in elections with low voter interest and weak DFL ticket leaders (as in 1994), the strength of Christian Right groups like MCCL and MFC lies in lobbying and public relations, not in mobilization to win elections. The best electoral potential should rest with the MNCC, but to date the MNCC has not shown the ability to generate the kind of grassroots groundswell that can swing elections to the GOP (Gilbert et al. 1996). In high-turnout elections, against the skillful organization of a Paul Wellstone or the popularity of a Bill Clinton leading the DFL slate, Christian Right organizations can succeed in Minnesota only by forming coalitions with broader cross sections of the Republican Party, a strategy favored by pragmatic politicians like Vin Weber but at odds with the ideological fervor that leads many Christian Right activists to engage in politics in the first place.

This conclusion should not be taken as a dismissal of the Christian Right in Minnesota. A typical Republican candidate needs the 25 percent to 30 percent of the electorate affiliated with Christian conservative causes to win. Moreover, this branch of the party played a vital role in defining who would represent the party both at the national convention and on the state primary ballot. The evidence from 1994 and 1996 points to one overarching conclusion: Christian conservatives are, above all else, issue driven. They may care deeply about candidates, but that is not the primary focus of their energies.

Understanding this leads to a series of corollary conclusions from the Minnesota experience. First, focusing on the top of the ticket is probably not the best way to examine the role of Christian conservatives. In Minnesota, the cursory evidence from the 1996 Senate and presidential races indicates that the influence of Christian conservatives has waned in the past two years. But at lower levels, their dominance of the endorsement process and control of party resources is insurmountable. Operating "under the radar" of media scrutiny, the quiet selection of delegates to San Diego represented the most decisive intraparty triumph of 1996.

A second corollary is that the media miss this role because of the traditional manner in which they cover politics, namely, focusing on the candidates themselves more than on party officials or issues. While the press continues to learn the nuances of reporting on religiously motivated candidates and groups, the evidence from 1996 suggests that the preferred form of coverage is still candidate centered, and therefore the role and significance of Christian conservative candidates and causes continue to be underestimated.

Christian conservatives will be mobilized and involved in Minnesota state politics no matter who runs for office under the Republican banner. When conditions are favorable—low turnout in midterm or special elections, weak DFL opponents, low-visibility activities like delegate selection, or targeting of state legislative districts in the Twin Cities suburbs—the potential for success will be high. While the Christian Right will continue to dominate the state Republican Party into the foreseeable future (barring some significant changes in the caucus-convention process), how much this carries over to general elections will depend largely on how involved others are in the elections. The 1996 race in the First Congressional District indicates that when Christian conservatives are truly energized behind a candidate and the setting is right, they can be successful despite the best effort of their opposition. Thus, the question in the future will be not, how strong are the Minnesota Christian conservatives? but rather, how strong is their opposition?

References

Baden, Patricia Lopez. 1994. "Religious Right Sees Its Influence in IR House Wins." *Minneapolis Star Tribune* (23 November).
———.1996a. "McKasy Ends His Quest for Senate Nomination." *Minneapolis Star Tribune* (24 July).
———.1996b. "McKasy Exudes Confidence in Uphill GOP Senate Battle." *Minneapolis Star Tribune* (3 July).
———.1996c. "Primary, Polls Rouse U.S. Senate Campaigns." *Minneapolis Star Tribune* (12 September).
Barone, Michael, and Grant Ujifusa. 1993. *The Almanac of American Politics, 1994.* Washington, D.C.: National Journal.
Bradley, Martin, et al., eds. 1992. *Churches and Church Membership in the United States.* Atlanta: Glenmary Research Center.

deFiebre, Conrad. 1996a. "GOP Backs No Senate Candidate." *Minneapolis Star Tribune* (2 June).

————.1996b. "The Race to Face Paul Wellstone." *Minneapolis Star Tribune* (29 February).

Elazar, Daniel, Virginia Gray, and Wy Spano. 1997. *Minnesota: The Government and Politics of the North Star State.* Lincoln: University of Nebraska Press.

Gilbert, Christopher P,. and David A. Peterson. 1995. "Minnesota: Christians and Quistians in the GOP." Chap. 9 in *God at the Grass Roots: The Christian Right in the 1994 Elections,* ed. Mark J. Rozell and Clyde Wilcox. Lanham, Md.: Rowman & Littlefield.

Gilbert, Christopher P., Jeffrey Gustafson, Joel A. Johnson, and Paul Mueller. 1996. "Strategy, Issues, and Voter Impact: Christian Right School Board Candidacies in Urban and Suburban Contexts." Paper presented at Midwest Political Science Association annual meeting, Chicago.

Haas, Cliff. 1992. "Life of the Party: Issues and Ideas Man Vin Weber Sets His Sights on Reviving GOP." *Minneapolis Star Tribune* (22 November).

Hoium, David, and Leo Oistad. 1991. *There Is No November.* Inver Grove Heights, Minn.: Jeric Publications.

Marshall, Thomas R. 1980. "Minnesota: The Party Caucus-Convention System." In *Party Renewal in America: Theory and Practice,* ed. Gerald M. Pomper. New Brunswick, N.J.: Eagleton Institute of Politics.

McGrath, Dennis, and Dane Smith. 1995. *Professor Wellstone Goes to Washington: The Inside Story of a Grassroots U.S. Senate Campaign.* Minneapolis: University of Minnesota Press.

Minneapolis Star Tribune. 1996a. Editorial. (2 June).

Minneapolis Star Tribune. 1996b. "The State Republican Convention." (1 June).

Ragsdale, Jim. 1996. "Wellstone Wins Big in Senate Rematch." *Saint Paul Pioneer Press* (6 November).

Schmickle, Sharon. 1996. "It's a Different GOP for McKasy and Boschwitz." *Minneapolis Star Tribune* (3 June).

Smith, Dane. 1992. "Tuesday's IR Losses Bound to Bring Changes in Strategy." *Minneapolis Star Tribune* (8 November).

————. 1993. "Carlson Must Speak Softly and Carry the IR Right." *Minneapolis Star Tribune* (13 September).

————. 1996a. "Boschwitz Would Buck Party, Run in Primary." *Minneapolis Star Tribune* (10 April).

————. 1996b. "Buchanan Wins Support from Quist and Others Who Had Backed Gramm." *Minneapolis Star Tribune* (17 February).

————. 1996c. "Decision on GOP Abortion Plank Pleases State Delegation." *Minneapolis Star Tribune* (7 August).

————. 1996d. "GOP Backs No Senate Candidate." *Minneapolis Star Tribune* (2 June).

————. 1996e. "McKigney Wins GOP Backing in Seventh." *Minneapolis Star Tribune* (28 April).

———. 1996f. "Moreno Vows to Stick to His Guns." *Minneapolis Star Tribune* (4 July).

———. 1996g. "The Race to Face Paul Wellstone." *Minneapolis Star Tribune* (28 February).

———. 1996h. "Republican State Convention." *Minneapolis Star Tribune* (30 May).

———. 1996i. "Rudolph Ely Boschwitz: Believer in the American Dream." *Minneapolis Star Tribune* (24 October).

———. 1996j. "State Delegates Will Be on the Right at GOP Convention." *Minneapolis Star Tribune* (4 August).

———. 1996k. "Zealous Young Candidate Stirs Up Senate Race." *Minneapolis Star Tribune* (27 April).

Triggs, Mike. 1994. "Zombie Conservatives Decimate IR Faithful." *Minneapolis Star Tribune* (12 April).

Whereatt, Robert. 1994. "Governor Hands DFL Its Biggest Defeat." *Minneapolis Star Tribune* (7 November).

———. 1996. "DFL Speaker Battle Begins." *Minneapolis Star Tribune* (7 November).

13

Kansas: The Christian Right and the New Mainstream of Republican Politics

Allan J. Cigler and Burdett A. Loomis

Kansas has a tradition of religious involvement in its political life. The Kansas-Nebraska Act of 1854 led to an influx of large numbers of Republican abolitionists from New England into Kansas as the territory became a central battleground for contending free- and slave-state forces. The victory of the former, linked to the establishment of what Daniel Elazar (1972) has termed the "moralistic culture," proved to be the catalyst for the 1861 creation of a Republican-dominated state. From statehood to the New Deal, Kansans played prominent leadership roles in various religious and moralistic movements, including abolition, populism, progressivism, and prohibition, all directly linked to the Republican Party.

Kansas's partisan tendencies survived even the powerful national forces that brought about the critical realignments of the 1890s and 1930s. In recent decades Democrats have been able to gain occasional short-run electoral advantage, especially at the gubernatorial level, by exploiting regionally based splits within the Republican Party, but there has been little evidence of the kind of durable voter shifts characteristic of partisan realignment (Cigler and Loomis 1992). Near the end of the twentieth century, Kansas remains staunchly Republican in its orientation, particularly in presidential voting, and it stands as the only state not to have elected at least one Democratic senator since the 1930s.

What has changed markedly in Kansas politics in recent years is the resurgence of long-quiescent religious forces within the Republican Party. Since the New Deal, Kansas Republicanism has been characterized more by fiscal than social conservatism. Nationally prominent Kansans such as former Senate majority leader and ex–presidential candidate Robert Dole and former senators Nancy Landon Kassebaum, James Pearson, and Frank Carlsen, in varying degrees, developed reputations as deficit fighters, uneasy with the expansion of government and the accompanying increasing tax burden, but not anxious to elevate social issues on the political agenda, despite their varying degrees of personal social conservatism.

The late 1980s and 1990s witnessed the rise of a new breed of party activist and politician on the state's political landscape: connected to the Christian Right, fiscally conservative, yet convinced that government action must be taken to reverse the perceived moral decline of the nation. The result has been an internecine conflict within the Republican Party that has greatly altered the style and intensity of the state's electoral politics. The 1996 election results represent the apex of the new trend.

The Growth of the Christian Right in Kansas

Kansas has long had a segment of its population that has been attracted to the broad social and economic agenda that has come to be labeled "Christian Right," a term often used to describe citizens who intensely hold conservative views on abortion, gay and lesbian rights, school prayer, sex education, school vouchers, and other issues that make up the "family values" political agenda. As elsewhere, Kansas Christian Right adherents are alarmed by unwholesome societal trends that they believe to be caused by the secularization of American culture, such as increases in crime, violence, sexual promiscuity, and social diseases and an erosion of the work ethic and performance in the public schools. The Kansas populist tradition is quite compatible with the Christian Right agenda, with its distrust of government, big business, political party, and mainstream media elites on one hand and, on the other, suspicion of the underclass, particularly racial minorities, ostensibly the major beneficiaries of welfare, child support, education, and other government initiatives. From the New Deal to the early 1970s, however, organized political efforts from religious sources were active only intermittently in Kansas, typically at the fringes of mainstream politics. The John Birch Society had a presence in Kansas, as did other groups whose message merged Christianity and anticommunism, such as the Defenders of the Christian Faith, the Christian Patriots, and the Mid-America League for Constitutional Government.

The 1973 Supreme Court decision in *Roe v. Wade* proved to be the galvanizing event that propelled the contemporary Christian Right movement in the state, as opposition to abortion gave Christian activists a sharp focus that they had previously lacked (Sigman 1996). The immediate post-*Roe* period saw the rise of a number of right-to-life groups, as well as the activization of individual Protestant church congregations and Catholic parishes. The target of the loosely coordinated efforts was usually the state legislature.[1]

In 1974, for the first time, antiabortion activists played a pivotal role in a major electoral contest. Senator Dole was strongly challenged by Democratic congressman William Roy, a physician who had previously performed a number of abortions while practicing in a Topeka hospital. Senator Dole had come under attack for his connection to the then-disgraced Nixon White House, and he trailed Representative Roy late in the race. Two days before the election, antiabortion activists engineered a massive grassroots "drop" of an anti-Roy pamphlet, which included a picture of an aborted fetus. Caught off guard by the last-minute charges, Congressman Roy failed to respond and lost to Dole by a small margin. Antiabortion forces, comprising both conservative Catholics and fundamentalist Protestants, had demonstrated their political might. More generally, however, social conservative forces, including antiabortion activists, stayed out of electoral politics during the 1970s. For example, Jerry Falwell's Moral Majority had virtually no impact upon the Kansas political scene.

The nature of social-issue politics changed markedly in the early 1980s. Until that time Kansas had on the books some of the most restrictive liquor and morality laws in the country, reflecting the religious, rural character of the state. But the declining rural influence in the legislature and the state's deteriorating economic condition combined to create a new context for morality issues. The Kansas economy was highly dependent for its economic growth on agriculture and the rural-based oil and gas industry, two sectors that did not experience economic recovery in the 1980s. As in the other Plains states, many small towns in Kansas dependent on the farm economy were in deep trouble, as grain commodity and energy prices remained low. Government officials turned their attention to diversifying the economy and attracting industry.

In order to compete with other states in attracting business, a number of government decision makers thought it necessary to remake the state's image. Morality issues again came to the forefront, in large part through the larger debate over economic development. The state did away with requirements to sell liquor only by the drink, adopted a lottery, and allowed for wagering on dog and horse racing, measures that were widely viewed as filling state coffers and contributing to an image of a more modern, more cosmopolitan Kansas.

Not surprisingly, the consideration of such intensely charged morality issues mobilized some sectors of the electorate. Kansas experienced a great proliferation of single-issue groups, of both culturally conservative and culturally liberal persuasions—a classic case of quiescent interests forced to respond when social issues are politicized (Cigler and Kiel 1993). Groups such as Kansans for Pari-Mutuel and the Kansas Greyhound Owners Association arose to challenge long-established morality groups such as Kansans for Life at Its Best. Antiabortion groups such as Right to Life of Kansas and Kansans for Life now faced well-organized opposition from state chapters of the

National Organization for Women (NOW) and Planned Parenthood. Even peak associations, such as the Kansas Chamber of Commerce and Industry and the Kansas Farm Bureau, often on opposite sides, became involved in the new highly charged issue context. Most of the battles were fought out in the Kansas legislature, rather than in elections.

By the late 1980s Kansas had in place a diverse collection of formally organized groups representing culturally conservative interests, most religiously based. A number of individual congregations were involved in the new issue context as well. The most visible was the Topeka Baptist church congregation headed by the Reverend Fred Phelps, who developed a national reputation for his crusade against homosexuality by demonstrating outside gay bars and picketing the state's higher-education institutions, which had funded gay and lesbian student groups. But there was little unity or even cooperation among the various elements of the Christian Right. Antiabortion forces, such as Randall Terry's Operation Rescue, based in Wichita, were more focused upon picketing abortion clinics than upon electoral politics per se. The Pat Robertson campaign in 1988 served as a catalyst for a more unified role for the Christian Right in Kansas electoral politics through the Republican Party.

The Christian Right and the Republican Party

While the Republican Party dominates state electoral politics in Kansas, state and local party organizations have always been weak (Mayhew 1986). The parties have traditionally played a relatively minor role in the recruitment of candidates, and "legislative candidates are pretty much on their own in running for office" (Grumm 1967, 51). The party organization has been open enough that concerted special-interest efforts to capture the formal organization have a high probability of success.

The first major effort by elements of the Christian Right to influence Republican Party politics directly came in the spring of 1988, when Robertson's Christian Coalition supporters, largely made up of members of individual congregations throughout the state, attempted to stack the Republican state and local caucuses entrusted with the selection of national convention delegates. Senator Dole, the acknowledged leader of the state party and himself a candidate for the presidential nomination, was more than mildly irritated by what he viewed as Christian Right efforts to embarrass him on his home turf. The Dole forces prevailed, thanks to a major mobilization of party regulars in the final two weeks, but tension between Republican moderates and insurgent Christian Right activists rose markedly.

Divisions between moderates and Christian Right adherents extended into the Kansas legislature in 1988 as well. A group of social-conservative legisla-tors, including state representative David Miller, who was critical of the Republican leadership for not pursuing a socially conservative agenda, were cut off from house Republican political action committee (PAC) money, with the blessing of Governor Mike Hayden, a Republican. Subsequently, this group of Republican "rebels" proved a consistent thorn in the side of Hayden and the mainstream legislative parties (Loomis 1994). Miller, who has also served as executive director of the Christian Coalition in Kansas, later left the legislature to become the political director of Kansans for Life, the state's leading antiabortion group, and he was instrumental in convincing Nestor Weigand of Wichita, a strong antiabortion advocate, to challenge incumbent governor Hayden in the 1990 Republican gubernatorial primary, with Miller as his running mate. Hayden won a close primary contest, but his efforts to deny his opponent access to the state party's voter-identification lists solidified Christian Right opposition to his candidacy. In the general election, a pro-life Democrat, state treasurer Joan Finney, defeated Hayden, in part because many Christian Right voters crossed party lines.

By the early 1990s important figures in the Christian Right, like Miller, had become convinced that Kansas politics could be changed only if religious activists and social conservatives captured the formal Republican Party organi-zation. Throughout the state, but particularly concentrated in suburban areas such as Johnson County (the Kansas City suburban area) and Wichita, a con-certed grassroots effort sought to take over the party. Since precinct committee positions in Kansas were often vacant and had to be filled by appointment, in many cases the key was simply to find a right-thinking individual to file for the position.

Johnson County, Kansas, provides a vivid example of how the Christian Right has altered the political party at the local level (Sullinger 1996b). Table 13.1 reports the changes in competition for precinct committee seats in the county since 1990.

Before 1992 there was virtually no competition for the lowest of party posi-tions. Starting in 1992 the Christian Right groups, led by the leading antiabor-tion group in the state, Kansans for Life, gained control of the county party committee, a position it consolidated in 1994. The group developed a slate of candidates and was active in communicating its preferences to voters sympa-thetic to its cause. Individual evangelical church congregations played a major role in the takeover as well, particularly the Full Faith Church of Love West, based in Shawnee. According to a longtime observer of Johnson County poli-tics, the takeover was not difficult, since establishment party officials had become "complacent and arrogant" and were "unwilling to work in the trench-es." The large number of contested races in 1996 reflects an attempt by the

Table 13.1
Competition for Precinct Committeeman/woman Positions,
Johnson County, 1990–1996

	Contested Races	Candidates
1990	10	330
1992	94	487
1994	221	759
1996	343	935

moderate GOP Club to recapture the party organization. As in their primary
and general election efforts in 1996 (see below), they were unsuccessful.

By 1994, Christian Right adherents were firmly in control of the state
Republican Party as well. David Miller was elected state party chairperson,
despite opposition from Republican governor Bill Graves and popular senators
Dole and Kassebaum. In 1996, Miller retained his control, to the extent that he
dominated the Kansas delegation to the Republican convention that would
nominate Dole as its presidential candidate.

The Christian Right in the Electoral Process

The Christian Right in Kansas is a diverse group of socially conservative orga-
nizations and individual church congregations, which now operate to achieve
their political goals through grassroots political activity. Many of the national
Christian Right groups like the Christian Coalition, Concerned Women for
America, and Eagle Forum have a presence in Kansas, but clearly the high-
profile groups in the statewide movement are the antiabortion groups, led by
Kansans for Life, an organization with eighty chapters throughout the state.
Kansans for Life is now led by Tim Golba, called by state representative Mark
Parkinson, a Johnson County moderate, "the grassroots leader of the far right"
in Kansas (Sullinger 1996a). With close connections to the Christian Coalition, Golba is active statewide in recruiting candidates for state and federal
office, conducting candidate training schools, helping to muster volunteer support for candidates, aiding in voter education, and getting out the vote on election day. The Christian Right electoral strategies in Kansas are the standard
ones of grassroots politics.

A few of the Christian Right organizations have political action committees. Kansas Right to Life, Inc., has a separate state political action committee,
KRTLPAC, that contributes to U.S. House and Senate campaigns in the state,
but the parent organization technically makes no endorsements in elections. It

does send to its members, however, the results of a candidate survey dealing with pro-life issues (most pro-choice advocates do not respond), including information about whether KRTLPAC has endorsed each candidate. Dissemination of voter guides is a common electoral strategy of Christian Right groups in the state.

In recent years Christian Right groups have worked closely with certain groups not normally thought of as part of the movement. In 1994 in Wichita, right-to-life groups coordinated their grassroots efforts with the National Rifle Association (NRA) to unseat U.S. Representative Dan Glickman, who had both supported abortion rights and voted for the Brady bill. The winner, state senator Todd Tiahrt, a political unknown and a substantial underdog in the race, was himself elevated from the ranks of Christian Right activists, a first for the movement in Kansas.

Not all Christian Right organizations in the state focus on the election of high-profile officials. Increasingly important is Kansas Education Watch Network (KEW-NET), a group dedicated to electing Christian Right candidates to the state board of education. The state board sets guidelines on curriculum and education; it has ultimate authority for goals and policies in public schools. The aims of the organization include electing candidates who would eliminate sex education classes, advocate abstinence as the only proper approach to sexual relations before marriage, and encourage Christian messages in public schools to give students a sense of right and wrong (Beem 1996).[2]

Despite the successes of the Christian Right in Republican Party politics, most Kansans, including Republicans, do not completely share the movement's views on social issues such as abortion and what should be taught in the public schools. Christian Right strategies in the general election, as a consequence, have maintained a low profile and have downplayed social issues. The 1996 elections illustrate vividly the difficulties encountered by Christian Right candidates when they face what is still a relatively moderate Republican electorate. Moreover, winning elections often has not led to major policy changes at the state level.

The Election of 1996: The Christian Right Ascendant

At 7:01 p.m. central standard time on 5 November 1996, the networks, to no one's surprise, called the Kansas presidential result for native son Bob Dole. Moments later, Representative Pat Roberts, a traditional Republican in the Dole mold, was declared the victor in his Senate race (for the seat held by retiring senator Nancy Kassebaum). With those two wins, "your father's Republican Party" essentially exited from Kansas politics. Despite this home-state victory,

Dole's presidential bid was already dead in the water, and Roberts, who was tolerated by the party's Christian Right wing, will probably serve two six-year terms, voting in a predictable, solidly conservative manner.

The rest of election night reflected the extent to which Kansas politics had changed since the late 1980s. Three of the state's four House seats went to candidates firmly in the Christian Right camp, and freshman representative Sam Brownback, a late but vigorous convert to the right's agenda, completed his rise to prominence by capturing the remaining two years of Bob Dole's Senate term. At the state level, Christian Right Republicans and their allies retained their control of the majority party in the Kansas house and have a chance to control the senate. All in all, the election demonstrated the extent to which Bob Dole's Republican Party had become—both organizationally and electorally—a party dominated by the pro-life Christian Right movement.

At the same time, moderate Republicans are not quite dead; led by popular governor Bill Graves and possessing an opportunistic willingness to combine with Democrats from time to time, the moderate faction remains a force to be reckoned with. For all the movement's electoral successes, no Christian Right agenda has come to define Kansas policy making.

Prologue: The 1994 Elections

In 1994, Kansas Republicans won a series of impressive but difficult-to-interpret electoral victories. After shrugging off a conservative challenge in the Republican primary, Secretary of State Bill Graves won an overwhelming, 30-percentage-point victory over a well-regarded Democratic opponent, moderate-to-conservative representative Jim Slattery. At the same time, Sam Brownback, a former state agriculture secretary with a moderate background (and a conservative, pro-life challenge in the primary) won Slattery's House seat convincingly over former governor John Carlin. Much to the discomfort of many moderate Republicans, Brownback enthusiastically embraced a thoroughly conservative agenda on both fiscal and social issues.

In the context of a strong Republican year, the Graves and Brownback victories were not all that surprising, but a shocking defeat was absorbed by Wichita's Dan Glickman, an eighteen-year House Democratic veteran, who lost to a first-term state senator, Todd Tiahrt. Even though Glickman had won important changes in liability laws that might well have saved the small-aircraft industry, he was excoriated for his votes to support abortion rights and gun control (Elving 1995).

Although Tiahrt ran in a favorable year for Republicans and benefited from redistricting that had increased the district's competitiveness, the energy and organization provided by the Christian Right–National Rifle Association combination proved enough to overcome Glickman. Even more than Brownback's victory, Tiahrt's win in the state's most Democratic congressional district bore witness to both the organizational and the electoral strength of the Christian Right, whose members had cut their political teeth on a decade of antiabortion protests in Wichita.

Candidates and Conservatives: The Republicans Tilt Right

The continuing presence of incumbent Republicans (and Kansas icons) Bob Dole and Nancy Landon Kassebaum in the U.S. Senate effectively squelched any possibility that an ambitious politician of either party could mount a successful challenge for one of their seats. Then, in 1995–1996, the political dam broke, first with Senator Kassebaum's declaring that she would not seek reelection and then with Senator Dole's resigning his seat in June 1996, to concentrate on his presidential campaign. Although Senator Kassebaum's decision was widely expected, Dole's abrupt departure pushed Kansas senatorial politics toward high drama. True to form for Kansas in the 1990s, the moderate–Christian Right split in the Republican Party stood at the center of virtually all decisions, most notably on candidate selection.

The Christian Right demonstrated both its sophistication and its clout in the candidate selection process. After first declaring himself out of the race for Kassebaum's seat and then reconsidering, Representative Pat Roberts was essentially given a pass by the social conservatives. A Washington veteran (as staffer and congressman), Roberts was scarcely the Christian Right's ideal outsider candidate. But he was a solid conservative and a consistent pro-life vote, as well as being an odds-on bet to win the seat. The religious conservatives kept their powder dry, and their patience was rewarded. Dole announced his resignation in mid-May, and Representative Brownback announced his candidacy almost immediately; in fact, he ran some hastily reworked television commercials within a week of his announcement.

Governor Graves took his time in selecting an interim Senate appointment and finally made a decision that confronted the Christian Right head on. He chose his lieutenant governor, Sheila Frahm, a former state senate majority leader and fiscal conservative who supported abortion rights. Frahm's appointment came less than three months before the 6 August primary, and although she reaped some initial favorable publicity, she had to contend with the dual tasks of learning at least some Senate ropes and running for the nomination. An effective, if less-than-colorful, politician in her past races, Frahm never found her footing in the 1996 race. The primary campaign was short and nasty; as the first seriously contested Senate race in eighteen years, the Brownback-Frahm contest demonstrated the harshness of the political rhetoric and the impact of money on politics, especially in a small state where media buys were relatively inexpensive.

Brownback's public, televised campaign relentlessly attacked Frahm on increasing taxes, thus raising questions about her fiscal conservatism. The private campaign emphasized social issues, as the Christian Right vigorously backed Brownback. Both Kansans for Life and the Christian Coalition distributed voter guides, often to church congregations. In addition, a less-than-anticipated turnout in the primary (506,000, compared to an expected 625,000) indicated that moderate Republicans were not rallying to the Frahm effort. Indeed, the low turnout and a 55 percent-42 percent Brownback victory raised serious questions about the electoral power of Republican moderates—a theme that would resurface in the general election.

Perhaps most noteworthy in the primary was the behavior of Republicans in the affluent Johnson County suburbs of Kansas City. Long a bastion of moderate Republicans, Johnson County voted 32,000 to 22,500 for Brownback; at the same time, its voters soundly defeated the moderate candidate to replace retiring representative Jan Meyers, a moderate Republican, and selected state representative Vince Snowbarger, who was strongly backed by religious conservatives. The Christian Right–conservative Republican forces emerged from the primary elections with a full slate of abortion opponents and either full-fledged social conservatives or candidates clearly acceptable to the right wing of the party. Looking at the Kansas results, Republican strategist Eddie Mahe made the general assessment that "Clearly, establishment Republicanism, and by implication, Dole, is not where the country's Republicanism is now" (Gugliotta 1996).

One compelling question remained outstanding: given a strong slate of moderate Democratic opponents, would Republicans clearly linked to the Christian Right be able to retain enough moderate Republican (and independent) support to win in November?

The General Elections: Whither the Moderates?

After the Republican primaries, Kansas Democrats expressed optimism, if not downright glee. Despite its tradition as one of the nation's most Republican states, Kansas has not been a place where winning the GOP nomination leads inevitably to victory in the general election. Since the 1960s, Kansas Democrats have consistently won one or two House seats (of five, prior to 1992) and have actually captured the governorship more than have Republicans. Still, both U.S. Senate seats have remained in Republican hands since the 1930s, and only twice in the last sixty years has even one state legislative chamber been held by a Democratic majority. Among registered voters, Republicans outnumber

Democrats by a 3-2 margin. Although the Christian Right has occasionally intervened in Democratic politics—for example, by offering some support to pro-life governor Joan Finney (1990–94)—for the most part Kansas Democrats have neither solicited nor received such assistance.

In 1996, Kansas Democrats sought to take advantage of the conservative primary victories as their candidates positioned themselves as social moderates (especially on abortion) on the one hand and fiscally responsible budget-balancers on the other. More important, the Democrats fielded a set of attractive, well-financed candidates who would be able to convey their moderate messages. U.S. Attorney Randy Rathbun ran against Representative Tiahrt; Judy Hancock, who had run impressively in the Third District (the Kansas City suburbs) in 1994, ran again, this time against Snowbarger; and, in the race for Brownback's seat, Topeka attorney John Frieden entered the race, promising to spend $250,000 of his own funds against former Kansas track star and darling of the Christian Right Jim Ryun. In the Senate elections, state treasurer Sally Thompson challenged Representative Roberts; and, in the glamour race of 1996, Representative Brownback found himself opposed by Wichita Democrat Jill Docking, a first-time office-seeker but the beneficiary of a storied Kansas political name (her father-in-law and his father both served as governor). Moreover, Docking was viewed as a personable candidate who might combine her private-sector experience as a stockbroker with the Kansas electorate's seeming preference for women officeholders (such as Senator Kassebaum, Governor Finney, and Representative Meyers). In short, Kansas Democrats put forward a strong slate of candidates, who explicitly sought to emphasize the alleged extremism—especially on social issues—of their Republican opponents.

In the end, all these races went to the GOP, although all were competitive and the Tiahrt-Rathbun margin was a mere 4 percent. Still, the Christian Right could rightfully argue that it did much of the heavy lifting in all of these races, to say nothing of playing major roles in retaining conservative control over the state house, making inroads in the state senate, and capturing several state board of education seats. The two most interesting, and most telling, races were the Brownback-Docking and Frieden-Ryun matchups. The former contest illustrated the capacity for a conservative Republican to court a wide range of voters, while the latter demonstrated the extent to which the politics of the Christian Right had become mainstream fare for Kansas Republicans.

Brownback versus Docking: Who's "Extreme"? More than seven of every ten Kansas voters (72 percent) in the 1996 general election did not consider themselves part of the religious right; if only they had voted, Jill Docking would have squeaked out a narrow victory. But almost three in ten did accept the religious right label, and among them the overwhelming majority (70 percent) cast their Senate ballot for Sam Brownback (Glass 1996). In short, Brownback's victory came as the result of two interrelated campaigns. Brownback sought to maximize turnout among the Christian Right with a quiet campaign that emphasized getting out his core supporters. At the same time, he ran a highly public campaign that attempted, with notable success, to neutralize the charge that he was an extremist—both as a Republican ally of Newt Gingrich and as someone who did not reflect Kansas values with his backing of social conservative positions.

Despite a well-funded campaign and the requisite advertisements, Docking simply could not convincingly paint Brownback as an extremist. In part this derived from Brownback's schoolboy demeanor (well-deserved, given his student-body presidency at Kansas State University in the 1970s). As the *New Republic* reported, at one campaign stop, "the genial forty-year-old . . . is the first to pick up a platter of cinnamon rolls and pass them around. With his support for campaign finance reform and a ban on congressional gifts, Brownback might be mistaken for a civic-minded businessman taking a little time off to knock some sense into the public sector" (Rubin 1996, 17). At the same time, Brownback turned the extremism label back onto Docking, who grew up in Massachusetts and had served as chair of the Kansas presidential campaign of Michael Dukakis. This was scarcely telling, but Brownback did effectively counter the extremist charge.

More important, perhaps, was the reaction of the Kansas electorate; although one Republican in five voted for Docking, one in ten Democrats crossed party lines to vote for Brownback, often on social issues, especially abortion (Glass 1996). In the end, the Christian Right was much more effective in getting out its vote than were moderates, who hoped to reap bushels of votes from Republican women. Brownback succeeded in breaking even among all women, while he won a sizable majority of the men's vote. Again, the extremist label failed to stick, in part because of his cordial style and in part because Kansas voters did not regard government cutbacks and a pro-life stance as extreme. Indeed, Brownback's campaign may well have defined a new mainstream in Kansas politics. If so, the Christian Right not only won an important seat but succeeded in shifting the political debate in its preferred direction.

Ryun versus Frieden: Testing the Limits of Republican Support. On 16 October 1996, the editor of staunchly Republican *Iola (Kansas) Register,* which had never endorsed a Democrat, signed an editorial that reflected on Jim Ryun's attitude toward courtship and his choice of lifestyle. The editorial read in part:

His views on fundamental family issues are so different from those held by 99.9 percent of the rest of us that I don't see how he could understand and represent the viewpoints of a typical Second District family on social issues.

Ryun and his family have taken elaborate pains to set themselves apart from today's society and values . . . [and] this determination to be different erects a formidable barrier between the Ryuns and everyone else. . . .

It is precisely because Ryun is unique that he seems to me to be uniquely unsuited for Congress. (Lynn 1996)

With widespread name identification and hero status to Kansans aged forty and older, Jim Ryun, former Olympian and longtime world record holder in the mile, would seem an ideal "amateur" congressional candidate (Canon 1990). Indeed, the single most effective television advertisement in all of 1996 was Ryun's initial effort, which showed him falling in an Olympic race, getting up, and gallantly attempting to rejoin the pack. Ryun was not simply supported by the Christian Right. Even more than Tiahrt, he was one of them. For more than twenty years he had helped support his family by being a motivational speaker, often before conservative religious groups. Although on occasion at odds with some groups and individuals within the Christian Right in Kansas, Ryun could rely on almost total support from this quarter. What he had to do was to meet the challenge articulated by the Iola editorial: demonstrate that he could represent others' points of view.

Ryun's words in print on a highly restrictive and patriarchal view of courtship and his occasional tendency to speak in tongues in public made this task a difficult one. He accomplished it in two complementary ways. First, he ran an extremely effective television commercial that featured his attractive family of five in a homey setting. As mundane as this sounds, it spoke directly to the idea that he and his family were somehow abnormal. Second, in contrast to his opponent, John Frieden, Ryun campaigned energetically throughout his district, which stretched from Nebraska to Oklahoma and included no single natural media center.

Many moderate Republicans who expressed lukewarm support for Sam Brownback had an even more difficult time backing the Ryun candidacy. Yet, with Bob Dole on the top of the ticket, with national funding coming into Kansas at record rates (both to the candidates and in independent expenditures), and with the natural Republican advantage in the state, as well as in the Second District, Ryun succeeded in linking himself to the conservative mainstream of Kansas politics in 1996. As with the Brownback race, moderate/traditional Republicans simply did not abandon their party's candidate in large enough numbers to elect even a well-funded, moderate Democrat. Jim Ryun proved that he could run effectively, not only on a track, but also in the slippery context of electoral politics. While acknowledging his Christian roots, often in highly visible ways, Ryun could and did present himself as someone who could identify and empathize with his constituents.

After the dust cleared in November 1996, Bob Dole had exited the Kansas political stage, and the social conservative–Christian Right element of the party, led by party chairman David Miller (ranked by one Topeka source as second only to the governor in political power within the state in 1997) had maintained its prominence. Strangely enough, however, state politics remains in the hands of the moderates, as social conservatives came up empty in terms of policies in the 1995, 1996, and 1997 legislative sessions. Even as Representatives Tiahrt, Snowbarger, and Ryun serve in the U.S. House and Senator Brownback readies himself to run for a full Senate term in 1998 (with the prospect of little opposition within either party), Governor Bill Graves, a pro-choice moderate, has reduced his disapproval ratings to single digits. Many members of the Christian Right, among them Republican chairman Miller, would love to challenge the governor, but the same forces that allowed Brownback and even Ryun to appear moderate enough to win broad support also allow Graves, a fiscal conservative, to appear conservative enough to prevail.

Kansas and Social Conservatives: The Limits of the Christian Right

The moderate-conservative division in the Kansas Republican Party mirrors its national divisions, in terms of the behavior and core beliefs of activists and voters alike. At one level, the frequently observed split between social and economic conservatives takes on deeper meaning, on the basis of fundamental philosophical differences. So-called "*neoconservatives* believe that America is special because it was founded on an idea—a commitment to the rights of man embodied in the Declaration of Independence. . . . The *theocon[servatives]*, too, argue that America is rooted in an idea, but they believe that idea is Christianity" (Heilbrunn 1996, 21). The split among Kansas conservatives, mostly within the Republican Party, runs along this fault line. As Kansas native and *Wall Street Journal* reporter Dennis Farney (1996, 1) wrote: "Currently, the religious right's central issue is abortion; in Kansas all six GOP candidates oppose it. But in a broader sense, the Christian conservative agenda is an across-the-board challenge to the central tenets to modernity: It champions home and religious schooling over public schooling, biblical literalism over social relativism, and individual responsibility over government social programs."

Especially within the congressional delegation, the 1996 elections produced a major change; Representatives Ryun, Tiahrt, and Snowbarger certainly fall on the religiously based "theocon" side of the divide, as do many of the core supporters of Senator Brownback, who personally has feet planted on both sides of the division. The Republican Party of the activists, led by David Miller and dependent on antiabortion support, is decidedly theoconservative, while Governor Graves and the state senate remain in the camp of the more secular neoconservatives with their emphasis on defined government functions and the protection of individual rights.

Yet the divisions are not all that simple to parse out, in that another, overlapping split comes into play. As a national 1997 Republican survey discovered, the party's voters fall into distinct camps on economic policy, with balanced-budget "deficit hawks" coming into conflict with advocates of deep tax cuts, in the supply-side economics vein (Dionne 1997). This second split among Republicans seems to have little to do with the Christian Right, yet in Kansas there has been considerable convergence between social conservative positions and the advocacy of substantial tax cuts; the government itself is seen as suspect, and the less the government does, save for moralistic initiatives, the better. Traditional Republicans in Kansas, always reasonably fiscally conservative, have taken on much of the responsibility of defending government, as they back prudent budgets and modest tax relief. In the end, ironically, the Christian Right has had more success indirectly, with its pressure for tax cuts, than it has had on straightforward social legislation.

Given the results of the 1996 elections, however, this element has taken its place as the strongest single interest in Kansas politics, as reflected in its capture of both national and state offices and its continuing domination of the Republican Party. The question that remains is whether the Christian Right can succeed within the state as well as it has in backing and electing like-minded candidates for the U.S. Congress.

Notes

1. Kansas has adopted relatively few restrictions on a woman's right to abortion; currently, there is an eight-hour waiting period after an initial consultation. Still, the abortion issue is continually on the state's legislative agenda, in that every year pro-life activists seek further restrictions.

2. In 1997, a number of Christian Right organizations turned their attention to endorsing candidates in city council and school board elections in certain Kansas cities and school districts. For example, Kansans for Life endorsed seventeen candidates in various Johnson County jurisdictions (Hobson 1997).

References

Beem, Kate. 1996. "Kansas Lobbying Group Triumphant in Elections." *Kansas City Star* (7 November): 2c.

Canon, David. 1990. *Actors, Athletes, and Astronauts: Political Amateurs in the United States Congress*. Chicago: University of Chicago Press.

Cigler, Allan J., and Burdett A. Loomis. 1992. "Political Realignment in Kansas: Two-Party Competition in a One-Party State." Pp. 163–78 in *Party Realignment in the American States*, ed. Maureen Moakley. Columbus: Ohio State University Press, 163–78.

Cigler, Allan J., and Dwight Kiel. 1993. "Kansas: Representation in Transition." Pp. 94–116 in *Interest Groups in the Midwestern States*, ed. Clive Thomas and Ronald Hrebenar. Ames: Iowa State University Press.

Dionne, E. J. 1997. "Republicans: A Party Splitting at the Seams," *Washington Post* (21 February): A1.

Elazar, Daniel J. 1972. *American Federalism: A View from the States*. 2d ed. New York: Thomas Crowell.

Elving, Ronald. 1995. *Politics in America*. Washington, D.C.: Congressional Quarterly Press.

Farney, Dennis. 1996. "With Many Hot Races, Politics Is Now Putting Kansas on the Map." *Wall Street Journal* (25 September).

Glass, Doug. 1996. "Kansas' Republican Base Rules." *Lawrence Journal-World* (6 November): A3.

Grumm, John G. 1967. "The Kansas Legislature: Republican Coalition." In *Midwestern Legislative Politics*, ed. Samuel Patterson. Iowa City: Institute of Public Affairs, University of Iowa.

Gugliotta, Guy. 1996. "Choices That May Help Democrats." *Washington Post* (8 August): A9.

Heilbrunn, Jacob. 1996. "Neocon v. Theocon." *New Republic*, 30 December. 20–24.

Hobson, Grace. 1997. "Anti-Abortion Groups Focusing on Local, School Board Elections." *Kansas City Star* (23 August): 1C.

Loomis, Burdett A. 1994. *Time, Politics, and Policy: A Legislative Year*. Lawrence: University Press of Kansas.

Lynn, Emerson, Jr. 1996. "Ryun Runs Alone." *Iola (Kansas) Register* (16 October).

Mayhew, David. 1986. *Placing Parties in American Politics*. Princeton: Princeton University Press.

Rubin, Alissa. 1996. "Right Turn." *New Republic*, 5 November, 16–18.

Sigman, Robert P. 1996. "The Religious Right Is More than Just an Army of Zealots." *Kansas City Star* (23 August): 1C.

Sullinger, James. 1996a. "Blue-Collar Politician Reshapes GOP." *Kansas City Star* (7 July): 4A.

———. 1996b. "Precinct Position Is Seen as Important amid Party Divisions." *Kansas City Star* (14 June): 1C.

14

Maine: Slow Growth in the Pine Tree State

Matthew C. Moen and Kenneth T. Palmer

When a systematic assessment of the Christian Right's impact in state Republican parties was released several years ago, Maine was identified as the only New England state where the movement had more than a minor influence; indeed, it was only one of two states in the entire Northeast with a "substantial" Christian Right presence, defined as 25 percent to 50 percent strength in the state party organization (Persinos 1994). That assessment was reasonable at the time, given the state's tradition of moralistic politics and its anti–gay rights referendum on the ballot the following year. Yet, closer scrutiny of the situation in Maine reveals that the degree of Christian Right influence in the state is easily overstated and misinterpreted. The Christian Right has an established role in Maine politics, which seems to be growing; however, its influence within the Republican Party is still relatively modest, its priorities differ somewhat from those of its related organizations in other states (reflecting Maine's unique political culture), and its focal points for attaining goals sometimes even lie outside the conventional party structure and processes. This chapter examines the characteristics and politics of the state of Maine and then proceeds to a discussion of the Christian Right's emergence and influence in the state.

Maine Politics

The state of Maine manifests the characteristics of New England and, because of its geographic isoltaion, possibly even exaggerates them relative to its sister states. Maine has historically been insulated from the twin pressures of urbanism and metropolitanism. It was formed by groups of (mostly Protestant) religious refugees, who agreed on fundamental ideas and settled in closely knit, small communities (Palmer, Taylor, and LiBrizzi 1992). Maine (with its four largest cities together accounting for only 13 percent of the state's population) is still a state of small towns, which are scattered over a large geographic area. One consequence of its unique residential living patterns is a high level of political participation; Maine traditionally has high voter-turnout rates, for instance, providing the highest turnout in the nation (64 percent) in the 1996 elections.

Before becoming a state in 1820, Maine was a district of Massachusetts. It served as a battleground for conflict between French (Catholic) and English (Protestant) settlers. As a result, the delegates to its state constitutional convention were sensitive to religious conflict and tried to diminish it by providing an absolute guarantee of religious freedom. The delegates agreed to language that made "no distinction whatever . . . between Protestants and Roman Catholics, Christians and non-Christians" (Banks 1970). With that guarantee, the Maine Constitution departed from the Massachusetts Charter of 1780 (under which the area had been governed), which had required church attendance and the taxation of all citizens for the support of public worship and "Protestant teachers of piety." According to a leading Maine historian, the language written into the Maine Constitution reflected "the liberal attitude of most of those at the convention" (Banks 1970).

At the same time, Maine has evinced interest in moral issues throughout its history. State politicians partly reconciled the guarantees of religious liberty with the emphasis on morality by approaching moral issues in moderate tones. They worked toward consensus on specific solutions, eschewing tactics apt to sharpen divisions in the electorate. A nineteenth-century businessman, Neal Dow, illustrates this point. He authored legislation in 1846 banning the sale and consumption of alcoholic beverages (Byrne 1985). In 1851, he tried to strengthen its enforcement in the legislature, partly by striking a deal to support Hannibal Hamlin's candidacy for the U.S. Senate in return for stricter enforcement of prohibition. In the same year, Dow was elected mayor of Portland, and he organized a group called the Watchmen of Temperance, whose sole purpose was to provide information to public officials about hidden liquor stocks. Dow's reputation declined when his obsession with eradicating liquor was connected with violence. A liquor stock being stored in city hall after it was seized became the source of conflict between a mob and Mayor Dow's militia, resulting in one death and several injuries. While Dow was legally absolved of blame, his popular appeal plummeted and he lost a bid for reelection.

Interestingly, Dow's temperance crusade was carried out with support from religious groups, but his relationship with them was not close. He did not attend church, and his tactics offended many clergy. Asa Cummings of the *Portland Christian Mirror* remarked that Dow was attempting "to dictate to ministers and churches" (Byrne 1985). Consistent with Maine traditions, Dow pursued his policy goals within the confines of the political process, positioning himself above all else as a citizen-politician. His loss in the mayor's race signaled the state's historic preference for moderation among its politicians.

Because of its substantial Franco-American community (about 20 percent of the population), as well as relatively equal numbers of Protestants and Catholics in modern times, Maine has always faced the possibility that religious tension will drive its politics. In the nineteenth century, for instance, Protestant resentment against Irish immigrants led to the burning of selected Catholic churches, and the nativist Know Nothing Party demonstrated popular appeal (Palmer, Taylor, and LiBrizzi 1992); in the 1920s, the Ku Klux Klan played a minor role in a gubernatorial election. Apart from those isolated examples, however, the norm has been the separation of religious and political issues in state politics.

A principal reason for this separation has been the state's overwhelmingly centrist political tendencies, which have worked to discourage politicians from advancing sectarian or moralistic appeals. The heavy concentration of Franco-Americans in certain cities (Saco, Lewiston, and Biddeford) and particular regions (northern Aroostook County on the Canadian border) has further mitigated conflict. Franco-American politicians have generally been satisfied with exercising influence in those communities and retaining seats in their regional delegations to the state legislature (Palmer, Taylor, and LiBrizzi 1992). Unlike other New England states, where ethnic politics is regularly practiced, Maine politics generally lacks those overtones. Relatively few Franco-Americans have run for the principal statewide offices, and probably only one has been elected governor in the state's history (in the late 1800s).

Perhaps the most striking conflict between Protestants and Catholics, involving some ethnic and regional differences, concerned public transportation of parochial students in the postwar period. In 1947, the Supreme Court ruled in *Everson v. Board of Education* that state law permitting public school buses to carry pupils to sectarian schools did not breach the "wall of separation" between church and state (330 U.S. 1 [1947]). Its reasoning was that the service benefited the child, not a church. The Maine legislature had no established policy on this matter, and several cities offered bus service to parochial students. The service was provided with little fanfare in Franco-American communities, but it provoked sharp protests in predominantly Protestant areas. The issue was particularly intense in Augusta, the state capital, where, in 1956, voters approved a nonbinding referendum that allowed transportation of parochial students at city expense. The following year, the city council provided a small appropriation for the program, causing a legal challenge that eventually was decided by the Maine Supreme Court.

In *Squires v. Augusta* (1959), the court ruled by a 4-2 margin that publicly supported transportation of non–public school students was illegal (153 A.2d 80 [1959]). Interestingly, the court found no barrier to the program in the U.S. Constitution; instead, it concluded that the city of Augusta exceeded its authority because neither the Maine Constitution nor the state's education statutes gave any power to local communities to provide such service (unlike the New Jersey case, where an authorizing state law existed). The majority on the court believed the state legislature could grant the power to local communities. In a lengthy dissent, two justices (both of whom were Catholics) argued that communities already had a police power that permitted them to transport parochial school students. In essence, the Maine Supreme Court narrowed the issue and also turned it over to the state legislature, where its intensity soon subsided (Sorauf 1977). This case is representative of the state's handling of religious and political issues.

The Christian Right in Maine Politics

The emergence of the Christian Right in American politics is often traced to the formal incorporation in the late 1970s of key organizations such as Christian Voice and the Moral Majority. Those groups spearheaded an expansionist phase of the movement, which ran from about 1979 through 1984 (Moen 1992). Its distinguishing characteristics were rapid organizational growth, fundamentalist leaders, and direct-mail solicitation; in a different vein, this phase was also marked by a lack of solid grassroots organization and by amateurish lobbying efforts on Capitol Hill (Moen 1995).

Maine mostly missed this first wave of political activism, largely because its electoral outcomes in the 1970s were almost the opposite of national trends. In 1974, as many states were electing more liberal politicians to office in response to the Watergate scandal, Maine replaced incumbent Democrat Peter Kyros in the First Congressional District with Republican David Emery, and it elevated political independent James Longley to the governorship. Longley campaigned on strongly conservative themes, such as reducing taxes and downsizing government, and he pursued very conservative policies during his tenure in office. Interestingly, the 1978 governor's race challenged that conservative direction with the election of the Democratic candidate, but in the process of doing so, it once again ran counter to the larger national trends that favored the Republican Party and presaged the Reagan landslide of 1980 (McIntyre 1979).

The 1978 gubernatorial race presented Maine voters with three distinctive choices. Joseph Brennan was a moderate Democratic nominee; Linwood

Palmer was a generally conservative Republican nominee; Buddy Frankland, a charismatic Baptist minister heading one of the largest congregations in northern New England, was a strongly conservative independent candidate. Frankland was widely known for his opposition to abortion and particularly to gay rights; he favored a reduction in the University of Maine's state appropriation when its administration extended formal recognition to a homosexual student organization (Fisher 1978). Even so, Frankland campaigned heavily on outgoing governor Longley's major themes, such as lenient environmental standards, lower taxes, and smaller government. He received Longley's formal endorsement late in the campaign, but Frankland drew only 25 percent of the total vote. His support came from Republican areas in eastern and northern Maine, cutting into the vote for Linwood Palmer and guaranteeing a landslide victory for Joe Brennan. In 1980, a year in which Republicans won control of the U.S. Senate for the first time in a generation and in which Ronald Reagan was elected president, Maine Democrats actually increased their margin of seats in both houses of the state legislature. Once again, state and national electoral trends diverged.

Maine also missed the first wave of national Christian Right activism because of its strong pro-choice sentiments, which basically denied religious conservatives within the state a critical mobilizing issue (Jorstad 1981). Maine is a strongly pro-choice state, with a high degree of consensus on that position, unlike many other states. Polls show that fully 70 percent of Maine citizens oppose a constitutional amendment to ban abortion, while 26 percent favor such an amendment (Campbell 1996). Those numbers are reflected in the public arena. Maine has experienced almost no abortion clinic violence over the years; every member of its congressional delegation and every governor since the late 1970s have been strongly pro-choice, with Senator Olympia Snowe often spearheading opposition to restrictive abortion language in Republican Party platforms, as she did in 1996. Furthermore, local communities such as Bangor have passed city ordinances that discourage picketing by right-to-life activists by requiring protestors to obtain a parade permit whenever three or more of them are involved in a formal protest, an ordinance so restrictive that it has been rewritten twice in response to successful legal challenges (Saucier 1997). The strong statewide consensus on abortion policy deprived religious conservatives in Maine of a coalescing issue in the late 1970s, and it still undercuts their ability to succeed in the 1990s, because it neutralizes the mutually reinforcing relationships that usually exist between powerful right-to-life groups and Christian Right organizations, such as the Christian Coalition (Berkowitz and Green 1996).

In the absence of mutually reinforcing networks, religious conservatives seem to have relatively discrete organizations in pursuit of their own agendas, with mixed-to-poor success. Right-to-life groups can claim few public policy successes. Home school networks have gained limited public attention compared to school funding issues and "magnet" schools for talented students. In his January 1997 drive to install educational standards for secondary schools in the state, for instance, Governor Angus King basically ignored the issue of home-school exemptions, arousing protest from home school advocates. Even the Christian Civic League, which is probably the most important organization connecting religiously conservative churches in the state, can lay claim to few tangible victories. Originally created as a temperance organization in 1897, the Christian Civic League modified and updated its agenda over the years to incorporate issues such as sex education, gun control, abortion, crime, gambling, and gay rights. Yet, at the end of the 1970s, as the Christian Right was starting to coalesce nationally, what a newspaper called "Maine's premier conservative group" was mostly moribund (Martin 1980). Few activists attended its annual meeting, and a cooperative relationship with the Maine Department of Education to offer sex education programs in the public schools gradually atrophied in the 1980s as its message of abstinence conflicted with school messages of moderation and safe sex.

Throughout most of the 1980s and into the 1990s, the league became closely identified with the political aspirations of its executive director, Jasper Wyman. He was the sacrificial nominee of the Republican Party in 1988 to contest the U.S. Senate seat held by popular incumbent Democrat George Mitchell, who defeated Wyman by 81 percent to 19 percent (a larger margin than any other winning Senate candidate in the nation that year); in 1994, Wyman pursued the governorship, placing third in a crowded Republican primary. In 1995, he left the state to work for the Prison Fellowship Ministry of Charles Colson.

During his tenure at the Christian Civic League, Wyman tried to moderate the organization's political agenda. He incrementally changed his position from a strict antiabortion stance to a more pro-choice position, in a manner consistent with statements from national Christian Right leaders at that same time (Moen 1996), on the grounds that the abortion battle had to be won in people's hearts rather than in the political arena. He criticized right-to-life groups for their "unreasonable and indefensible opposition to birth control" (Rawson 1995). He repudiated his stance on an antiobscenity referendum in the state in 1986 (Weinstein 1994), and he promoted themes of compassion and tolerance in the midst of an anti–gay rights referendum in 1995 (while remaining opposed to gay rights). Those positions created deep fissures in the Christian Civic League, prompting Wyman's chosen successor actually to ban him from its office (Rooks 1995). The larger point is that religious conservatives in the state have often exhibited fissures among themselves and have claimed relatively few tangible policy victories, while demonstrating some ability to set the political agenda, a pattern often evidenced at the national level (Moe 1989; Fowler 1993; Wald 1997).

For the most part, religious conservatives in the state have also not been well connected to the major national organizations. Moral Majority never exhibited a wide following nor an ability to influence elections and policy in Maine; the Reverend Jerry Falwell is probably best known in the state for his role in helping to rescue the Bangor Baptist Church when former gubernatorial candidate Buddy Frankland resigned as its minister amidst scandal in the mid-1980s. The Christian Coalition seems to have only a small following in the state, demonstrated by the fact that it lacks an Internet website as a state affiliate on the Christian Coalition's home page and that only one of sixteen county chapter chairpersons attended its annual Road to Victory conference in 1994 (author observation 1994). These conclusions are buttressed by studies of Christian Right organizations showing that their membership rolls are routinely exaggerated (Hadden et al. 1987; *Church & State* 1996).

The lack of supportive networks and powerful organizations of religious conservatives in the state, in comparison to those operating in some other states (Rozell and Wilcox 1995), at times translates into activity outside conventional party structures and processes. Religious conservatives have cleverly taken advantage of Maine's highly participatory traditions by appealing directly to the people through referendum measures. That approach allows religious conservatives to sidestep organizational stagnation or factionalism and a mostly moderate, pro-choice Republican Party. Two notable examples illustrate this tactic. In 1986, religious conservatives promoted an antiobscenity referendum. It emerged from an ordinance approved by the city of Portland that inhibited the growth of adult bookstores; religious conservatives sought to extend and apply that ordinance to the entire state by referenda. Their campaign encountered resistance from educators, who claimed that it not only constituted censorship but actually encouraged "book burning" (Rooks 1995). The referendum measure failed by a wide margin, but it set a tactical precedent.

In 1995, religious conservatives advanced an anti–gay rights referendum, the only one of its kind in the nation that year. Gay rights had been a hotly contested issue in Maine for years, going back at least as far as a 1984 campaign against the Equal Rights Amendment on the grounds that it would promote homosexual rights. In 1991, the issue reverberated when the state legislature passed an antidiscrimination bill, only to have it vetoed by Republican governor John McKernan, whose political calculations necessitated a move to the right (Rooks 1995). Subsequently, some of the more highly populated cities in Maine, such as Lewiston and Portland, voted on local ordinances prohibiting discrimination on the basis of sexual preference. The Portland ordinance passed. That outcome prompted an organization called Concerned Maine Families, headed by Carolyn Cosby, to gather the necessary signatures to place a measure on the statewide ballot. The measure would have superseded any local antidiscrimination ordinances. It was patterned after Amendment 2 in Colorado, the referendum that prohibited the extension of protected status to gay people; Amendment 2 passed with 53 percent of the vote, but it was subsequently struck down by the courts (Morken 1994). The Maine referendum—called Amendment 1—used less elaborate language toward a similar end. It prohibited the extension of the Maine Human Rights Act to any new classes, including homosexuals; although certainly intended to limit gay rights, the referendum was technically neutral with respect to any particular class of citizens; this strengthened its appeal relative to the Colorado provision. No single group of citizens was singled out in the Maine referendum.

A group called Maine Won't Discriminate spearheaded opposition to Amendment 1. It enjoyed the backing of virtually every prominent politician in the state, including Governor Angus King, and it outspent Concerned Maine Families by a large margin (Associated Press 1995). The group also had the backing of many prominent organizations, such as the Maine Chamber of Commerce, the Maine AFL-CIO, the Roman Catholic Diocese in Portland, and various human rights groups. Given those endorsements, the lopsided financial advantage, and a history of antidiscrimination legislation passing in the state legislature as well as in local communities, one might have expected a larger victory margin than the 54 percent to 46 percent vote against Amendment 1. On the other hand, Amendment 1 opponents won eleven of sixteen counties (Vegh 1995) and effectively obstructed the efforts of religious conservatives to bypass the regular state legislative channels through the referendum process, at least on this issue.

Arenas for Activism

The weakness of the political party structures in Maine makes their "takeover" by religious conservatives simple in theory but much less meaningful in practice, since the potential reward may not be commensurate with the effort. Moreover, the Maine Republican Party, which is the obvious focal point for the Christian Right, has traditionally resisted the influence of religious conservatives because of its moderate character (a point made earlier) and its unpleasant electoral experiences with conservative leadership. Democratic victories in the state during the 1950s and 1960s, under the leadership of Edmund Muskie, basically turned Maine into a two-party competitive state. Republicans meanwhile responded in 1967 to those Democratic successes by elevating Cyril Joly to the position of state party chairperson; he was a strong conservative who had supported the 1964 presidential bid of Barry Goldwater, even though Goldwater was unpopular in the state party (Palmer 1997).

The Republican organizational shift to the right cost the party. It lost gubernatorial races in 1966, 1970, 1974, 1978, and 1982, as well as losing control of the state house of representatives in 1974 and the state senate in 1982 for protracted periods. In contrast, the GOP was winning with moderate congressional candidates who were running independent of the state party apparatus, such as Olympia Snowe and William Cohen. The stark contrast between the party's fate in state elections and its fate in congressional elections prompted all three Republican members of the congressional delegation to write a letter in 1982 to all state committee members encouraging the election of an experienced and moderate state party activist as party chairperson. The recommendation prompted the election of Lloyd Sewall, who proved to be an effective leader, as Republicans won control of the governorship in 1986 for the first time in twenty-four years (Palmer 1997).

Since the mid-1980s, moderates have been in control of the party structure, and they have turned back occasional efforts by conservatives to seize control of the state chairmanship. Telling evidence of control by moderates is found in the inclusion of an Equal Rights Amendment plank in the state platform in 1984, a year in which the national GOP did not endorse the ERA and in which the president virtually ignored the general subject of women's rights in his annual State of the Union address (Moen 1990); likewise, the state party included a pro-choice plank in its 1988 platform, in contrast to the national party. According to one longtime activist and member of the state Republican executive committee, a clear minority of the current state committee is pro-life, and very few (if any) people are actually members of the Christian Coalition (Bott 1997).

The unattractiveness of fighting to seize control of a somewhat weak party structure, coupled with an inability to do so, is part of the reason that the Christian Right has focused much of its effort on the referendum process. David Lackey, press secretary to Republican senator Olympia Snowe, said in an interview on 10 January 1997 that he estimates that about one-third of all Maine Republicans may be favorably disposed to the Christian Right. That proportion is sufficient to help get referenda placed on the ballot by petition, but it is insufficient to win the final vote, as noted earlier. The future for referendum votes on social issues appears increasingly dim for the Christian Right, not only because of past defeats, but also because of criticism of the referendum process itself. In 1996, a petition aimed at capping statewide property taxes failed when the secretary of state discovered bogus names and graveyard signatures, leading to an indictment of the leader of the effort (*Brunswick*

Times Record 1996). Also in 1996, the voters approved a referendum measure that requires that a politician's opposition to congressional term limits be displayed on future ballots for state legislative and congressional seats. The measure passed despite the obvious constitutional questions it raised. Cognizant of these and previous referenda issues, a well-known journalist wrote, "What used to be a selectively applied lawmaking tool has set loose a flood of petition drives concerning every half-baked idea that pops into some energetic advocate's head" (Brunelle 1996). Recent abuses of the referendum process, in other words, are likely to inhibit Christian Right leaders from pursuing that avenue in the years ahead. One exception to that rule may be a referendum that defines marriage in heterosexual terms, a measure similar to those considered by Congress and other states to ban gay marriages ruled constitutionally permissible in Hawaii. In the absence of any state legislative action, Carolyn Cosby, of Concerned Maine Families, announced in January 1997 that her organization gathered 20 percent more than the necessary number of signatures to place the issue on the ballot (*Bangor Daily News* 1997).

Given the moderate nature of the state Republican Party and the declining attractiveness of the referendum process, religious conservatives have been left with relatively few venues to pursue their goals. Perhaps the most significant outlet for activism in Maine at this time is local school boards in predominantly rural areas. This outlet is attractive for several predictable reasons. First, school board races are low-salience elections where it is possible for a particular faction with a high turnout to prevail. Second, school board races and politics train people in the art of politics at the lowest level, giving them the experience and connections necessary to work in high-profile campaigns. Third, school board races keep the Christian Right grounded in local communities, where the pressures of a pluralistic political process are often minimized. Fourth, school board races and politics are central to the Christian Right's broad goal of instilling appropriate values in the next generation of citizens,

For all of those reasons, religious conservatives have been increasingly active in that arena, although in selected locales. In the town of Gardiner in 1991, for instance, a prolonged debate occurred over the *Impressions* reading series in the town's middle school, leading to its eventual abandonment by school officials; in Harpswell in 1994, an intense fight transpired over outcome-based education (OBE), leading religious conservatives to consider nominating a school board member and prompting an (unsuccessful) effort to scuttle the OBE standards. In Palermo in 1996, religious conservatives gained control of the school board, and used their power to eliminate sex-education programs and guidance counseling, as well as to refuse to apply for federal grant monies for selected special and remedial education programs on the grounds that they brought interference from federal authorities into local school affairs (Chutchian 1996). (Local citizens directed the board to apply for the grant by a 150-20 vote at a public meeting.) In recognition of these controversies over school board issues and races, a report authored by a professor that was highly critical of Christian Right goals and tactics created a firestorm statewide (Davis 1996). In spite of the salience of these issues, though, the school board fights are largely restricted to a subset of small towns in rural areas of the state. Even acknowledgment of a link to the national Christian Right organizations by local activists is injurious to their efforts because it undercuts the sanctity of the principle of local control, which is their basis for pressing claims, Kenneth Chutchian told the author in a 6 January 1997 interview. Accordingly, while religious conservatives have made some inroads into school boards across the state, their influence has been unevenly manifested and sometimes ephemeral.

A second and newly emerging outlet for activism by religious conservatives seems to be in the state legislature, in the guise of informal weekly prayer breakfast meetings of like-minded members. According to a representative who has attended, about ten legislators gather on such occasions (roughly 7 percent of the total state house membership); the event has parallels to the prayer breakfasts on Capitol Hill—mostly a social event among like-minded members, rather than a strategy session for pursuing particular goals, the representative said in an interview on 9 January 1997. Republican members attending the breakfast, however, will probably be the vanguard of opposition to bills legalizing the medical use of hallucinogenic drugs and legalizing euthanasia, two issues expected to surface in the current legislative cycle.

The same members will also probably spearhead opposition in the state legislature to independent governor Angus King's education reform proposals. King seeks to replace existing high school graduation requirements, which are mostly met by taking a prescribed set of courses, with a set of learning outcomes. The governor's 1996 bill included six guiding principles, ninety-nine content standards, and nearly nine hundred performance indicators; it would have mandated state standards for the first time in Maine public schools by specifying what every student should know and be able to do at each grade level. Carolyn Cosby, of Concerned Maine Families, which had spearheaded support for the anti–gay rights referendum in 1995, orchestrated the opposition to the bill at a public hearing (Beem 1996). The effect was to scuttle the content standards and performance indicators, leaving only the guiding principles intact when the bill was eventually signed into law. In the summer of 1996, a committee of legislators tried to restore benchmarks in a revised bill. They received input from Michael Heath of the Christian Civic League, who praised the process as "much more inclusive of different interest groups and their concerns" than had been the case during deliberations on the original bill (Saltonstall 1996). However, in early 1997, as the governor's revised package began to undergo a series of public hearings around the state, religious conservatives were still scrutinizing and questioning it. The activities concerning education standards confirm many of the propositions laid out by scholars in recent years about the Christian Right—its shift toward state and local issues, especially education, and toward mainstream political tactics and rhetoric (Moen 1995; Rozell and Wilcox 1996; Oldfield 1996).

1996 and Beyond

The Christian Right fared rather poorly in Maine in the 1996 election cycle, particularly at the congressional level. In the U.S. Senate race to fill the seat being vacated by Bill Cohen, moderate Republican Susan Collins defeated Democratic stalwart Joe Brennan. While religious conservatives preferred Collins to Brennan, their relationship with her is uneasy. In 1994, a social conservative named Mark Finks filed a legal challenge to Collins's residency in her bid for the governorship, because of her service in a government post outside the state of Maine. Collins won the GOP nomination, but the protracted dispute helped undermine her candidacy, and she was outpolled by both an independent and the Democratic candidate in a three-way race. In 1995, Collins came out against the anti–gay rights referendum. In 1996, she defeated social conservative John Hathaway (and others) in the GOP primary before defeating Brennan in the general election. She campaigned openly as a moderate, pro-choice Republican in the tradition of Olympia Snowe and Bill Cohen (for whom she once worked), and she beat Brennan by an 8 percent margin.

In Maine's two races for the U.S. House of Representatives, the Christian Right fared miserably. First-term incumbent Democrat John Baldacci—one of only thirteen Democratic freshmen elected to the House in 1994 and recipient of a 13 percent approval rating by Christian Coalition for votes in the 104th Congress—easily won reelection in a noncompetitive race. In contrast, first-term incumbent Republican James Longley—one of Speaker Gingrich's most avid supporters and recipient of a 66 percent approval rating by Christian Coalition—was defeated by a liberal Democrat. Longley was the son of the conservative independent governor by the same name in Maine in the 1970s, and his defeat after one term signaled the reinstitution of the state's traditional political outcomes.

The Christian Right fared only slightly better at the state legislative level. In 1996, the Maine Christian Civic League sent out 314 questionnaires to candidates competing for the 151 seats in the Maine House of Representatives.[1] Eighty-nine candidates responded, with 60 (49 Republicans, 7 Democrats, 4 independents) expressing support for two-thirds or more of the Civic League's nineteen agenda items, which dealt with abortion, gay rights, liquor, gambling, divorce, education reform, and taxes. (It is reasonable to assume that the 225 candidates who never bothered to respond to the Civic League's questionnaire were not very supportive of the league's agenda). Of the 60 who supported Civic League positions, only 25 Republicans and 5 Democrats won, translating into about 20 percent of the total seats in the house of representatives. The picture is even less favorable in the state senate. Questionnaires were sent to 71 candidates. A total of 21 responded, with two-thirds (14) of the candidates expressing support for two-thirds or more of the Civic League's agenda; of those 14, only 3 won election. The Christian Right is a minority faction within a minority party in both chambers of the current state legislature.

Looking ahead, the prospects for the Christian Right are not particularly bright. Every member of the congressional delegation is pro-choice, as is the governor; the Republican Party structure is clearly in the hands of moderates rather than religious conservatives; the attempt to use referenda to bypass the party structure and conventional means for making policy has failed on two major occasions, and the process itself is now under scrutiny; the ratio of opponents to sympathizers in the state legislature is strongly tilted against the Christian Right; the state's long tradition of centrist and nonsectarian politics presents a set of formidable obstacles to the Christian Right. The ranking of Maine as a state with a "substantial" Christian Right influence in the Republican Party (Persinos 1994) is probably now overstated, and certainly it misses the major focal point for activism at present, which is the school board in small towns scattered across rural areas. The Christian Right is a sometimes vocal, and perhaps slowly growing, movement, trying to win converts and form alliances with secular conservatives in Maine. Yet, the seeds of activism that it sows fall on barren soil more often than they lead to bountiful harvest in the Pine Tree state.

Notes

The authors wish to thank Ryan P. MacDonald for his excellent research assistance.

1. The information reported in this paragraph is calculated from *Maine Senate and House of Representatives,* pamphlet distributed by the Christian Civic League of Maine, 1996; and *General Election Tabulation, State Senator and Representative to the Legislature,* Bureau of Corporations, Elections and Commissions, Election Division, State of Maine, 1996.

References

Associated Press. 1995. "Gay Rights Funds Outstrip Anti-Gay Coffers 10 to 1." (2 November).

Bangor Daily News. 1997. "Group's Petition Seeks Ban on Gay Marriage." (21 January): B3.

Banks, Ronald F. 1970. *Maine Becomes a State.* Middletown, Conn.: Wesleyan University Press.

Beem, Edgar Allen. 1996. "What You Don't Know Can Hurt You." *Maine Times* (21 March): 2.

Berkowitz, Laura A., and John C. Green. 1996. "Christian Right Activism at the Grass Roots." Paper presented at the conference "The Christian Right in Comparative Perspective," Calvin College, Grand Rapids, Mich., 4–5 October.

Bott, John. 1997. Interview by author, 8 January.

Brunelle, Jim. 1996. "Voter Initiatives Taken Over by Professionals and Zealots." *Portland Press Herald* (14 March).

Brunswick Times Record. 1996. "State Indicts Tax Activist on Charge of Petition Forgery." 21 October.

Byrne, Frank L. 1985. "The Napoleon of Temperance." Pp. 244–53 in *Maine: A History through Selected Readings,* ed. David C. Smith and Edward O. Schriver. Dubuque, Iowa: Kendall-Hunt.

Campbell, Steve. 1996. "Poll: Mainers on the Issues." *Portland Press Herald* (29 September): 8A.

Church & State. 1996. "Ralph Reed's Mission Million." (January):15.

Chutchian, Kenneth Z. 1996. "A Rude Awakening: Is It Democracy in Action or a Stealth Takeover?" *Maine Times* (19–25 September): 2–5.

Davis, William E. 1996. "Impact of the New Religious Right on Public Schools." Monograph distributed by the College of Education, University of Maine.

Fisher, Peggy. 1978. "Longley's Heir." *Maine Times* (28 July): 14–15.

Fowler, Robert Booth. 1993. "The Failure of the Religious Right." Pp. 57–74 in *No Longer Exiles: The Religious New Right in American Politics,* ed. Michael Cromartie. Washington, D.C.: Ethics and Public Policy Center.

Hadden, Jeffrey K., Anson Shupe, James Hawdon, and Kenneth Martin. 1987. "Why Jerry Falwell Killed the Moral Majority." Pp. 101–15 in *The God Pumpers,* ed. Marshall Fishwick and Ray B. Browne. Bowling Green, Ohio: Bowling Green State University Popular Press.

Jorstad, Erling. 1981. *The Politics of Moralism.* Minneapolis: Augsburg.

Martin, Lucy L. 1980. "Maine's Premier Conservative Group: Has the Christian Civic League Gone Soft?" *Maine Times* (7 November): 16–18.

McIntyre, Thomas J. 1979. *The Fear Brokers.* With John C. Obert. Boston: Beacon Press.

Moen, Matthew C. 1989. *The Christian Right and Congress.* Tuscaloosa: University of Alabama Press.

———. 1990. "Ronald Reagan and the Social Issues: Rhetorical Support for the Christian Right." *Social Science Journal* 27(2): 199–207.

———. 1992. *The Transformation of the Christian Right.* Tuscaloosa: University of Alabama Press.

———. 1995. "The Fourth Wave of the Evangelical Tide: Religious Conservatives in the Aftermath of the 1994 Elections." *Contention: Debates in Society, Culture, and Science* 5 (Fall): 19–38.

———. 1996. "The First Generation of Christian Right Activism." Paper presented at the conference "The Christian Right in Comparative Perspective," Grand Rapids, Mich., 4–5 October.

Morken, Hubert. 1994. "No Special Rights: The Thinking behind Colorado's Amendment #2 Strategy." Paper presented at the annual meeting of the American Political Science Association, New York, 1–4 September.

Oldfield, Duane M. 1996. *The Right and the Righteous: The Christian Right Confronts the Republican Party.* Lanham, Md.: Rowman & Littlefield.

Palmer, Kenneth T. 1997. "Maine." Pp. 132–38 in *State Party Profiles: A Fifty-State Guide to Development, Organization, and Resources,* ed. Andrew M. Appleton and Daniel S. Ward. Washington, D.C.: Congressional Quarterly Press.

Palmer, Kenneth T., G. Thomas Taylor, and Marcus A. LiBrizzi. 1992. *Maine Politics and Government.* Lincoln: University of Nebraska Press.

Persinos, John. 1994. "Has the Christian Right Taken Over the Republican Party?" *Campaigns & Elections,* September, 21–24.

Rawson, Davis. 1995. "Wyman Picks Religion over Politics." *Waterville Morning Sentinel* (3 September).

Rooks, Douglas. 1995. "No Room Left for Jasper Wyman in Maine." *Maine Times* (7 September).

Rozell, Mark, and Clyde Wilcox. 1996. *Second Coming: The New Christian Right in Virginia Politics.* Baltimore: Johns Hopkins University Press.

Rozell, Mark, and Clyde Wilcox, eds., 1995. *God at the Grass Roots.* Lanham, Md: Rowman & Littlefield.

Saltonstall, Polly. 1996. "Learning Standards Revamped." *Kennebec Journal* (18 August).

Saucier, Roxanne Moore. 1997. "Bangor Requests Picketing Hearing." *Bangor Daily News* (3 January): B1.

Sorauf, Frank J. 1977. *The Wall of Separation: The Constitutional Politics of Church and State.* Princeton: Princeton University Press.

Vegh, Steven G. 1995. "Gay Rights Foes Turn Attention to Blocking Bill." *Portland Press Herald* (9 November): 1.

Wald, Kenneth D. 1997. *Religion and Politics in the United States.* 3d ed. Washington, D.C.: Congressional Quarterly Press.

Weinstein, Joshua L. 1994. "Wyman Bucks Stereotypes to Reshape Image." *Portland Press Herald* (7 May): 1.

15

West Virginia: In Search of the Christian Right

John David Rausch Jr. and Mary S. Rausch

On 5 November 1996, voters in West Virginia elected Cecil Underwood, a Republican, as governor, the first GOP chief executive in more than twenty years. Republicans unseated two liberal Democratic state senators to bring the total number of GOP senators to nine. These victories were surprising in a state that is a "modified one-party Democratic state" (Bibby and Holbrook 1996), especially in a year when President Clinton was able to capture over 50 percent of the state vote.

Although West Virginia is a Democratic stronghold with strong influence by the United Mine Workers (UMW), it is also a morally conservative state with large numbers of evangelical Christians. A number of Christian Right organizations are active in the state, operating in an environment of Democratic dominance. How have these Christian Right organizations developed? What obstacles have challenged the groups? What is the role of the Christian Right in the parties? Can we attribute Cecil Underwood's victory to aggressive campaigning by the Christian Right?

To answer these questions, we first describe the context of politics in West Virginia. We then examine Christian Right organizations in detail and their role in the 1996 elections. We conclude by considering the future of the Christian Right in West Virginia.

Political Context

Although most research identifies West Virginia as a one-party state (see Bibby and Holbrook 1996), Fenton (1957) reports that there are four political "parties": three Democratic factions and the Republican Party. The "liberal faction" draws support primarily from labor, especially the UMW. The "Bourbon," or conservative, faction is largely rural and its strength tends to be in

239

central West Virginia and the eastern panhandle (Brisbin et al. 1996, 38). The statehouse/courthouse faction is based largely on patronage and has weakened as the state has more completely adopted the merit system.

The Democratic factions were significant political actors until the late 1980s (Brisbin et al. 1996, 38–39). In the 1988 and 1992 elections, Democratic gubernatorial candidate Gaston Caperton was able to unify the party. However, a new alignment within the party emerged with the 1992 elections, pitting a reform faction against a status quo faction. Charlotte Pritt, a state senator from Charleston, challenged Caperton in the 1992 Democratic gubernatorial primary. Running on a platform of reforms (Marsh 1996), Pritt almost defeated the incumbent, then refused to endorse Caperton and instead allowed a general election write-in campaign to be conducted on her behalf.

Pritt's campaign left the party deeply divided. A group of Democrats in the state legislature tried to build party cohesion by organizing the Democratic Legislative Council (DLC) to assist Democratic legislative candidates. The council's effectiveness has been limited by philosophical issues involving the historical dispute between labor and management illustrated by the debate over workers' compensation reform in 1995 (Seiler 1996b).

Moreover, although the principal split in the Democratic Party is between a liberal, reformist faction and those who resist the reform agenda, there is also a cleavage on sociomoral issues. Many Democrats support issues typically found on the Christian Right's agenda (see Blatnik 1996). This fact, combined with the current disarray of the Democratic Party, may allow the Christian Right some influence in West Virginia.

The Democratic Party dominates the political process in West Virginia, winning all but 7 of 121 terms of statewide public office contested from 1932 to 1994. The Democrats also have been the majority party in both houses of the state legislature since 1930 (Brisbin et al. 1996, 35). The Republican Party is unable to move into majority-party status because of "atrophy of party organization" (Key 1963, 13–16). In many local and statewide races, Republicans are not able to recruit a candidate. In 1996, state auditor Glen Gainer was unopposed, as were the First and Third District congressmen. In state legislative races, the party contested twelve of seventeen races in the Senate and seventy-five of the one hundred seats in the House of Delegates. The party suffers from internal disputes, poor leadership, and a lack of public support. There is no evidence, however, that any of the disputes within the party are caused by Christian Right attempts to wrest control of the party.

While the party organization is weak, the future of the party may hinge on the Republican Legislative Committee. When Democratic legislators created the DLC in preparation for the 1996 election cycle, they copied the RLC (Seiler 1996b). In the RLC, there is some Christian Right influence.

After the 1990 elections, there was one Republican in the state senate, Donna Boley (R-Pleasants County). Meeting as the "phone booth caucus," Boley became the minority leader (Ruckle 1996b). In 1992, the size of the Republican caucus doubled and Boley continued as leader. Boley hired Robert Gould as counsel. Gould, self-recruited to run as a Republican for state attorney general in 1992, came to the state after working at the Department of Housing and Urban Development during the Reagan administration. He also worked for several months on Pat Robertson's 1988 presidential campaign (Owens 1992). Gould's first job was to assist Boley in developing legislation, particularly pro-life measures. He also organized and directed the Republican Legislative Committee, while managing his own political consulting firm on the side.[1] Since 1993, the Republican senate caucus has expanded to nine, including Republicans who defeated the senate president and four liberal Democrats. All of the new Republicans are conservative and committed to a pro-life position on abortion and a "pro-family" agenda. Clearly, the RLC is one locus to watch to judge the growing influence of the Christian Right.

The Cultural Context

West Virginia is a rural state, with nearly 60 percent of its population living outside metropolitan areas. Charleston, the state capital and largest city, has fewer than 60,000 residents. The population of 1.8 million is largely white (96 percent) and ethnically homogeneous. Brisbin et al. (1996, 2) report that the population is largely descended from "North Briton stock, including Lowland Scots (Scotch-Irish), and English from the northern shires." Less than 3 percent of the population is African American.

West Virginia also is a heavily Protestant state with a significant concentration of Catholics in the steel towns of the northern panhandle. According to Rice and Brown (1993), the early immigrants to the region were Scotch-Irish who were largely Presbyterian. Since there were few educated ministers in the region at the time, most settlers organized more evangelical congregations. These churches tended to be highly sectarian and, owing to the isolation caused by the topography, tended to remain independent of other congregations. Nonetheless, one study of religions found that "United Methodists or American Baptists were one of the two largest denominations in every county of the state" (Bradley et al. 1992, 416–23; Brisbin et al. 1996, 17). Overall, nearly 40 percent of state residents attend churches of evangelical denominations, and Methodists in the state often hold evangelical doctrinal beliefs.

This means that there is a strong religious constituency for the Christian Right in West Virginia.

The people of West Virginia have been described as a "backcountry culture" (see Brisbin et al. 1996, 6–7; see also Welch 1984). Backcountry people, according to Weller (1965), embrace tradition because of fear of change; do not join groups with which they have no natural ties, like family; and adopt a fatalistic view that may hinder involvement in groups designed to "fix" society. If this cultural interpretation is correct, then West Virginia residents may be supportive of the values of the Christian Right because of their moral traditionalism but less likely actually to join movement organizations.

West Virginians believe in an activist government; fully 38 percent agree that "the proper role of government is to bring about what it believes is good," while only 8 percent think "the proper role of government is to interfere as little as possible with the way things are" (Brisbin et al. 1996, 38). On social issues, however, West Virginians are generally conservative. A Mason-Dixon Political/Media Research poll of March 1996 found that 55 percent of West Virginians opposed legalizing casino gambling. Of those who favored legalizing casinos, 57 percent saw the issue as one of economic development. About 39 percent of those who opposed gambling saw it as a question of morality ("West Virginia–April 1996" 1996). In October 1996 the *Charleston Gazette* reported that 87.2 percent of West Virginians were opposed to legalizing same-sex marriages and 58.2 percent did not want to provide Medicaid funds to women to have abortions (*Charleston Gazette* 1996). Norrander and Wilcox (1995) reported that West Virginia is among the most conservative states on abortion opinion. In the 1996 state exit poll, fully 29 percent of voters identified themselves with the "Religious Right," compared with only 17 percent nationwide.

In general ideology, one study found that West Virginia was the most liberal of all states (Erickson, McIver, and Wright 1987, 801). Other studies report that state citizens identify themselves as conservatives. Photiadis (1985) found that rural Appalachians "tend to classify themselves politically as more or less conservative" (106). The 1996 Voter News Service exit poll found that 47 percent of West Virginia voters consider themselves "moderate," while 36 percent are "conservative."

The Christian Right faces significant obstacles. The West Virginia Republican Party offers little organizational structure on which to build. A number of residents are apolitical and shy away from joining groups. While West Virginians approve of an activist government, significant numbers also hold positions similar to those of the Christian Right. Despite the complex and somewhat uninviting political environment, the Christian Right has gained a toehold in West Virginia.

Christian Right Organizations

While the cultural predispositions of West Virginians may keep them out of the political sphere, threats to their local community and family values often mobilize citizens to action.[2] This is best illustrated by the protests that accompany the opening of an adult bookstore or a topless bar. The most famous of these protests is the Kanawha textbook controversy. In 1974, a group of parents challenged the English textbooks adopted by the Kanawha County School Board. While Charleston is in Kanawha County, the county in the 1970s was very diverse in terms of socioeconomic status. There were "two distinct populations of whites: the reasonably well-educated middle-class citizens of Charleston and the rural Appalachians" (Martin 1996, 117). Alice Moore, the wife of a fundamentalist minister and a member of the school board, led the protest, which eventually grew to include a boycott of the schools, a miners' strike, and some violence. Moore and her followers opposed the books because they were "disrespectful of authority and religion, destructive of social and cultural values, obscene, pornographic, unpatriotic, or in violation of individual and familial rights of privacy" (Jenkinson 1979, 18). There is no evidence that anyone involved in the controversy was concerned about future political activity, and none of the principals in that event appear to play significant roles in current Christian Right organizations.

According to two observers, fundamentalist Christians have become more proactive since the early 1990s, aggressively seeking to enact their agenda (Harman 1996; Blatnik 1996). The leading Christian Right organization in West Virginia is the West Virginia Family Foundation (WVFF), founded by Sam Cravotta in 1990. Cravotta was the Republican challenger to U.S. Representative Bob Wise in the Second District in 1992 and 1994. He also directs West Virginia Gun Owners of America, an affiliate of Gun Owners of America (*Charleston Gazette* 1995b). Cravotta publishes a bimonthly newsletter, the *West Virginia Family News,* in which he provides space for other organizations to present their agendas and solicit funds. In election years, the newsletter also provides voter information in the form of voter guides. Through its newsletter and board of directors, the WVFF ties together most of the pro-family, pro-life, antitax, and anti–gun control groups in the state, a source of significant power. At one time, the WVFF was formally affiliated with the American Family Association, but the WVFF lost that status in 1995 after the West Virginia secretary of state questioned the AFA's political activities. The WVFF is registered as a charity with the secretary of state, and, as such, the group may not participate in partisan politics.

The West Virginia Christian Coalition (WVCC) was active in select areas of the state in the 1994 and 1996 elections. There are chapters in a number of counties, with the most active in Kanawha, Mercer, Jackson, Putnam, and Harrison Counties. Since the organization was legally incorporated in 1991, its history has been marked by challenge. In the spring of 1995, former state senator Mark Anthony Manchin (D-Kanawha County) resigned as chairman of the group. Manchin, a son of former secretary of state and almost-impeached treasurer A. James Manchin, announced that he wanted to devote more time to his family. He revealed that his resignation was not linked to his cousin's gubernatorial campaign or to the fact that he was a Democrat in a primarily Republican organization. In fact, before leaving office, Manchin "suggested [to the Christian Coalition's national office that] it ought to get a more moderate voice in West Virginia" (Seiler 1995b).

Charleston political consultant Chuck Hamsher argues that Manchin left because of a dispute over how to respond to new state election law requirements on the disclosure of financing for voter guides and scorecards that are distributed outside the group's membership within sixty days of an election. While other WVCC leaders wanted to go to court, Manchin saw a legal challenge as unnecessary "because the coalition had nothing to hide" (Seiler 1995b). The law, enacted by the legislature in 1995, was ruled unconstitutional by a U.S. district court in March 1996 (see *West Virginians for Life v. Smith* 1996). The current chairman of the WVCC is Bill Harvey, chairman of the Mercer County Christian Coalition. He was appointed to lead the state chapter in part because his county chapter produced the most thorough voter guides in 1992.

The WVCC is independent of the national Christian Coalition. The national headquarters made the determination in February 1995 while renewing its charitable registration with West Virginia secretary of state Ken Hechler, a Democrat (Seiler 1995a). Hechler has had a significant impact on the development of the Christian Right in the state. His office is responsible for overseeing charities and political action committees (PACs). Spurred by the independent investigations of political consultant Hamsher (see Seiler 1995a), Hechler's office has challenged the status of charities that try to influence politics. It would be illegal for the WVCC, as a charity, to receive funds from the national organization because the national office was not registered as a charity in West Virginia. In order to give the secretary of state greater power to regulate voter guides and scorecards, the legislature in 1995 changed election regulations to require greater public disclosure. One senator, foreseeing the argument raised by Christian Right organizations in their suit against the law, argued that it "would make it difficult for the 'church people' and the 'gun people' to support candidates" (McCarthy 1995). Conflict with the Christian Right was not an issue in Hechler's reelection bid in 1996.[3]

The WVFF and the WVCC appear to be the two largest Christian Right organizations, although membership numbers are hard to obtain. A number of other groups operate primarily at the local level. Most groups are on the WVFF Board of Directors either as voting members or in a "nonvoting advisory capacity." In fact, several observers reported that "there couldn't be more than a dozen or so leaders" in the Christian Right in West Virginia. "When I go to different groups' meetings, I see the same people," one observer noted. The WVFF board includes Concerned Citizens of West Virginia (in Scott Depot), Concerned Citizens for Community Values (Morgantown), the West Virginia Family Council (Scott Depot), and various county and regional chapters of the Christian Coalition and the American Family Association.

West Virginians for Life (WVL), founded in 1975 and headquartered in Morgantown, is the oldest Christian Right group in the state. Unlike other Christian Right groups, WVL has been able to maintain its close affiliation with the National Right to Life Committee. Unlike other Christian Right groups, WVL has an internal political action committee, allowing it to endorse and financially support pro-life candidates. The PAC has been successful. In 1994, no pro-life incumbent lost to a pro-choice challenger. Five of six challenged pro-choice incumbent senators lost to pro-life challengers. In 1996, pro-life activists were able to help defeat pro-choice state senator Thais Blatnik (D-Ohio County), a Catholic.

WVL tends to be pragmatic and bipartisan in its politics. During the 1996 session, the state House Constitutional Revision Committee was considering a proposed antiabortion amendment to the state constitution. On the day of a key vote, West Virginians for Life, supported by the National Right-to-Life Committee, published fliers calling on legislators to oppose the amendment (Seiler 1996c). They did not see the necessity of conducting a potentially expensive referendum campaign that might distract attention from electing pro-life legislators (Adkins 1996). A number of Christian Right leaders, including Cravotta, were understandably angry at the WVL's change of tactics.

Other groups, such as the Concerned Women of West Virginia and the Eagle Forum of West Virginia, have been active in the state. These groups were very active during the debate over reauthorizing funds for the West Virginia Women's Commission, a target of Christian Right groups because of its research on women's issues.

The 1996 Election

Primaries

The primaries were a disappointment for the Christian Right. By the 14 May West Virginia primary, Bob Dole had secured the Republican presidential nomination. Dole was not the first choice of many Christian Right activists. Jay Wolfe, a Clarksburg businessman and pro-life Republican candidate for the U.S. Senate in 1988, directed the Phil Gramm campaign in the state. When Gramm left the race, Wolfe became the state coordinator for Pat Buchanan (Wolfe 1996).[4] In the Democratic U.S. Senate primary, incumbent senator John D. Rockefeller IV handily defeated the Reverend Bruce Barilla, director of the Christian Heritage Week Ministry in southern West Virginia. Second District congressman Bob Wise (D-Charleston) easily defeated a pro-life opponent in his primary.

The races in which the Christian Right was most active were the Republican primary in the Second Congressional District and the Democratic and Republican gubernatorial primaries. In the summer of 1995, Cravotta announced that he was going to seek the Republican nomination in the Second Congressional District. Cravotta had been Representative Wise's opponent in the 1992 and 1994 general elections. In November 1995, seven of the eight Republicans then serving in the state senate endorsed another candidate, Greg Morris (*Charleston Gazette* 1995a).

The Christian Right played an active role in both gubernatorial primary campaigns, providing favored candidates with endorsements. On the Democratic side, front-runner Charlotte Pritt was challenged by Marion County state senator Joe Manchin and nine other candidates. Pritt had been a state senator from Kanawha County until she challenged incumbent governor Gaston Caperton in the 1992 Democratic primary and almost won. Senator Manchin was "endorsed" by the Christian Coalition, West Virginians for Life PAC, and the National Rifle Association. Manchin regularly introduced pro-life legislation and supported other pro-family issues as a senator. In a much maligned attempt to weaken Manchin's relationship with the Christian Right, Pritt's campaign ran a commercial in which "a preacher of a church [Pritt] rarely attended [gave] public testimony to her piety" (Deutsch 1996).

The GOP primary pitted two Christian Right favorites against a former governor. Former GOP party chair David McKinley of Wheeling was the first entrant into the race, followed closely by former astronaut Jon McBride of Lewisburg in Greenbrier County. Before declaring his candidacy, McBride commissioned a poll to determine whether he should run as a Democrat or Republican, or take a chance as an independent candidate. He chose Republican, angering McKinley, who saw 1996 as his year. Both contenders were surprised, and a little frustrated, when just after Christmas 1995, former governor Cecil Underwood announced he would try to retake the mansion he left in 1961.

Both McKinley and McBride had the enthusiastic support of the Christian Right. The West Virginians for Life newsletter printed the pro-life views of both men. It was noted that McKinley had a 100 percent pro-life voting record while serving in the state house of delegates. Cecil Underwood did not return the group's survey and was considered "pro-abortion" (*Life Matters* 1996b). Christian Right endorsements were so important to McKinley and McBride that the candidates bickered over who had endorsed whom. McKinley's campaign "questioned McBride's claims to endorsements by Americans for Tax Reform, West Virginia Family Foundation, and West Virginians for Life." McBride's campaign chairman, Bob Gould, responded that McBride had the support of these groups (*Charleston Gazette* 1996b). Finally, the Christian Coalition's voter guide indicated that both McKinley and McBride answered "correctly" on the "1996 State Issues Survey."

To examine the impact of the Christian Right on primary election voting, we regressed county vote totals for Manchin and for Underwood on county demographic and religious characteristics. To our surprise, Manchin did significantly less well in counties with significant concentrations of members of traditional evangelical denominations, and evangelical membership had no impact on voting in the GOP primary. Manchin did best in the Democratic primary in more affluent counties, as did the two candidates backed by the Christian Right in the GOP primary. It is not immediately clear why membership in evangelical denominations does not predict support for Christian Right candidates, but it may well be because of the prevalence of evangelical doctrine in mainline Protestant churches, especially among Methodists.

The Christian Right played a less important role in state legislative primaries. Few Republican primaries were contested. On the Democratic side, contested races were either open seats or incumbents who were challenged because of their votes on workers' compensation reform. The Christian Right lost an ally in the Democratic primary in Summers County with the defeat of Delegate Arnold Ryan, who had guided the effort to abolish the Women's Commission in 1995 and headed the effort to place a pro-life amendment in the state constitution (*Charleston Gazette* 1996a).

General Election

The Christian Right, while almost shut out in the primaries, played a significant role in the general election. We are able to use the Voter News Service (VNS) exit polls to learn about the choices of Christian Right voters. These data complement the county-level contextual data used in the multivariate models. We do, however, recognize that the VNS uses a potentially unreliable method of measuring Christian Right affiliation.

In the campaigns for federal offices, little was heard from the Christian Right. Of course, the Christian Coalition, West Virginia Family Foundation, and West Virginians for Life identified Republicans Bob Dole and congressional candidate Greg Morris as the proper choices on voter guides. Senator Rockefeller's challenger, Betty Burks, was largely invisible and could not be found by the Christian Coalition. The VNS exit poll found that 29 percent of the West Virginia electorate considered themselves part of the conservative movement "known as the Religious Right." Bob Dole received 54 percent of the "Religious Right" vote with Clinton getting 37 percent. Clinton received 55 percent of the "non–Religious Right" vote. Rockefeller received 61 percent of the religious right vote and 83 percent of the non–religious right vote.

The gubernatorial contest between Pritt and Underwood revolved around economic issues. Marc Harman, Underwood's campaign manager, revealed that while moral issues are important to many voters, the campaign's polls indicated that West Virginians were concerned about economic development, health care, and education (Harman 1996). Nonetheless, moral issues did enter the picture. While Congress debated the Defense of Marriage Act, the media asked how the candidates would handle similar state legislation if elected. Underwood responded quickly that he would sign a state Defense of Marriage Act. Pritt hesitated, waiting almost ten days to answer that she would also sign similar legislation.

The campaigns let other groups raise moral issues. Democrats for Underwood worked to keep conservative Democrats out of the Pritt camp. A series of television and radio commercials detailing Pritt's state senate votes on issues dealing with children, pornography, and flag-burning were paid for by the Republican Senatorial Committee, a national organization (Ruckle 1996a). Christian Right activist Jay Wolfe established a political action committee called "Just the Facts, Ma'am!" and circulated Pritt's voting record on moral and pro-family issues. In an unusual development, Underwood had the "correct" answers on the Christian Coalition's voter guide despite the fact that he had not responded during the primary.

Cecil Underwood was not the Christian Right's candidate in the primary, but he was definitely a more favorable choice than Pritt. The VNS exit poll found that Underwood received 67 percent of the votes of those who identified with the religious right; however, Pritt was able to garner the support of only 50 percent of non–religious right voters. Underwood was elected governor with 52 percent of the votes. In a sterling example of pragmatism, West Virginians for Life proclaimed "WV elects a pro-life governor" (*Life Matters* 1996a).

To assess the importance of the Christian Right, we return to our multivariate model. Once again, the percentage of evangelicals in a county was not a significant predictor of vote choice. That evangelicalism did not influence vote choice even in the general election is striking, for evangelicals are more supportive of GOP candidates in nearly every state.

The most significant Christian Right influence in 1996 was felt in races for the state senate. Two incumbent Democrats were defeated by opponents endorsed by Christian Right organizations. In Kanawha County, David Grubb was defeated by state house member Vic Sprouse. Grubb was a target of the Christian Right because of his visible support for abortion rights, gay rights, and gun control. Late in the campaign, Grubb stated his support for same-sex marriages on a Charleston talk radio program, sealing his fate. As a member of the house of delegates, Republican Sprouse supported the attempt to abolish the Women's Commission and to place a pro-life amendment in the constitution. He went as far as to call on Governor Caperton to call the legislature into special session to debate a state Defense of Marriage Act. Senator Grubb, despite labor support, was defeated. Sprouse garnered 51 percent of the vote. This marked the second consecutive election in which a Kanawha County Democrat lost his senate seat to a conservative Republican. In 1994, Republican Jack Buckalew defeated incumbent Democrat Jim Humphreys, also a "friend of labor."

In two other races, the Christian Right won one and lost one. Democratic incumbent senator Thais Blatnik of Wheeling was defeated by Andy McKenzie by a margin of 53 percent to 47 percent (Gallagher 1996). According to former senator Blatnik, the pro-lifers distorted her voting record and drew attention to her repeated support of abortion rights. "They put disgusting handbills under windshield wipers and slipped them under doors. Some of the pictures of fetuses, I didn't want my grandkids to see," Blatnik explained. Even the priest at her Roman Catholic church was less than kind during the campaign (Blatnik 1996). Of course, her highly visible support for riverboat gambling proposals did not win her many friends with fundamentalist Protestants either. In the other targeted race, incumbent Democrat Bob Dittmar was reelected in the fourth senatorial district. Dittmar, a conservative, was depicted as a liberal by his opponent, Bobby Brown. Brown was endorsed by West Virginians for Life and the West Virginia Family Council, a new organization loosely affiliated with the national Family Research Council. In 1996, the Republican Party won two senate seats but lost five seats in the house of delegates. The party had fared better in 1994, winning six seats in the senate and gaining ten in the house.

Conclusion

The Christian Right faces substantial obstacles in its attempt to influence West Virginia politics. West Virginians for Life president Charlotte Snead said:

Our greatest challenge . . . is getting the working class, although traditionally church-going and conservative, to vote against union dictates. Many simple folks, not highly educated or politically savvy, vote as they are instructed, and their closest leaders are in their unions. . . . So, pro-lifers vote in block [sic], when they are knowledgeable, but the impact is dulled by devotion to Party and union. (Snead 1996)

Recent trends may work to limit party and union voting. First, union membership is declining as the number of jobs in manufacturing decreases. Service industries are not as easily unionized. The second trend is reflected in the number of new voters who register as independents. While it is difficult to determine how these new independents vote, the Democratic Party cannot depend on a large body of straight-ticket voters in the future.[5]

Other groups in the Christian Right would benefit from following the lead of West Virginians for Life and becoming more pragmatic and less purist. The greatest stumbling block to attracting significant numbers of union families, who are social conservatives, to the Christian Right banner is the call for "right to work." If the West Virginia Family Foundation and the West Virginia Christian Coalition could convince union members that "Republican" does not necessarily equal "right to work," then we would see more support for the Christian Right in the state.

Furthermore, factional divisions within the Democratic Party create the possibility of a truly bipartisan Christian Right strategy in the state. Many Democratic voters and even officeholders are cultural conservatives, so the weakness of the state GOP need not mean that the Christian Right cannot influence state policies. Although at the national level the Christian Right has firmly established itself as a Republican movement, in West Virginia it might be better served by adopting a less partisan stance.

There remains a substantial base of support for culturally conservative politics in West Virginia, but the statistical analysis described above suggests that the political system does not provide a mechanism for this constituency to express its views. Conservative Democratic candidates appeal to conservative Christians, as do many Republican candidates. The evangelical vote is split in West Virginia between the GOP and the conservative factions of the Democratic Party.

We must caution against attributing too much of the West Virginia Republican Party's recent success to the Christian Right. The prima facie evidence suggests that the trends seen in state legislative elections mirror the national trends: the state GOP did better in 1994, a Republican year, and was less successful (except for Underwood) in 1996, a Democratic year. For the Christian Right to be identified as truly influential in West Virginia politics, a significant event will have to take place—for example, Republicans need to gain a number of seats in the senate in a "Democratic" election year, or a Christian Right leader must be appointed party chair. A realignment of the parties would help. The GOP organization would not benefit significantly from a Christian Right takeover. The Republican Party is in debt, and the Christian Right would add little to its coffers.

Finally, change comes slowly in West Virginia. The Christian Right became increasingly active in many states in the early 1990s, but its influence has not truly been felt on a large scale in West Virginia. Former senator Blatnik, a victim of the Christian Right, suggested that we should continue watching "them" closely. "In the next 18 months or so, they will become much more powerful," she said (Blatnik 1996). The 1998 election cycle could be a defining moment for the Christian Right in West Virginia.

Notes

We would like to thank a number of people for helping us with this research. Chuck Hamsher of Knight Phillips Associates in Charleston provided some of his research and a significant amount of time. Professor Chuck Smith of West Virginia State College also directed us to important information on Christian Right organizations in the state. The persons we interviewed were generous with their time and insights on West Virginia politics. They are identified in the references. Chris Davis, a former student, assisted in locating legal information presented in this research. Finally, the Voter News Service exit poll data were purchased by Rausch Consulting of Fairmont.

1. Much of the legislative staff is hired for the duration of the legislative session. Many have other jobs, including positions with lobbying firms.

2. This section relies on research conducted by political consultant Chuck Hamsher of Knight Phillips Associates of Charleston.

3. Executive officials (e.g., secretary of state, treasurer, commissioner of agriculture) are elected in West Virginia.

4. West Virginians remember Wolfe for his commercials, "graphic portrayals of a fetus in front of an American flag" (*Fairmont Times–West Virginian* 1988).

5. It should also be noted that any movement leader who refers to voters as "simple folk" who are poorly educated and who follow the orders of union leaders will have a difficult time reaching out to the broader electorate.

References

Adkins, Melissa. 1996. "1996 Legislative Session: New Challenges to Overcome." *Life Matters* (WVL newsletter), March/April.

Bibby, John F., and Thomas M. Holbrook. 1996. "Parties and Elections." In *Politics in the American States: A Comparative Analysis,* 6th ed., ed. Virginia Gray and Herbert Jacob. Washington, D.C.: Congressional Quarterly Press.

Blatnik, Thais. 1996a. "Commentary: Does the West Virginia Legislature Really Have Two Parties?" In *Government and Politics in West Virginia,* ed. James R. Forrester. 3d ed. Needham Heights, Mass.: Simon & Schuster Custom Publishing.

————. 1996b. Interview by author, 21 November.

Bradley, Martin B., et al., eds. 1992. *Churches and Church Membership in the United States, 1990.* Atlanta: Glenmary Research Center.

Brisbin, Richard A., Robert Jay Dilger, Allan S. Hammock, and Christopher Z. Mooney. 1996. *West Virginia Politics and Government.* Lincoln: University of Nebraska Press.

Charleston Gazette. 1995a. "Cravotta Not GOP State Senators' Preference." (15 November).

————. 1995b. "Cravotta to Take on Wise Again." (19 July).

————. 1996a. "Charade." Editorial. (8 February).

————. 1996b. "State GOP Chairman Critical of Comment by Underwood." (26 April).

Deutsch, Jack. 1995. "Voters Pick Pritt, for God's Sake." *Charleston Daily Mail.* (17 May).

Erikson, Robert S., John P. McIver, and Gerald C. Wright Jr. 1987. "State Political Culture and Public Opinion." *American Political Science Review* 81: 797–813.

Fairmont Times–West Virginian. 1988. "Controversy Surrounds Wolfe's Ads." (3 November).

Fenton, John H. 1957. *Politics in the Border States.* New Orleans: Hauser Press.

Gallagher, A. V. "GOP Gains Two Seats in State Senate." *Charleston Daily Mail* (6 November).

Harman, Marc. 1996. Interview by author, 30 September.

Jenkinson, Edward B. 1979. *Censors in the Classroom.* New York: Avon.

Key, V. O., Jr. 1963. *American State Politics: An Introduction.* New York: Knopf.

Life Matters. 1996a. November/December.

————. 1996b. "WVL-PAC Announces Endorsements for Statewide Races." March/April 1996.

Marsh, Don. 1996. "Pritt Shakes Up the Country Club Set." *Graffiti* (Charleston), September.

Martin, William. 1996. *With God on Our Side: The Rise of the Religious Right in America.* New York: Broadway Books.

McCarthy, Jack. 1995. "Bill Forces Religious Groups to File Reports of Election Activities." *Charleston Gazette* (11 March).

Owens, Paul. 1992. "GOP Hopeful Has to Beat the Odds." *Charleston Daily Mail* (26 May).

Photiadis, John. 1985. *Community and Family Change in Rural Appalachia.* Morgantown: West Virginia University Center for Extension and Continuing Education.

Rice, Otis K., and Stephen W. Brown. 1993. *West Virginia: A History,* 2d ed. Lexington: University Press of Kentucky.

Ruckle, Stacey. 1996a. "Radio Spots Attack Pritt's Patriotism." *Charleston Daily Mail* (29 October).

———. 1996b. "Senator Will Not Fight for Leadership Position." *Charleston Daily Mail* (20 November).

Seiler, Fanny. 1995a. "Christian Coalition Calls State Group Independent." *Charleston Gazette* (24 February).

———. 1995b. "Manchin to Give Up Post with Christian Coalition." *Charleston Gazette* (28 April).

———. 1996a. "Kiss, Labor Leaders Discuss Philosophical Makeup of House." *Charleston Sunday Gazette-Mail* (27 October).

———. 1996b. "Manchin Letter Slams Pritt's Qualification, Integrity." *Charleston Sunday Gazette-Mail* (3 November).

———. 1996c. "Weapons Bill Advances." *Charleston Gazette* (8 February).

Snead, Charlotte. 1996. E-mail message to John David Rausch Jr., 4 April.

Wald, Kenneth D. 1992. *Religion and Politics in the United States.* 2d ed. Washington, D.C.: Congressional Quarterly Press.

Welch, Janet Boggess. 1984. "A Study of Appalachian Cultural Values as Evidenced in the Political and Social Attitudes of Rural West Virginians." Ph.D. diss., University of Maryland.

Weller, Jack. 1965. *Yesterday's People: Life in Contemporary Appalachia.* Lexington: University of Kentucky Press.

"West Virginia-April 1996." 1996. http://www.nando.net/newsroom/nt/Elex96/polls/wv496.html. 16 October.

West Virginians for Life v. Smith. 1996. 919 F. Supp. 954.

Wolfe, Jay. 1996. Interview by author. 26 October.

16

Conclusion: The Christian Right in Campaign '96

Mark J. Rozell and Clyde Wilcox

The essays in this volume show that the Christian Right was active and organized in 1996 but that its strengths and successes varied from state to state. In some states, the Christian Right is organized and effective, in some others it is not a significant player in politics. In this chapter, we focus on the Christian Right in national politics, beginning with an examination of the role of the movement in the 1996 presidential election. We then discuss the success of the Christian Right with the GOP Congress and examine divisions within the movement and between the Christian Right and moderate Republicans. Finally, we assess what the Christian Right has achieved and speculate about its prospects.

After the 1994 elections, it appeared that the Christian Right was an important insurgent force in American politics, especially within the Republican Party. Many analysts agreed with Ralph Reed's claim that Christian conservatives had been a key element in the winning coalition that had swept to power a GOP majority in both the House and Senate for the first time in a generation. An article in *Campaigns & Elections* credited the Christian Right with having dominant or substantial influence in some thirty-one state Republican parties, and Pat Robertson openly called to increase that number to 100 percent (Persinos 1994). At the 1995 Christian Coalition convention in Washington, D.C., all but one of the GOP presidential hopefuls made an appearance and appealed for support.

After the 1996 elections, the status of the Christian Right in the GOP and in American national politics is more ambiguous. Clearly, 1996 was not a stellar year for the Christian Right. Although Bob Dole, the Republican presidential nominee, had strong credentials as a social conservative, he refused to campaign on those issues, choosing instead to stress his proposal to cut income and other taxes. Americans reelected as president a man who was detested by Christian Right activists, who had vetoed legislation that would ban certain late-term abortion procedures, and who had supported increased civil liberties protections for gays and lesbians. Moreover, Republican moderates were beginning to organize in an effort to regain control of state and local party organizations. Finally, after two years of Republican control of Congress, the Christian Right had made little progress in achieving its policy goals.

Yet the news was not all bad for the Christian Right. Its strongest supporters in the House of Representatives had won reelection about as often as other Republicans, and the party retained control of that chamber. Moreover, the retirement of a number of moderate GOP senators resulted in the elections of members sympathetic to the Christian Right. And after the 1996 elections the Christian Right was probably more entrenched in GOP party organizations and was dominant in more places than it had been two years previously.

The Presidential Nomination Campaign

Although in late 1994 Clinton's flagging popularity had raised GOP hopes of regaining the White House in 1996, the president moved quickly and effectively to shore up his political support and to negate traditional GOP advantages on issues such as crime and values. On crime Clinton continued his support of the death penalty, worked to increase the number of beat officers across the country, and worked for gun control, thereby winning the support of many police groups that had in the past endorsed Republican nominees. His position on gun control also helped him shore up votes among liberal activists, many of whom were deeply disappointed with his support of a GOP-led welfare reform measure. Clinton seized control of family values, advocating school uniforms, a V-chip and a voluntary rating system to help parents regulate the amount of sex and violence their children view on television, and stricter regulation of tobacco.

As Clinton moved early to preempt the social issues and to build his popularity, a number of important social conservatives such as William Bennett, Dan Quayle, and Jack Kemp announced that they would not seek the presidency in 1996. Christian conservatives had three candidates willing to champion their issues: television commentator Patrick Buchanan, former Reagan administration UN ambassador Alan Keyes, and California congressman Bob Dornan. Although each of these men appealed to different constituencies in the Christian Right, none of them had a real chance to win the GOP nomination, much less the presidency. Texas senator Phil Gramm also hoped to attract Christian conservative votes, but when Ralph Reed and James Dobson visited him to complain that he was not making social issues a focus of his campaign, he reportedly snapped, "I am not running for preacher. I am running for president." (Reed 1996, 240). Dobson's anger at this encounter helped assure that Gramm would not get the backing of Christian Right organizations.

Buchanan trounced Gramm in the Louisiana caucuses, despite the Texas senator's strong financial and time commitment to that state. In Iowa, Buchanan gave Dole a real scare, eventually losing by only 3 percent of the vote, and in New Hampshire he narrowly defeated Dole. At that point, Ralph Reed reportedly decided to back Bob Dole, who had a long record of opposition to abortion but who was most clearly identified as part of the moderate wing of the party. Reed's decision was primarily pragmatic—Dole was still the favorite to win the party nomination, and early support by Christian conservatives might ensure that they would have more say in a Dole administration. Moreover, all three candidates who most ardently appealed to Christian Right voters came with certain baggage that made it difficult to unite the movement behind them, and none had as good a shot as Dole at defeating Clinton in November. The South Carolina primary victory was the key turning point for Dole, and many analysts credited Reed and other pragmatic Christian conservative leaders with having helped the front-runner secure enough Christian Right votes to defeat Buchanan handily.

The decision to back Dole was not universally supported by Christian conservatives. Although Dole managed to enlist a number of activists from Robertson's 1988 presidential bid, some Christian Coalition activists signed on for Patrick Buchanan, and exit polls showed that Dole trailed Buchanan among self-identified supporters of the "religious right" outside the South but that his substantial margin among more secular conservatives propelled him to victory. In many states in the South, however, Dole carried a narrow majority of the votes of Christian conservatives as well, possibly because fundamentalist Baptists were reluctant to back Catholic Buchanan.

Ultimately, the decision by leaders of the Christian Coalition to back Dole helped legitimize his candidacy among many Christian conservatives who were nervous about his unwillingness to emphasize social issues in his campaign. After Dole clinched the nomination, Christian conservatives pressured him both on the platform and on his selection of a running mate. Party moderates, in contrast, urged him to move quickly to the center and to avoid the combative rhetoric that characterized "family values night" at the party's 1992 presidential convention.

Dole indicated support for a move that would embody the concept of a "big tent" in the Republican platform by calling for tolerance for those with divergent viewpoints on abortion. Christian conservatives strongly opposed this language, however, and they had powerful and vocal advocates on the platform committee in Bay Buchanan, Ralph Reed, Paul Weyrich, Gary Bauer, and Phyllis Schlafly. Ultimately, Dole's proposed language on tolerance was defeated, although Christian conservatives did allow him to include it in an appendix that contained defeated proposals. Christian conservatives then made the choice of a pro-life running mate a litmus test for their support. Although Dole initially resisted this pressure, he eventually chose Jack Kemp, a choice that excited social and economic conservatives alike.

Although members of the Christian Right won on the platform and were satisfied with the selection of Kemp, they had less to applaud at the GOP convention in San Diego. The main speaker on opening night was Colin Powell, who publicly professed his pro-choice credentials to some scattered boos. New Jersey governor and pro-choice Republican Christine Todd Whitman was cochair of the convention, and pro-choice representative Susan Molinari the keynote speaker. Dole's speech touched on family values without referring directly to any of the issues central to the Christian Right. Patrick Buchanan, whose rousing "culture wars" speech in 1992 was widely believed to have cost Bush votes, was not allowed to speak. When reporters asked Dole and party chair Haley Barbour how they might square the inclusive message of the convention with the party's repudiation of a tolerance plank in the platform, both men responded that they had not read the platform. As Republicans for Choice chair Ann Stone described it, "Dole ultimately gave the platform to the conservatives and the convention to the moderates" (Stone 1996).

During the general election campaign, Dole focused on a variety of themes and messages, but he never explicitly embraced the social agenda of the Christian Right. When Jack Kemp visited Pat Robertson, Robertson sent a message to Dole imploring him to speak out on abortion, education, or any other issue that might excite Christian Right activists. Dole ignored this advice, as did Kemp himself, who instead focused his efforts on broadening the Republican base to include minority groups. In October, with Dole still trailing by double digits in the polls, Christian conservatives began to call publicly on him to focus his campaign on values, mostly to no avail. Dole did signal his support for Christian Right values by scheduling a brief speech to the Christian Coalition annual leadership meeting. One of the few times that Dole actually mentioned an issue of special interest to Christian conservatives was in the final presidential debate, when the candidates were asked their views on legislation that would protect gays and lesbians from discrimination in the labor force. Dole first denounced "special rights" but then quickly emphasized that discrimination was wrong and said that his Senate office had never discriminated in hiring on the basis of sexual preference.

Although Dole did better on election day than most polls had predicted, his lackluster campaign and Clinton's easy victory led to the usual round of recriminations in the party, and Christian conservatives were quick to argue that Dole lost precisely because he refused to embrace the social issues their supporters most cared about. If only Dole had more directly and passionately championed a pro-life stand, or school choice, or traditional moral values, they claimed, he could have beaten Clinton by igniting the enthusiasm of social movement activists. Party moderates replied that it was the actions of the Christian conservatives that weakened Dole; by refusing even to allow language about tolerance in the platform, they argued, the party had signaled that it was controlled by uncompromising religious fanatics.

In fact, there is probably very little that Dole could have done to win the election. Clinton had spent the previous two years carefully stealing one Republican issue after another, and the economy was doing remarkably well. Even affluent Republicans were celebrating a surging Dow that refused to become a bear, and it is historically very difficult to defeat an incumbent president in the midst of good economic times. The Clinton campaign also had an enormous financial advantage in the late spring and used that money to portray Dole as too old and too lacking in new ideas to be president. In many ways, Clinton's reelection victory echoed Reagan's 1984 triumph—a contest in which voters signaled that they wanted more of the same (Herrnson and Wilcox 1997).

Dole failed to campaign on Christian Right issues not because he was a closet social liberal—his long career in the Senate proves that he is a genuine social conservative—but because his pollsters told him that these issues were losers for him, that he would divide his party, alienate independents and moderates, and frighten younger voters if he campaigned on a very conservative social agenda. For much the same reason, the GOP in 1994 did not include abortion in its Contract with America, and even the Christian Coalition did not call for banning abortion in its Contract with the American Family. When the GOP platform is to the right of the official program of the Christian Coalition, it seems unlikely that that platform is the ticket to winning an election.[1]

Overall, the presidential campaign was a setback for the Christian Right, for it was effectively shut out of the campaign. On the other hand, Christian conservatives can correctly argue that Dole ignored their issues and their constituency, and lost the election. Thus movement activists will continue to pressure candidates in the year 2000 to campaign on values. And with Vice President Al Gore weakened by a campaign finance scandal, Republicans, including such Christian Right favorites as Dan Quayle, now appear to be lining up to run.

Taking Stock of Christian Right Successes in the GOP Congress

Since 1978 the Christian Right has devoted most its energies to influencing and perhaps even capturing the Republican Party. Although the Christian

Coalition claims to be nonpartisan in order to maintain its tax-exempt status, in fact Pat Robertson, Ralph Reed, and other Christian conservative leaders are highly visible Republicans, and the movement has made major efforts to move white evangelicals even more quickly into the Republican camp. As a result, white evangelicals are an important electoral constituency for the GOP, providing 38 percent of Bush's votes in 1992 (Green et al. 1994).

When the Republicans won control of Congress in 1994, most analysts attributed their victory in part to the mobilization efforts of Christian conservatives, gun enthusiasts, and other cultural groups. Although the Republicans' Contract with America avoided divisive social issues and focused instead on economic policy, Newt Gingrich assured Ralph Reed and others that the House would turn to these issues after it finished its work on the Contract. He promised a vote on school prayer by the Fourth of July. In the meantime, the Christian Coalition continued to support the party, contributing funds and energies to help write and promote legislation for the GOP Contract.

In May 1995, the Christian Coalition released its own Contract with the American Family (figure 16.1). Like the Republicans' Contract, the Coalition's platform was carefully tested with polling and focus groups and included only items that research showed might gain popular support. The document made

Figure 16.1
The Christian Coalition's "Contract with the American Family"

1. Allow communal prayer in public places such as schools, high school graduation ceremonies, and courthouses.
2. Abolish the federal Department of Education.
3. Establish vouchers for parents to use to send their children to private and parochial schools.
4. Establish a $500 tax credit for children, favor "in concept" a flat tax, remove the "marriage penalty" in tax laws, and allow homemakers to contribute $2,000 annually toward an Individual Retirement Account.
5. Limit abortion, ban certain abortion procedures, end use of Medicaid funds for abortion, cut off federal funding for groups such as Planned Parenthood.
6. Limit access to pornography on cable television and the Internet.
7. Abolish federal funding for the National Endowments for the Arts and Humanities, the Corporation for Public Broadcasting, and the Legal Services Corporation.
8. Eventually turn over welfare programs to private charities.
9. Enact a "Parental Rights Act" and reject the UN Convention on the Rights of the Child.
10. Use federal funds to encourage states to require prisoners to study and work, and require restitution to victims subsequent to release.

Source: Washington Post, 18 May 1995, A6

no mention of gay and lesbian rights, and called for banning only "certain abortion procedures" and for limiting access to pornography on cable television and the Internet. The document outlined what was in many ways a curious agenda, for most Christian Right activists seek far more sweeping changes to policy in these areas (Wilcox 1996).

Moreover, the Contract with the American Family showed that Reed continued to be a good party regular: although the first three elements of the Contract deal with educational issues of great interest to Christian conservatives, the fourth plank calls for a flat tax, the eighth calls for eliminating welfare, and the final plank calls for prisoners to make restitution to their victims. Although white evangelicals have become conservative on economic issues (Fowler and Hertzke 1995), these issues are more central to the agenda of secular conservatives than to Christian Right activists. Presumably Reed included these items in part to cast his platform as a mainstream GOP document and perhaps to increase support for these items among Christian conservatives. He must have anticipated that in exchange the GOP would back the items of most concern to the Christian Right.

The GOP did take up some of the Christian Coalition program. The House and Senate passed a ban on "partial-birth" abortions but could not muster the votes to override Clinton's veto. They also passed restrictions on Internet pornography, in language so broad that it is unlikely to survive a ruling by the Supreme Court. Individual Retirement Accounts (IRAs) for homemakers were expanded. And the Defense of Marriage Act became law, despite its absence from the Christian Coalition Contract.

Early in 1997, the Christian Coalition released a report detailing twenty-three Christian Right victories in the GOP Congress. The list of victories contained many items that are merely a part of the mainstream GOP agenda, including welfare reform and limits on the Legal Services Corporation—hardly issues centrally identified with religious conservatives. Most of the items that dealt more explicitly with social issues were very tiny victories indeed: for example, providing asylum for victims of forced abortion, and banning the use of federal funds for abortions for federal prisoners.

But overall, the Republican Congress spent more time catering to its economic constituency than its social supporters. Misreading the meaning of the 1994 election results, the GOP Congress acted with a mandate mentality and moved quickly and aggressively to try to relax environmental regulations, weaken consumer protection laws, cut domestic spending, and help corporations—all actions that were highly unpopular and plunged Congress's approval rating to levels below even that of the Democratic Congress that the public had replaced. Among cultural conservatives, it was the gun enthusiasts who perhaps did best, at least in the House, which voted to repeal the ban on assault weapons and held hearings where the National Rifle Association identified and interviewed witnesses and for a time sat with the committee staff. Although the repeal of the gun ban did not pass (principally because Dole was running for president and did not want to spend the entire campaign defending the repeal), the House action did demonstrate that the GOP was willing to spend a lot of political capital to pay back its core supporters.

Although pragmatists such as Ralph Reed put a positive spin on Christian conservative victories in the GOP Congress, other movement activists are understandably less positive. Former Moral Majority leader Cal Thomas has written in great frustration that after eighteen years of working for the Republicans, it appears to him that the party values tobacco farmers more than Christian conservatives and is more concerned with cutting taxes than with stopping abortion (Thomas 1996a). There is increasing talk among many movement purists that it may be time to form a third party or to join with the American Taxpayer Party. Some maintain that perhaps they can achieve more through private actions in their own communities than through laborious work in party politics.

In his book *Active Faith,* Reed details the disappointment that movement activists eventually felt with the Reagan administration. He notes that Reagan lobbyists made only token efforts to implement the policy agenda of Christian conservatives, despite significant rhetorical support (Reed 1996). Indeed, Reagan's policy payoffs to the economic conservatives in tax cuts and to defense conservatives in increased spending were truly substantial, but his policy offerings to the Christian Right were mostly symbolic. Over the next two years, we will see if the Christian Right can do any better with the GOP still in control of Congress. If the Congress also gives Christian conservatives mostly small symbolic victories, then the movement may face the dilemma of either calling the party to account for its policies and possibly withholding support or continuing to support a party more interested in economic than social policy. Either strategy has its dangers: should the Christian Right withdraw its support for a time from the GOP, it risks political marginalization, but if it continues to back Republicans despite few concrete achievements in public policy, it risks alienating its activist core and therefore losing its most valuable resource. We will discuss this dilemma in more detail below.

In March 1997 the Christian Coalition announced strong support for Representative Ernest Ishtook's proposed constitutional amendment to allow prayer in public schools. The Coalition announced plans to spend as much as $2 million to promote the amendment and to lobby Congress and the public to build support. A great deal may ride on the fate of this amendment. If it passes the House and Senate, then it may spur considerable grassroots mobilization as a by-product of the effort to pass it in the states. If it fails to pass the House and Senate because a few Republicans join a united Democratic Party in opposition, then the Christian Right may continue to work enthusiastically on behalf of the GOP. But if Republican support is perceived as lukewarm, it may be increasingly difficult to persuade movement purists that support for the GOP is meaningful.

The Christian Right in the Republican Party

In 1996, the Christian Right was arguably stronger in the party than in any previous election. Its adherents made gains in controlling state and local party organizations and dominated the GOP platform committee. In previous years they had won intraparty nomination battles almost entirely where these decisions were made by caucus or convention, but in 1996 they won important primary elections as well. After the November elections, the Christian Coalition was a key player in the selection of the new GOP party chair, which for the first time put a movement sympathizer at the head of the national party.

Yet the GOP remained deeply divided between Christian conservatives and party moderates. Although the selection of Jack Kemp and Dole's choice of tax cuts as the central issue of his campaign led to a harmonious convention, the tensions between moderates and the Christian Right were evident in San Diego. Although there remain a number of politicians who can appeal to both wings of the party, such as Governor George W. Bush of Texas, Governor George Allen of Virginia, former vice president Dan Quayle, and Senator Rod Grams of Minnesota, the divide between the two factions is large. Surveys show that in some states, party moderates prefer Democrats to Christian Right candidates, and in a few cases Christian Right Republicans prefer Democrats to party moderates (Rozell and Wilcox 1996; Green, Rozell, and Wilcox 1996).

Moderates charge that Christian Right activists are uncompromising and unelectable and point to candidates such as Ellen Craswell of Washington, Lon Mabon of Oregon, Oliver North of Virginia, and Alan Quist of Minnesota. Christian conservatives argue that moderates are eager to get the votes and financial resources of Christian conservatives, but when conservative candidates win fair intraparty battles, the moderates often take a walk. Christian conservatives point to Senator John Warner's refusal to back Christian Right candidates nominated by the GOP in Virginia and note with dismay the obvious efforts by Bob Dole to distance himself from social conservatives.

Factional divisions are not new to American parties—indeed, they are the way our system processes multiple issue cleavages within a two-party system. A healthy competition between two groups of partisans with different policy preferences can at times strengthen parties, but bitter factional feuding can be a disaster. It appears that the Republicans do best at the polls when they nominate candidates who can speak the language of Christian conservatives and who offer some policy initiatives on matters of special concern to the Christian Right but who take mainly centrist positions and focus on economic issues. Such candidates do not engender a countermobilization of moderate and liberal voters and can often win the votes of even pro-choice Republicans who trust that they will not aggressively seek to implement a conservative social agenda.

Pragmatists in the Christian Right are willing to be part of this kind of coalition, reasoning that they will make incremental progress in at least some policy areas. William Kristol, writing of Ralph Reed's pragmatism, noted that "Ralph understands that the Christian Right can be part of a governing coalition, but it can't govern the nation, and that means a certain amount of compromise and accommodation" (Edsall 1996, A18). Yet movement purists increasingly question whether they get sufficient policy payoffs for their electoral and financial support of GOP candidates. Thus the split within the Republican Party in turn exacerbates an ideological and tactical division within the Christian Right between pragmatists and purists.

Purists and Pragmatists: Divisions within the Christian Right

As Christian conservatives evaluated their role in the Republican Party, the split between movement pragmatists and purists appears to have widened. Reed is the most visible pragmatist. In 1996 he made moderate pronouncements only to backtrack quickly when his comments provoked a firestorm of protest from movement purists. This was most evident on abortion, where Reed variously appeared to support replacing the abortion plank with language recognizing the right to life of all citizens, adding tolerance language to the abortion plank, allowing exceptions to the proposed constitutional amendment to ban all abortions, and making no changes to the longtime GOP call for a constitutional amendment to ban abortions. In his book *Active Faith,* Reed called for a change of language and focus on abortion, gay rights, and other issues (Reed 1996).

Reed's pragmatism has drawn sharp criticism from James Dobson, Gary Bauer, Bay Buchanan, and other Christian conservative activists, who accuse him of compromising key moral issues in order to gain access to political power. Buchanan proclaimed, "There is no question that he no longer represents those of us who feel very strongly about family values, and life, and the importance of the Republican platform" (Edsall 1996, A18.) James Dobson has openly criticized Reed's pragmatic approach to the abortion issue, and Dobson undoubtedly speaks for many movement purists who continue to support absolute policy pronouncements and strong moral and religious condemnations of behavior they believe to be sinful.

The division goes beyond Reed and his critics and is about ideas more than personalities. Consider the difference between the tactics of Smith in Oregon, who repackaged himself and moved some distance from the Oregon Citizens Alliance, thereby drawing a challenge from movement purist Mabon, and the candidacy of Craswell in Washington, who refused to compromise even to pass legislation of great interest to conservative Christians. Although many activists in the Christian Right have adopted a pragmatic approach of compromise that is essential to succeed in U.S. politics, others retain an unyielding approach to public policy.

In late 1996 and early 1997, purists in the movement questioned not only their involvement in the Republican Party but also the legitimacy of the American government itself. In a controversial symposium in *First Things,* many Christian conservatives argued that a government that countenanced abortion could not count on the support or loyalty of Christians. Charles Colson wrote that Christian conservatives must consider whether this flawed republic was really "their country" (Thomas 1996b). Echoing their arguments, former Moral Majority leader Cal Thomas reminded his readers of the words of the Declaration of Independence that "it becomes necessary for one people to dissolve the political bands that have connected them with one another" (Thomas 1996a). Although none of these writers advocated revolution or secession, they did deliberately and consistently raise the issues. In contrast, movement pragmatists advocate continued compromise and incremental progress within Republican Party politics.

Such disputes are common in social movements and are often institutionalized into different social movement organizations. In the civil rights movement, the Black Panthers advocated different policies and tactics than the Southern Christian Leadership Conference, and in the gay rights movement ACT UP advocates different policies and tactics than either the Human Rights Campaign or the Log Cabin Republicans. Sometimes these differences are reflected in struggles over the leadership of a single organization, as the many elections for leadership of the National Organization for Women demonstrate. Yet they can pose serious difficulties for a movement and possibly even create divisions deep enough to undermine any semblance of cohesion. The future of the Christian Right will depend critically on how this internal division is resolved.

The Christian Right in the Next Millennium

As the Christian Right prepares for the final national elections in this millennium, its future is uncertain. To date, the Christian Right has paradoxically been one of the most successful social movements in terms of electoral politics, while it has achieved less in concrete policy terms than many other movements in this century. The labor, civil rights, and feminist movements transformed American society and politics in ways that were almost unimaginable when the movements began. The gay and lesbian rights movement has already made impressive gains and may well end up having a profound effect on society as well. To date, the Christian Right has accomplished far less than these earlier movements (Rozell and Wilcox 1996b).

To put the achievements of various social movements in the twentieth century into context, imagine a Rip Van Winkle who fell asleep in 1952 only to awaken during the 1996 GOP convention. Rip would have been shocked to see an African American man make the most important speech on opening night and to learn that this man had been head of the Joint Chiefs of Staff. He would have stared in amazement at the enthusiasm of Colin Powell's reception and of the reaction to J. C. Watt later in the meeting. Rip would have been equally shocked to see a young mother who had retained her own name and who worked full time in the House of Representatives give the keynote address, while her husband held their young child on his knee. But on social policy, what would have surprised him most would have been the open support for abortion rights proclaimed by Powell, Whitman, and a few other Republicans and, later, the sight of the GOP nominee announcing in a presidential debate that he would never discriminate in hiring a gay or lesbian applicant.

The current wave of Christian Right activity began in 1978–79 with the formation of the Moral Majority and Christian Voice. Over the past eighteen years, the Christian Right has achieved some marginal success in policy—for example, waiting periods and parental notification on abortion, and the rights of student religious groups to meet on public school property. Yet the movement has achieved little of its core agenda, and on many issues, policy has moved in the opposite direction. Public policy and private institutions now make it easier for women to enter the labor force even when they have young children, and even many conservative major companies now pay spousal benefits to the partners of gays and lesbians.

Why has a movement that has been so successful in establishing itself in the GOP achieved so little in concrete policy terms? The policy demands of the Christian Right are different in kind from those made by the labor, civil rights, feminist, and gay and lesbian rights movements. Labor unions early in this century demanded decent pay, blacks demanded the right to vote and to attend college and to eat in any restaurant, women asked for access to higher education and meaningful careers, and now gays and lesbians ask for the right to live their lives free of discrimination based on whom they love. In each case, movement activists asked to be treated fairly—to have access to the same privileges and responsibilities as other Americans.

When the Christian Right has made similar demands, the movement usually has been successful. This is most evident in education, where nervous principals had in a few cases denied students the right to read Bibles in study hall
or offer a private prayer before lunch or organize a student religious group.
Support for free exercise of religion by religious conservatives is strong in
America, even among those who are not themselves religious (Jelen and
Wilcox 1995).[2] Where Christian conservatives suffer real discrimination or
disadvantage, the Christian Right will probably continue to achieve victories.
It is likely that Congress will enact IRA reforms to help homemakers save for
retirement, for example, and possibly enact a substantial tax credit for each
child in a family.

Recent efforts by Christian Right leaders to frame many issues in terms of
discrimination against Christians, however, may prove counterproductive. It is
difficult to convince most Americans, themselves Christians, that the large
Christian majority in America suffers from widespread discrimination. Such
indiscriminate claims of prejudice risk reducing the credibility of all claims,
even in instances where discrimination may have occurred. Moreover, the inci-
sive conservative critique of the culture of victimization applies to efforts of
Christian conservatives to cast every dispute in terms of religious prejudice by
seculars.

Yet the core of the Christian Right agenda is not about fair treatment for
Christian conservatives but about moral conduct by all Americans. What
Christian Right activists seek is not the freedom not to have abortions themselves but laws prohibiting all Americans from having abortions. They seek,
not the freedom for Christian conservative women to stay home with their children, but legal arrangements that may make it more difficult for mothers to
work. Although some activists seek only to excuse their children from using
school texts their parents find objectionable, others seek to include religious
materials, antigay propaganda, and creationism in the public school curriculum. Many Christian conservatives want to remove books from public
libraries, not merely to protect their children from being forced to read them.

For such policies to succeed, Christian Right leaders and activists must
engage the culture and persuade the country that their moral values are superior.
To date, this has not occurred. Indeed, the General Social Survey reveals that
Americans are more liberal today on abortion, gay rights, women's rights, sex
education, and similar issues than they were in the late 1970s when the Christian Right was beginning to mobilize. And more important, the most conservative Americans on these issues are the oldest cohorts, who are steadily being
replaced by a younger generation that is far more liberal on these issues. It is
quite possible that the Christian Right is fighting the tides of history.

As America approaches the new millennium, the Christian Right has achieved considerable electoral success. The movement is far more sophisticated than any earlier incarnation of the Christian Right in America, and it has made real strides in trying to ease the religious prejudices that doomed earlier Christian Right efforts (Rozell and Wilcox 1996a). Yet the movement today may well have peaked. Polls show that the Christian Right has the support of slightly more than half of white evangelicals—a figure that is especially impressive because a substantial minority of evangelicals are moderate on many issues, and many are Democrats. Recent efforts to attract Catholic support have paid off among conservative intellectuals, but there is little evidence that it is working in the parishes. Catholics may share with the Christian Right an opposition to abortion and to some types of gay rights, but they have very different views of social justice, women's roles, and economic policy. Similarly, Ralph Reed's highly visible efforts to win blacks to the Christian Right will probably not succeed so long as the movement remains an integral part of the GOP coalition. It is possible that the Christian Right might expand its support a bit more in the near future, perhaps to a figure approaching one-fifth of the population. But it is more likely that the movement's upper boundary is 15 percent of the electorate (Wilcox 1996). This represents a powerful political force—larger than African Americans and comparable to labor unions—but it is nowhere near a real "moral majority."

It now appears quite possible that the movement will begin to fragment, with moderates building permanent institutions both within the GOP and outside it, in the form of organized interest groups. Most social movements do spawn at least one large, mainstream, national organization such as NOW or the NAACP, and the Christian Coalition seems likely to be on the political scene for some time. It will attract the more pragmatic elements of the movement and will continue to work for incremental achievement of its policy goals. But the purist elements of the movement appear to be growing increasingly dissatisfied with "normal politics" and may well spin off into a series of more radical organizations that leave the Republican Party for the solitary pleasures of independent candidacies or a third party.

Notes

1. Dole was not well positioned to run on values issues, given his opposition to the V-chip and industry ratings for television content, his opposition to the assault weapons ban, his support of the tobacco industry, and the fact that he was very far from the median voter on the issue of abortion. His charges against the values of Hollywood did strike a responsive chord among many but then opened him up to ridicule when he confessed to not having seen the movies he had condemned and when he praised *True Lies,* a film that was very violent and had misogynistic overtones.

References

Edsall, Thomas. 1996. "Conservatives Win First Conflict over GOP's Antiabortion Plank." *Washington Post* (12 May): A18.

Fowler, Robert Booth, and Allen D. Hertzke. 1995. *Religion and Politics in America.* Boulder, Colo.: Westview.

Green, John C., James L. Guth, Lyman A. Kellstedt, and Corwin Smidt. 1994. "Murphy Brown Revisited: The Social Issues in the 1992 Elections." In *Disciples and Democracy,* ed. Michael Cromartie. Washington, D.C.: Ethics and Public Policy Center.

Green, John C., Mark J. Rozell, and Clyde Wilcox. 1996. "Religious Coalitions in the Christian Right: The Decline of Religious Particularism." Paper presented at the Tenth Citadel Conference on Southern Politics, Charleston, S.C.

Herrnson, Paul, and Clyde Wilcox. 1997. "The 1996 Presidential Election: A Tale of a Campaign That Didn't Seem to Matter." In *Toward the Millennium: The Elections of 1996,* ed. Larry Sabato. New York: Allyn & Bacon.

Jelen, Ted G., and Clyde Wilcox. 1995. *Public Attitudes toward Church and State.* Armonk, N.Y.: M. E. Sharpe.

Persinos, John F. 1994. "Has the Christian Right Taken Over the Republican Party?" *Campaigns & Elections,* September, 21–24.

Reed, Ralph. 1996. *Active Faith.* New York: Free Press.

Rozell, Mark J., and Clyde Wilcox. 1996a. *Second Coming: The New Christian Right in Virginia Politics.* Baltimore: Johns Hopkins University Press.

———. 1996b. "Second Coming: The Strategies of the New Christian Right." *Political Science Quarterly* (Summer): 271–94.

Stone, Ann. 1996. Speech at American University. 4 September.

Thomas, Cal. 1996a. "The Religious Right's Faith Is Tested and Found Wanting." Watch97@aol.com. 3 July.

———. 1996b. "Which Way for the Religious Right and the GOP?" *Washington Times* (23 October): A14.

Wilcox, Clyde. 1996. *Onward Christian Soldiers? The Religious Right in American Politics.* Boulder, Colo.: Westview.

Index

About the Contributors

ANDREW M. APPLETON is assistant professor of political science and associate director of the Division of Governmental Studies at Washington State University. He is coeditor of *State Party Profiles* and author of *Party Politics* (forthcoming).

JOHN M. BRUCE is assistant professor of political science and director of the Social Science Research Laboratory at the University of Mississippi. His research interests are in the areas of political parties and mass behavior.

CHARLES S. BULLOCK III is Richard B. Russell Professor of Political Science at the University of Georgia. He has done extensive research on southern politics and is the coeditor (with Keith Gaddie and John Kuzenski) of *David Duke and the Politics of Race in the South*.

ALLAN J. CIGLER is Chancellor's Club Teaching Professor of Political Science at the University of Kansas. His research and teaching interests include political parties, participation, and interest group politics.

JOEL FETZER is a visiting scholar with the Center for International Studies/Pacific Council on International Policy at the University of Southern California. His research focuses on immigration and on religion and political behavior.

DANIEL FRANCIS is a graduate student in political science at Washington State University. His dissertation research focuses on the New Christian Right and organizational changes in the Republican Party.

CHRISTOPHER P. GILBERT is associate professor of political science at Gustavus Adolphus College, St. Peter, Minnesota. He is the author of *The Impact of Churches on Political Behavior*.

JOHN C. GREEN is director of the Ray Bliss Institute of Applied Politics at the University of Akron. He has written extensively on religion and politics, including most recently as coauthor of the book *Religion and the Culture Wars: Dispatches from the Front*.

JAMES L. GUTH is professor of political science at Furman University, Greenville, South Carolina. His work on religion and politics has appeared in the *Journal of Politics, American Journal of Political Science, American Politics Quarterly, Western Political Quarterly, Social Science Quarterly, Sociology of Religion,* and many other journals and collections. He is coauthor of *Religion and the Culture Wars: Dispatches from the Front.*

BURDETT A. LOOMIS is professor of political science and interim director of the Robert J. Dole Institute for Public Service and Public Policy at the University of Kansas. He has written extensively on legislatures, interest groups, and public policy.

WILLIAM M. LUNCH is professor of political science at Oregon State University and political analyst for Oregon Public Broadcasting. He has written and broadcast on the Oregon Citizens Alliance and the Christian Right in the Northwest for a decade.

MATTHEW C. MOEN is professor and chair of the Department of Political Science at the University of Maine. His latest book on the Christian Right is *The Transformation of the Christian Right.*

KENNETH T. PALMER is professor of political science at the University of Maine, teaching in the area of state politics, federalism, and constitutional law. He is coauthor of *Maine Politics and Government* and book review editor of *Publius: The Journal of Federalism.*

JAMES M. PENNING is professor of political science at Calvin College, Grand Rapids, Michigan. He is coeditor with Corwin Smidt of *Sojourners in the Wilderness: The Christian Right in Comparative Perspective.*

DAVID A. M. PETERSON is a graduate student in political science at the University of Minnesota. His research interests are religion and politics, political behavior, and mass media influences on public opinion.

JOHN DAVID RAUSCH JR. is assistant professor of political science at Fairmont State College in West Virginia. His research interests include legislative term limits, direct democracy, and religion and politics.

MARY S. RAUSCH is catalogue librarian at Fairmont State College. Her research interests include political culture, West Virginia politics, and library automation.

MARK J. ROZELL is associate professor of political science at American University in Washington, D.C. His latest book on the Christian Right is *Second Coming: The New Christian Right in Virginia Politics* (with Clyde Wilcox).

RICHARD K. SCHER is professor of political science at the University of Florida and the author of *Politics in the New South* (2d ed.).

CORWIN E. SMIDT is professor of political science at Calvin College, Grand Rapids, Michigan. His research focuses on religion and politics. He is coauthor of *Religion and the Culture Wars: Dispatches from the Front.*

CHRISTIAN SMITH is assistant professor of sociology at the University of North Carolina–Chapel Hill. He is the author most recently of *Resisting Reagan: The U.S. Central America Peace Movement.*

MARK C. SMITH is a graduate student in political science at the University of Georgia. He has an M.A. in the history of Christianity from Trinity Evangelical Divinity School, and his research focuses on religion and politics.

ORAN P. SMITH received his Ph.D. from the University of South Carolina in 1995 and is the author of a number of papers and articles on religion and politics in the South. He is also the author of *The Rise of Baptist Republicanism* (forthcoming).

J. CHRISTOPHER SOPER is associate professor of political science at Pepperdine University. His latest book is *The Challenge of Pluralism: Church and State in Five Democracies.*

RAY SWISHER is a doctoral student in the Department of Sociology at the University of North Carolina–Chapel Hill. His current research interests include determinants of voting with the Christian Right, secularization, and the effects on mental health of economic change and stratification.

KENNETH D. WALD is professor of political science at the University of Florida. He is the author of *Religion and Politics in the United States* (3d ed.).

CLYDE WILCOX is professor of government at Georgetown University. His latest book on the Christian Right is *Onward Christian Soldiers? The Religious Right in American Politics.*